QUANZHOU TAIZUQUAN

泉州太祖拳

QUANZHOU TAIZUQUAN

THE ART OF FUJIAN EMPEROR FIST KUNG-FU

By
Zhou Kun Min

Translated by
Carol Lyngarde-Lane
Simon T. Lailey

Additional Translation by
Zhang Xiaofeng

www.TambuliMedia.com
Spring House, PA USA

DISCLAIMER

The author and publisher of this book DISCLAIM ANY RESPONSIBILITY over any injury as a result of the techniques taught in this book. Readers are advised to consult a physician about their physical condition before undergoing any strenuous training or dangerous physical activity. This is a martial arts book and details dangerous techniques that can cause serious physical injury and even death. Practice and training require a fit and healthy student and a qualified instructor.

Original Chinese edition published in October 2007 by Heaven Earth Books Limited Company/Corporation (www.cosmosbooks.com.hk)

First Tambuli Media edition July 01, 2017

©2017 Tambuli Media

ISBN-13: 978-1-943155-26-2
ISBN-10: 1-943155-26-7

All Rights Reserved. No part of this publication may be reproduced or utilized in any form or by any means, electronic or mechanical, including photocopying, recording, or by any information storage and retrieval system, without prior written permission from the Publisher.

Photography by Chen Ying Jie
Translated by Leijiang Translations: Carol Lyngarde-Lan (Wu Jiang Ying) and Simon T. Lailey
Edited by Mark V. Wiley
Interior and Cover Design by Summer Bonne

TABLE OF CONTENTS

Publisher's Foreword..vii

Translator's Foreword ix

Preface by Mr. Zheng Dao Qi xvii

Preface by Mr. Xu Cai xix

Preface by Mr. Chen Zu Chang xxii

Preface by Mr. Han Jian Zhong..xxiv

Chapter 1. Origin of Quanzhou Taizuquan 1

Chapter 2. The System of Taizuquan 21

Section 1: Empty Fist (Kong Quan) 22

Section 2: Weaponry (Jiasi) 27

Section 3: Duida and Juji 32

Section 4: Nei Gong, Wai Gong, and Chuan Chen 37

Chapter 3. Taizu Training Theory 41

Chapter 4. The Framework of Quanzhou Emperor Fist 55

Hand Techniques Within Taizuquan 55

Foot Positions (Horse Stances) — Buxing (Ma) 59

Stepping Method 62

Body Method (Shenfa) 65

Chapter 5. Introduction and Illustration of Taizuquan Forms 69

    Sanzhan (Three Battles) 69

    Shizi (Cross Pattern) 84

    Dantou..108

Chapter 6. Essence of Taizuquan Technical Hands 137

Chapter 7. The Book of Discussions on the Fist Art............................ 193

    Section 1: How to Distinguish Wuzuquan 193

    Section 2: The Key Points of Wuzuquan 201

    Section 3: Monk Chang Kai Discusses Nanshaolin Taizuquan.......222

Postscript...227

Epilogue..229

Translator's Notes 235

PUBLISHER'S FOREWORD

It gives me great honor to present this Tambuli Media English translation of Master Zhou Kun Min's excellent Chinese-language cannon on Taizuquan, otherwise spelled Tai Cho Kun and known as either "Grand Ancestor Boxing" or "Emperor Fist" kung-fu.

To quote from his biography, "Master Zhou Kun Min began training at the Quanzhou Wushu Research Society in 1961, and in 1963 he joined the Xiamen University Wushu Team, where he was trained by the celebrated martial arts masters of the Minnan area, including Master Dai Huo Yan, Lin Qi Yan, and Lin Du Ying. In due course, Master Zhou was appointed Chairman of the Quanzhou City Wushu Association and Deputy Chairman of the Fujian Province Wushu Association. In 2005, he was appointed 10th Chairman of the International Southern Shaolin Wuzuquan Fellowship General Association." This, of course, is but a small portion of his larger accomplishments but sheds enough light on them that his analysis of history and the fist-art instruction found within these pages are to be taken seriously.

This impressive book details the origins and development of Taizuquan and Wuzuquan through the centuries, often shedding new light on previously accepted ideas. Complementing the invaluable historical content are deeply detailed chapter discussions on Qi Energy, Body Mechanics, Stances, Fist Methods, Partner Training, Five Element Defenses, Weapons, several Fist Forms and Applications. This volume is the only English edition of the Chinese masterpiece by one of the most respected masters in Fujian province.

Quanzhou Taizuquan provides deep insights and details on posture, movement, body structure, and energy. It is thorough in its history, analysis and instruction. Without doubt, Zhou Shifu has indeed written one of the most important books on Southern Fist kung-fu, and I am personally elated to be its English-language publisher. *Quanzhou Taizuquan* is an important treatise on the martial arts of Fujian Province, China, and a "must have" for all practitioners and historians of the Chinese and Okinawan martial arts.

Tambuli Media is indebted to Sifu John Graham, himself a very accomplished Wuzuquan master and former Chairman of the International South Shaolin Wuzuquan Association, for connecting us with Zhou Kun Min Sifu. We also are extremely grateful for the nimble translating of the original Chinese edition by Carol Lyngarde-Laneand (Wu Jiang Ying) and Sifu Simon T. Lailey; and additionally grateful to Sifu Zhang Xiaofeng for his "insider" interpretation of difficult sections of the text, and to Sifu Henry Lo for helping coordinate the efforts. And, once again, our designer Summer Bonne has done a great new cover and interior layout. (We only wish we had the original photos, as the ones presented here were scanned from the printed Chinese edition, and so the quality is not as crisp as we would have liked).

Enjoy this treasure of Fujianese martial culture. Please spread the word of its availability among friends and colleagues. It is only with continued patronage that we can continue to publish important books like this on lesser-known styles in the West.

Dr. Mark V. Wiley
Publisher, Tambuli Media
President, International Beng Hong Athletic Assoc.

TRANSLATOR'S FOREWORD

The year is 2010 and the location is Quanzhou, Fujian Province in southeast China. As the 2010 "Quanzhou City Five Ancestor Fist International Meeting" drew to a close I was presented with three copies of the, then, just recently-published hardback publication entitled, *Quanzhou Taizuquan*.

Written by the Chairman (at that time) of this association, Master Zhou Kun Ming, he very kindly signed one copy of his book for me and it is this copy that I was to, later, spend more than a year translating for the Tambuli Media edition you now read. The other two copies I gave away; one to my senior kung-fu student of that time, and the other to Master Mark V. Wiley.

Five years later Master Wiley asked me to translate a book written, by hand, in Chinese on Fujian Feihequan (Fujian Flying Crane Fist style kung-fu). This I excitedly did and it was very soon after I had completed that project that Master Wiley then asked me to translate the book you are now holding in your hands!

But I cannot, must not, and will not take all the credit for translating these two literary works, for I could never have done this without the help of my Chinese Culture teacher, Miss Carol Lingarde-Lane (Wu Jiang Ying), who I most certainly must thank because it was through her tireless efforts — during her spare time and during my weekly one-to-one lessons with her — that the essence of this relatively unheard of Fujian kung-fu style (Taizuquan) is now before you.

As a joint-venture, translating this book has represented, for me, a unique journey all of its own and one from which I have come to understand, more deeply, both Ngo cho kun (Fujian Five Ancestor Fist kungfu) and Fujian Taizuquan (Fujian Emperor Fist kung-fu) as well Chinese culture, itself… by way of Carol's help.

It is my feeling that with the publication of this book (which Master Zhou Kun Ming has very kindly allowed to happen) the next couple of years leading up to 2020 is going to mark the beginning of a new and exciting era for Taizuquan that, so far outside of Mainland China —indeed, outside of Fujian — has not happened.

Having translated this book I, for one, am now most certainly on the Taizu trail as this past fifteen months of translating and associated, inevitable and hugely enjoyable research has inspired me to seek, find and explore this unique art for both its own sake and that of Ngo cho kun (Wuzuquan).

Six months into translating this book I began to think along the lines of given Carol and myself a joint-venture publications/translations title. Presenting one or two titles to Carol we together came up with "Leijiang Translations."

With "Lei" being the first Chinese character of my Chinese name, Lei Si Men, and with "Jiang" being the first Chinese character used in her given name (Jiang Ying), I had decided to work these two names into our title.

One of the names I had come up with had actually used Carol's Chinese name first (this was me behaving in a polite and typically Chinese manner and was thus in-keeping with Chinese tradition and Chinese etiquette) but Carol, being Chinese, responded in a way that was also typically Chinese and so presented me with a title that actually put my Chinese name character first!

"Leijiang," she said, "sounds like the name of a Chinese river - the River Lei - and so suggests something that is moving, flowing, and constantly evolving. So this name, I think, would be very suitable." I could not have agreed more so "Leijiang" it was and "Leijiang" it is! "Leijiang Translations."

So now, make yourself comfortable and enjoy this publication — the very first book on Taizuquan to have ever been published in English! Enjoy it and learn well from it as indeed have I.

Sifu Simon T. Lailey
"Leijiang Translations"
Isle Of Wight, England
June 2017

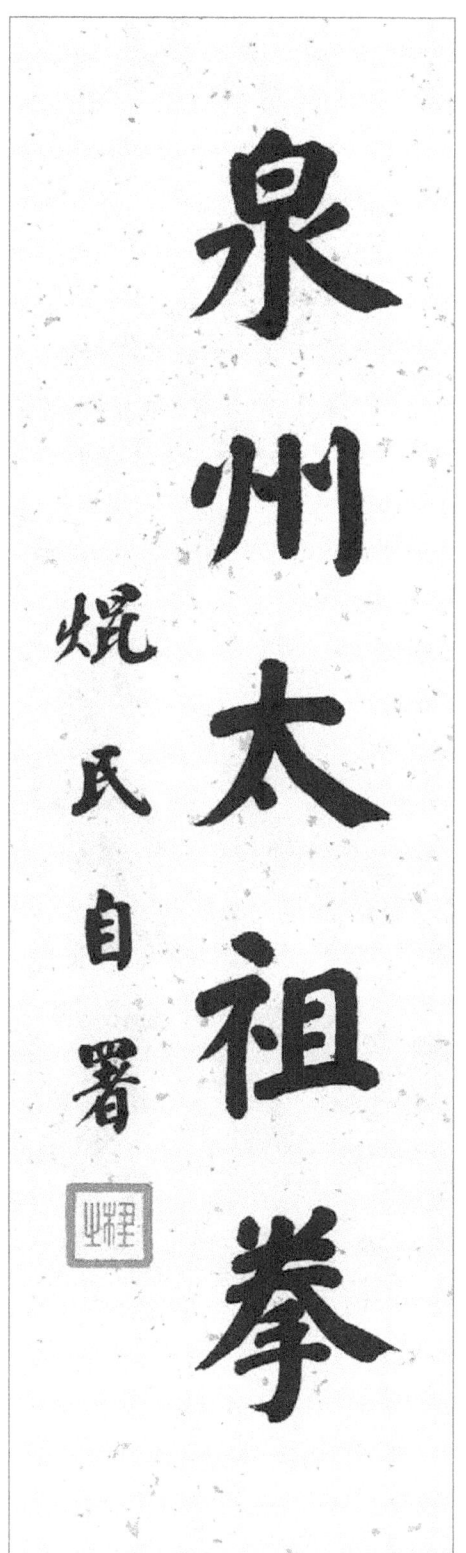

"Quan Zhou Tai Zu Quan Kun Min"

The Emperor Fist style of Chinese martial arts from Quanzhou in Fujian (Mainland China)

Written and signed by the author of this book, Zhou Kun Min

Zhou Kun Min

Zhou Kun Min was born in Quanzhou City in Fujian province. In 1961 he started to train at the Quanzhou Wushu Research Society, and in 1963 he joined the Xiamen University Wushu Team, where he was trained by the celebrated martial arts masters of the Minnan area, including Master Dai Huo Yan, Lin Qi Yan, and Lin Du Ying.

In due course, Master Zhou was appointed Chairman of the Quanzhou City Wushu Association and Deputy Chairman of the Fujian Province Wushu Association. In 2005, he was appointed 10th Chairman of the International Southern Shaolin Wuzuquan Fellowship General Association.

In the past, Master Zhou has assumed the position of Chief Editor for the "Quanzhou City Evening Newspaper" and the Secretary-General to the Communist Party Quanzhou Municipal Party Committee. He has also previously been Deputy Head to the Quanzhou City Standing Committee and was the Deputy Mayor to the Quanzhou City People's government.

Master Zhou is now enjoying his retirement.

Mr. Wei Guo Qi.

Mr. Dai Huo Yan

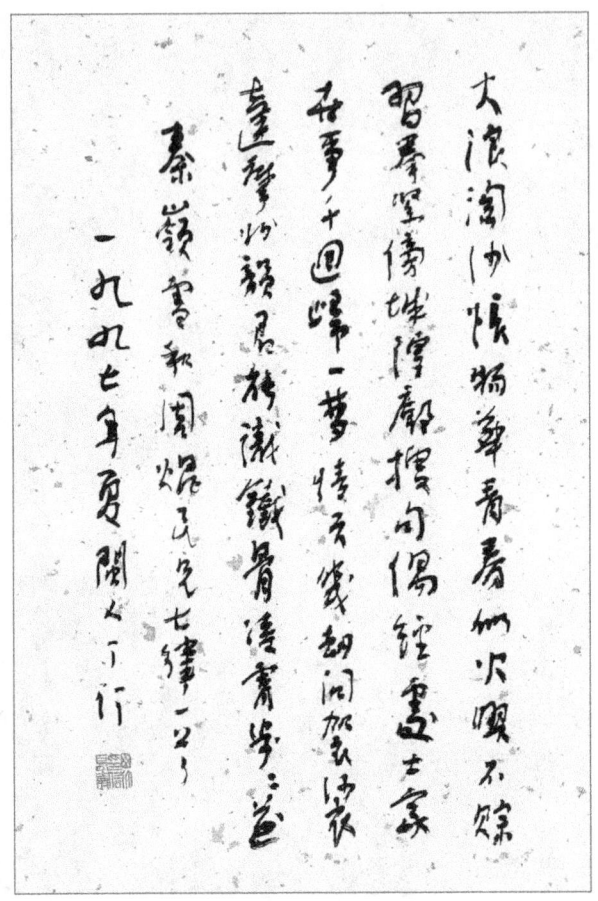

Composed by Zhou Kun Min and the Hong Kong poet, Qin Ling Xue. The calligraphy is by Mr. Ding Ling.

1997 Summer

PREFACE BY MR. ZHENG DAO QI

More than 1,300 years of history and development has forged its own culture embracing both splendour and glory within Quanzhou City. Rich in substance and cultural heritage as well as an intangible heritage, Quanzhou City has become a core region of abundance when speaking of the Minnan[1] culture.

The Minnan culture is a valuable and important aspect of the Chinese way of life and has clearly shown that the people across the Taiwan Straits (the Taiwanese) are from the same roots and share a common origin. Inseparable from the south-eastern Chinese seaboard that is Fujian, the Taiwanese maintain an amiable connection with the southern Fujianese (the Quanzhou people) while acting as a moral pillar that keeps Taiwan inextricably linked to Fujian's third largest city (Quanzhou). In view of this, I once made a proposal at the National People's Congress that the Western Straits Culture Reserved District be established in Quanzhou City. At the present time, the Minnan Culture Ecology Reserved Experimental Area/District has been declared and confirmed by the local culture department, as being the very first "Culturally and Ecologically Reserved District" in China.

The Quanzhou City People's Government has issued a name-list of the first group of city-level intangible cultural heritage in March 2007, including nine major categories and 68 items/classifiers with the Southern Shaolin martial arts being one of these. Quanzhou City has, for a very long time now, been well-known as the origin of Southern Shaolin martial arts and with Wuzuquan as its representative. Indeed, it has passed through centuries —from ancient times to the present — and so has been introduced into Taiwan, Hong Kong and Macao as well as other overseas countries and regions. For many years now, groups and individuals from around the world have come to Quanzhou in order to seek the roots and origins of Chinese martial arts.

As for myself, I have always been passionate about Chinese martial arts; therefore, I was very pleased — in fact, delighted — to see that the Southern Shaolin martial arts have been booming and thriving among the Quanzhou people. It has not only had a huge people-base but has been promoted to a *spiritual culture* level amongst its people. Together with the Minnan sound, Minnan music, Minnan Opera and the Minnan construction arts, the Minnan martial arts have become an important and meaningful aspect of Quanzhou City and so have left their mark when spoken of in relation to other cities across the country.

Southern Shaolin martial arts reflect the splendour of the local people while developing awareness, love and passion amid the native land as a native clan-spirit. Therefore, I consider Quanzhou Southern Shaolin martial arts to be a cultural treasure which enjoys ongoing development. In this way the locals of Quanzhou City build and develop what I choose to call the "soft power" of the city.

This book, *Quanzhou Taizuquan*, is a recent work of Mr. Zhou Kun Min. By way of his deep research, Mr. Zhou has introduced one of the important quanfa (fist-types) of Southern-style Shaolin martial arts. It is my sincere hope that by way of this book many will come to realize the common view-point so that more will participate in this kind of pursuit — not just to protect themselves, but in order to protect and preserve the culture while promoting the tradition and respecting its history.

Mr. Zheng Dao Qi
Secretary of Quanzhou City Municipal Committee
Date: September 21st 2007

PREFACE BY MR. XU CAI
A TRIBUTE TO QUANZHOU MARTIAL ARTS

Quanzhou City has always been well-known to the world as an historic and cultural city. I first visited this city more than 40 years ago and even then I was deeply attracted to, influenced by, and affected by its history and its very rich culture; not to mention its beautiful landscapes. My short stay in the city gave me a taste of its true meaning and its reputation as, "the coast of a prosperous culture," "the coastal starting-point of the *Silk Road*," "The world-wide religious museum," and "The country of Southern Gaojia Opera." Therefore, Quanzhou City has made a deep impression upon my memory ever since, which made me often think of Quanzhou and my longing to go back for another visit.

Casting my mind back I am so pleased to have received many opportunities to visit Quanzhou where I came into contact with the charm of Quanzhou martial arts. My knowledge of this subject has been improved during those visits and my subsequent inquiries that I have come to recognize Quanzhou City as being not only a well-known historical and cultural city but a business city since ancient times. Here, then, I am taking this opportunity (by way of Master Zhou Kun Min's excellent book, *Quanzhou Taizuquan*) to provide some of my own humble views relating to the subject.

Mr. Zhou has been an old friend of mine for years. Over 10 years ago I came to Quanzhou City to participate in the Southern Shaolin International Martial Arts Conference. At that time Mr. Zhou was the Secretary-General of the Municipal Committee of Quanzhou City as well as the Chairman to the Quanzhou Martial Arts Conference. I was delighted when I learnt about this fact—that this leader and of such a high position was in charge of the development and promotion of local martial arts and local martial societies and groups.

But there was also another reason that drew me close to Mr. Zhou and this was that he had once worked as the Chief Editor of the "Quanzhou Evening Newspaper," for I had also worked for newspapers and so realized the great need for help from within the media when it came to promoting and developing Quanzhou martial arts.

Over a decade went by where Mr. Zhou not only worked as a cautious and conscientious political leader (making valuable contributions within this field of work) but also cared so much for and, indeed, loved the local martial arts even after his retirement, which I find so admirable! This encouraged me to relate closely to those well-known words of a poem (written by the famous poet, Wang Bo) which refers to, "An extraordinary land with remarkable people." Quanzhou City is certainly such a good place.

During the Jia Jing years (during the reign of Emperor Jia Jing of the Ming dynasty) the invasion of the Japanese pirates led to utter disaster. Mr. Yu Da You, a young man of some 20 years, bravely involved himself in the battles to defend against those pirates. His battlefield was so vast that it included Jiangsu province, Zhejiang province, Fujian province, Guangdong province, and Hainan province. Mr. Yu became a famous general because of these battles and was thus recognized as a national hero. But not only was he a military leader he was also an outstanding scholar. An expert in poetry and verse his eventual passing meant that he would leave behind some precious works that have been handed down and preserved over the years. The famous book, *Sword Manual* (which has built the base for southern Shaolin martial theory) is considered one of the "classics" of Chinese martial arts history. As Mr. Zhou once said, "The traditional Quanzhou martial arts, regardless, whether fist-arts or weapons-based arts, are traceable to the same stock as described within the book, *Sword Manual*."

Even now there are large groups of famous martial arts lovers (such as Mr. Zheng Dao Xi, Secretary to the Quanzhou Municipal Committee, who has been passionate about martial arts ever since his university days) and Mr. Zhu Ming (the Mayor of Quanzhou City), as well as Mr. Zhou Kun Min. These individuals are not only familiar with martial arts but are also experts at being leaders when it comes to promoting these martial arts.

In ancient times the government carefully selected quality for both literary personnel and military personnel and suggested that education should cover both literary skills and martial skills. From this viewpoint the rich martial arts culture and traditions among the Quanzhou people were cultivated and so they transformed Quanzhou City into a "brand new city of martial arts." Hereby, then, I consider Quanzhou City as a city that has raised extraordinary people and as a city of glory.

During one of my visits to Quanzhou I was attracted to a place named Chongwu (literally, "worshipping martial"). Asking the locals about its name I was informed that this was, indeed, a place of worshipping and esteeming martial provisions. This place of Chongwu was once a place where Mr. Qi Ji Guang led his troops in order to fight against the Japanese pirates and swept them away. This was during the Ming Dynasty. For this reason he, together with a Mr. Yu Da You (they were known, together, as "Tiger Qi and Dragon Yu") were renowned for their heroic deeds and contributions to defending their country and have since been recorded in history as such. Therefore, I felt obliged to pay a visit to this somehow mysterious island and finally had a good look at the ancient fortress on this half-island.

This ancient fortress is only 2.4 kilometres long and 6.9 kilometres high. Military fortifications were built upon the walls of this fortress while Mr. Qi Ji Guang made perfect the defence structure while intensifying the drilling of the troops. Thus the Japanese invasion was quashed. It was also here, at Chongwu during the Qing dynasty, where Mr. Zheng Cheng Gong (of Nan'an County, Quanzhou) began to dispense his troops where they sailed across the Taiwan Straits to Taiwan to drive out the Dutch invaders thus restoring Taiwan to China. Nowadays the Quanzhou people have built two memorial halls — one for Mr. Yu Da You and one for Mr. Zheng Cheng Gong — so that people can always remember their heroic deeds and patriotic moral character.

Looking back at the historic tales and patriotic poems of Quanzhou one can see clearly how they relate to the martial arts along with the fact that modern-day Quanzhou people still have a passion towards the martial arts and their promotion. I thus feel obliged to sing my praises of these unique disciplines.

Mr. Xu Cai
Previously appointed as deputy-chief of China national level, central government physical education committee

Presently he is consultant of Chinese national level physical education general conference and honorary chairman of Asia martial art fellowship conference

Date: September 21st, 2007

PREFACE BY MR. CHEN ZU CHANG

My homeland (Fujian, China) has always been known for its rich literature as well as for its martial arts. Indeed, when I was a child I was told that Quanzhou Nanshaolinquan was famous the world over.

For a decade now I have been living overseas, in the Philippines. Through my experiences during these past ten years I have come to realize there are two things in the Philippines that represent the quintessence of Chinese culture: one is "strings and chords" (music) and the other is Fujian Five Ancestor Fist style kungfu (Wuzuquan, Ngo Cho Kun).

In Binondo (Manila's "Chinatown") there are well-known martial schools such as the Kong Han, the Beng Kiam and the Xing Han. These schools have not only been teaching Chinese martial arts but have been taken very seriously by the overseas Chinese communities. The origins of the martial arts they teach are all from my homeland: Fujian.

Through the links between the Quanzhou Wuzuquan international exchanges and the martial arts groups of the Philippines I have come to know Mr. Zhou Kun Min as a quanfa master and one who is devoted to the interaction between quanfa groups worldwide. Our national martial art(s), or guoshu as it is sometimes called, is an original creation from Mainland China and has served to strengthen the soul of the nation.

Not so long ago the outside world looked down upon our nation and referred to our people as, "The Sick Men of Asia"— in Mandarin Chinese, Dongya Bingfu, which literally translates to "East Asia Sick People." This greatly demoralized our nation's people but, at the same time, made them resolute in changing such a negative and offensive perspective. Now, thanks to our highly-praised and hugely-respected guoshu, our country is far more prosperous; with national pride forever on the increase and the life of the people noticeably bettered, we now stand shoulder-to-shoulder with and amongst the rest of the world. Thanks to our guoshu we no longer bear the brunt of shame!

In my opinion there are three main reasons why Chinese martial arts should be taken so seriously: firstly, as a skill over and beyond the call for military war and civilian unrest, the martial arts is a wonderful way to train if only for health and physical fitness which should never be neglected; secondly, be it Quanzhou nanquan or northern-style shaolin kung-fu, both involve essential skills and extensive disciplines that date back thousands of years and so represent the very blood vessels of our nation as well as our unique cultural heritage; and thirdly, over the years the Chinese martial arts have regretfully lost part of their originality and so it is our responsibility to restore and preserve this ancient and very special practice.

While xiangpu (sumo), kongshoudao (karate-do) and taiquandao (taekwondo) are all rooted in our own jiaodi (ancient wrestling) and shoupu (hand-flapping) skills, it is also with regret that our national arts have not yet been accepted into and included amongst the Olympics Games. Even more reason, therefore, that we should make huge efforts and go to extraordinary lengths to promote our very own Chinese martial arts — so that they will not perish and will never be forgotten.

Mr. Zhou, therefore, by way of his accumulation of knowledge, has written this book as a reference to the origin of Quanzhou Taizuquan from the Wuzuquan Sect angle and has thus accounted for quanfa theory and practical usage instead of keeping it a closely-guarded secret, which is the attitude of previous generations of Chinese traditionalists. Giving out this information for the very first time, Mr. Zhou is thus encouraging a tremendous martial spirit and so, for myself, I am deeply appreciative of his work and achievements and so look forward to its eventual publication.

Chen Zu Chang
Founder and Head of the Song Qing Ling Charity Foundation
Binondo, Manila (Luzon, Philippines)
July 2007

PREFACE BY MR. HAN JIAN ZHONG

Mr. Zhou Kun Min is a great friend, who is both wise and modest. As they say, "Still water runs deep" (ning jing zhi yuan). This is Mr. Zhou Kun Min. The Chinese martial arts is the bridge by which Mr. Zhou Kun Min and I became acquainted.

I heard, over a decade ago (in 2002), that Mr. Zhou was considering the idea of writing this book. Back then he was attending numerous everyday affairs as the position of mayor of Quanzhou City while I was busy working for the benefit of charitable activities within the martial arts domain. As a result, we barely had the opportunity to sit down and discuss further this project, this book; and it was not until last year (2006) that I was invited by CCTV (China Central Television) to attend the up-and-coming wulin ("martial arts social circles") "General Assembly." In fact, it was not until Mr. Zhou Kun Min travelled to Beijing where he led a delegation of twenty skilled Wuzuquan (Five Ancestor Fist) kung-fu athletes from Quanzhou that he and I would eventually get to meet, sit down together, and talk over martial arts matters while drinking traditional Chinese tea. Currently, I am reading through the manuscript of this book, *Quanzhou Taizuquan*, and have thus become more aware of the sense of "cultural status" reflected through the works of Mr. Zhou. Now I feel the need to put down on paper some of my own words through such an inspiration.

Mr. Zhou Kun Min has made a deep impression upon me as a learned and refined individual. He is the mayor of Quanzhou city and a scholar who has majored in Chinese Language studies. He has a *"full forehead and a straight back,"* as we say. Behind his golden-framed spectacles he wears a genuine smile upon his face while exuding warmth and confidence. Talking to Mr. Zhou is inspiring, refreshing and relaxing. He is modest and positive, gentle and patient. He never forces his opinions upon others although he does make his own viewpoint crystal-clear. When speaking he does so with logic and clarity while providing vivid verbal illustrations that captivate his audience with sheer and absolute magnetism. Mr. Zhou once told me:

> *The development of Southern Shaolin martial arts in Quanzhou carries the banner of an immensely strong Chinese cultural legacy. For countless citizens in Quanzhou, learning the ways of the "Quan" (Fist Arts) has long been the local culture as well as a daily exercise, a way of*

> *life and an invaluable combination of upbringing, wisdom, spirit and creativity.*

South shaolin martial arts from Quanzhou City have been well-known for such a long period of time, while Five Ancestor Fist has been the most celebrated style of all which is why, in 2007, it was chosen to be the focus of the opening demonstration-piece during a martial contest organized by CCTV. Not surprisingly it proved to be a huge hit amongst the viewers.

Five Ancestor Fist kung-fu is a style based upon five distinct disciplines of classical Chinese kung-fu, one of these being the celebrated (martial) art called Emperor Fist (Taizuquan), which is renowned for its uniqueness and its longest historical standing. Regarding this extraordinary art Mr. Zhou Kun Min has written and illustrated every possible detail within this book which is not only eye-catching amidst Five Ancestor Fist forums but written in such depth.

Undoubtedly a masterpiece as well as being the very first book *ever* to be written (on the subject) in Chinese, *Quanzhou Taizuquan* is a comprehensive introduction to this unique art. Indeed, one can sense the author's solid cultural accumulation of both skill and knowledge which is the result of decade upon decade of dedication, experience and diligent training. Judging from Mr. Zhou's writing skills I can only conclude that he must have built a solid foundation of knowledge within the areas of Chinese literature and Chinese history as well as Chinese philosophy; which means that when he began to study Chinese martial arts he did not simply learn the physical aspect but embraced the philosophy, the aesthetics, the history and the associated literature that essentially, inevitably and crucially goes hand-in-hand with the physical pursuit.

As is typical of a genuine master, Mr. Zhou has pursued his chosen craft and so accomplished his work with extreme diligence. Focusing upon himself amidst a world of ancient culture, Mr. Zhou has read the ancient texts and studied the historical records while enquiring about, through word and deed, those masters and grandmasters from past generations. Through such a cultivated energy Mr. Zhou has acquired a depth of understanding that has broken all boundaries and so led to a personal viewpoint that goes way beyond all restrictions of out-dated opinions that individual martial arts sects might normally encourage. This has prompted a greater perspective and a far wider field of vision on his part that is well-appreciated by and within academic circles.

With an all-too-clear understanding that *one must never forget one's cultural roots,* one also has to familiarize oneself with it as well as preserve it but, at the same time, bring forth new ideas from it! Otherwise, how can one cultivate oneself and go on to become a true master in such a chosen area of study?

Genuine martial artists have always despised the exaggerated, theatrical and impractical side to modern-day martial arts. While "martial dances" are now fashionable upon a global scale, Quanzhou City has retained the old-school classical and traditional aspect of self-cultivation through training by way of regular annual international events amongst which Five Ancestor Fist has always been the essential focus. In the same way that "Southern Music" and "Southern Opera" have been at the forefront of south China culture, the "Southern Fist" arts have also held their place thus completing this essential trilogy.

Aside from promoting his chosen discipline within Quanzhou City, Mr. Zhou has travelled outside China in order to fulfil this same self-set mission. During his visit to the Philippines in 1989 Mr. Zhou was a huge driving force that led to the founding of the "International Southern Shaolin Five Ancestor Fist Fellowship General Conference," which has since become an international event held in Quanzhou every two years. So far, practitioners of Five Ancestor Fist from close to forty countries and worldwide regions now attend (or have attended) this regular and ongoing event.

I very much admire those that are passionate about promoting Quanzhou's traditional martial arts. Some of these supporters are political leaders, others are martial artists. Some are from educational bodies, others are small business owners. But whatever their background and whatever their agenda, they are all focused upon developing martial arts that are local to Quanzhou. One will, therefore, have to admit that sometimes the efforts of one single person can elevate a subject to a far greater level and a level that is truly beyond all stretches of the imagination. Mr. Zhou is one such single person.

Although Mr. Zhou Kun Min is now retired, his name was put forward as — and has since become Chairman to — the International South Shaolin Five Ancestor Fist Fellowship Association. He is also Chairman to the Quanzhou Calligraphers Association, owing to the fact that his personality and style is also reflected by way of his skills in shufa (the "writing" of Chinese characters) which reflects a natural, unrestrained, elegant and unconventional style of "writing" that is symbolic of the grace of both the Wei and Jin dynasties (265-420 AD and 386-549 AD, respectively), from an age-old

China as well as elegance from China's Tang and Song dynasties (618-906 AD and 906-1279 AD, respectively).

Amongst martial arts enthusiasts from the present age I have not seen many that can compare with Mr. Zhou upon the sensibility of the art and the ability to judge and appreciate numerous types of calligraphy sects. I do believe that Mr. Zhou's profound experience with both martial techniques and shufa is like the merging of *jade and pearl* whereby each improves by association with the other* thus producing a "magic key" that has unlocked the door and so led to such achievements.

Mr. Zhou Kun Min originates from a celebrated martial sect that has allowed him to understand very well how much hard work (gongfu) is involved in learning and teaching Quanzhou's quanfa (fist-based arts). During his initial teaching years Mr. Zhou inspired and encouraged each and every student of his to become a success in Chinese culture. Constantly providing personal advice as well as methodical and patient guidance he worked them hard — from the early morning until late at night — to the point where they would be dripping and drenched in their own sweat thus becoming united as one peaceful and supportive family.

Later on, Mr. Zhou became a government official and, resultantly, he suspended teaching quanfa for three decades. However, he never did abandon the martial society but, in fact and instead, managed to push forward the local martial arts so as to develop and advance the cultural aspect. So far, among the students that Mr. Zhou Kun Min has taught, these include the current abbot of the Quanzhou Shaolin Temple[2], the headmasters of various martial schools, the Overseas Chinese people, doctors, industrialists... and so the list goes on. Endlessly. With each student taking their quanfa studies and the associated morals with the utmost seriousness, these individuals have become the very backbone to his *quanfa* group. Keeping abreast of and paying strict attention to global changes within the international quanfa society, I believe that such awareness — such focus, care and attention — was initiated by way of their learning from Mr. Zhou Kun Min.

To this day I remain grateful and feel privileged that I had such good fortune to meet with this man, this master. I truly realise that as a scholar and a government official, what he has learnt has, indeed, been put to the test. As a scholar, one's own individual character can be exerted to the maximum. However, as a more eminent goal one has to condense one's own specific individuality to an absolute minimum. Over and above dealing with the hectic life of governmental matters, Mr. Zhou Kun Min has focused more upon the noble cause of integrating martial techniques with the culture of a forever-expanding city. As a modern-day thinker and with his sharp scientific mind, Mr. Zhou's knowledge of both martial theory and historical depth allows for a freshness he delivers with an emotive language and vivid description that reflects an accurate and precise logic with a narrative using a powerful and unconstrained voice and style.

But don't take my word for it! Enter this book and see for yourself as you enter the world of Quanzhou Emperor Fist. It will be like *entering a field of wheat in the autumn season* — with its serenity and calmness penetrating through thickness and solidity while warmth and heartiness is sent forth amongst a golden glow. As pleasant as the scent amidst autumn breezes — a scent that has been hardened by the years showing the depth of harvest following ploughing and weeding beneath Fujian skies. Mr. Zhou's writing sparkles with the brilliance of intellectuality as well as the beauty of sensibility and a pure heart that oozes strength. This is my friend Mr. Zhou Kun Min, a portrayal of "still water that runs so deep."

Mr. Han Jian Zhong
China People's Public Security University
Professor and Police Commissioner Class III
Chief Judge of the CCTV's "Martial Masters Competition"
28th July, 2007, Beijing

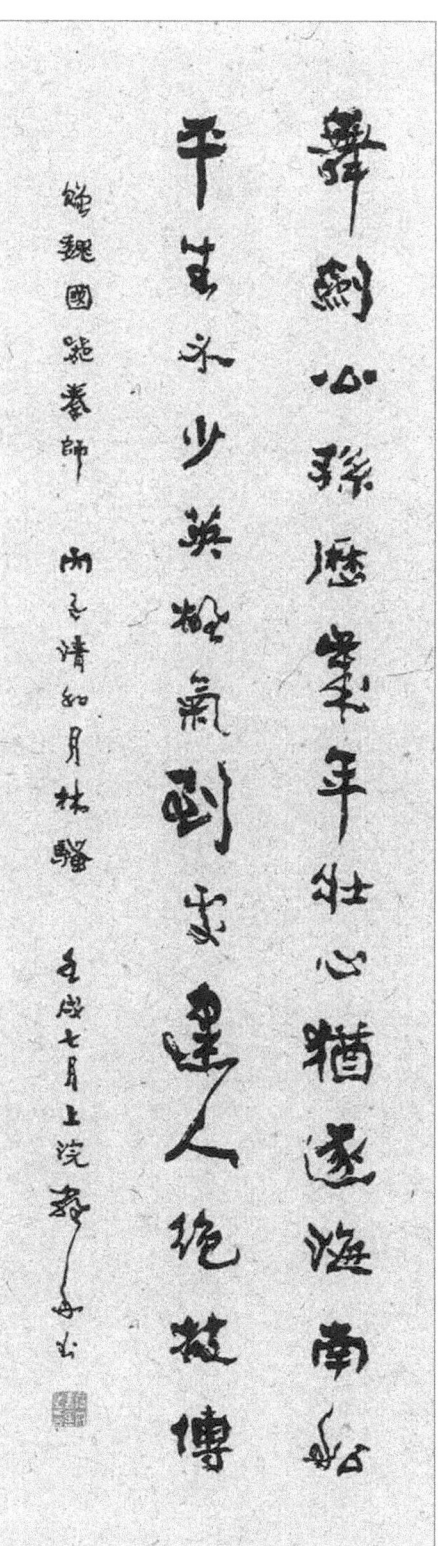

Lin Sao, the successful candidate in imperial exams from the past Qing Dynasty, composed this poem for Master Wei Guo Qi. Calligraphy by Luo Dan.

The translation of the poem reads:

Years of training with mastery skills as Lady Gong Sun[1] practiced and mastered sword dances

His magnificent aspiration is still yet to chase the vessels from Hainan Island[2]

In his life he performed plenty of heroic deeds

Everywhere he went he taught his supreme secret skills.

泉州太祖拳

CHAPTER 1

ORIGIN OF QUANZHOU TAIZUQUAN

Taizuquan is one of the five "quanfa" styles that make up the composite art we call Five Ancestor Fist (Wuzuquan, Ngo Cho Kun). It has a long historic standing that has spread to vast regions and has distinctive features all its own. This book focuses upon Taizuquan, although I have purposely added "Quanzhou" to this book's title for the simple reason that there does exist a Taizuquan kung-fu style outside of Quanzhou and, indeed, outside of Fujian (which is the provincial home of Quanzhou City). These "alternative" Taizu styles differ greatly in terms of their techniques… but more of this later.

As the author of this book I consider myself to have a very limited knowledge of the Taizu fist-art as it appears outside of Fujian — indeed, outside of Quanzhou — so to avoid speaking inaccurately and documenting false information thus exposing myself to ridicule I have decided to talk about Taizuquan with regard only to Quanzhou's interpretation.

Quanzhou Dongchan Shaolinsi (front entrance main door)

Quanzhou is now famous for its Southern Shaolin Temple as well as for its own indigenous (southern Shaolin) martial art. Mr. Huang Jing Fang, the Minister of Revenue from the Ming Dynasty (1368–1644 ad), refers to Quanzhou in his book, titled *Wenling Jiushi* ("The Past Aspects of Wenling"), where "Wenling" is an ancient name for Quanzhou. In his book he states that: "The martial art that is unique to Quanzhou is the most wonderful of all those martial arts within the whole of China."

In Quanzhou during the 1980s a survey was conducted regarding traditional and non-governmental quanfa where it was determined that even though the world had undergone so many changes there still remained over twenty kinds of quanfa (according to the registered information). Some types of quanfa were initiated in the name of "Heavenly Celestials" (or Buddha) while others were far more recent—since the past three generations. But only Taizuquan can be traced back as far as the emperor of China who reigned during the Song Dynasty (960–1279 ad).

The famous Ming Dynasty general named Qi Ji Guang (1528–1588) compiled a book, titled *Jixiao Xinshu* ("New Treatise on Military Efficiency/Strategy"), wherein chapter fourteen ("Quanjing Jieyao" or "Scripture of the Fist and Key Points") states, "Among ancient and current quanfa sects there exists Song Taizu (Grand Emperor from Song Dynasty) and his Thirty-two Long Fist, Six Steps Fist, Monkey Fist, and Decoy Bird Fist. But even though the names of the movements are different they all bear the same general resemblance."

Mr. He Liang Chen, one of Qi Ji Guang's contemporaries who lived through the reign of two Chinese emperors (known as the "Years of Emperor Jia Qing" and "Years of Emperor Wan Li from Ming Dynasty") also wrote a military book. This was titled *Zhen Ji* and included similar recordings. He Liang Chen wrote: "Among the quanfa created by Song Taizu (such as Thirty-six Long Fist, Six Steps Fist, Monkey Fist and Decoy-Bird Fist) these may carry different names yet they all prove victorious in combat by way of the same means."

Jianjing (sword manual)

These records adequately prove that Taizuquan matured during the Ming Dynasty and was taught among the military troops and so enjoyed great fame; otherwise it would not have been mentioned within two military books authored by two eminent generals!

During the Song Dynasty, martial arts became distinctively separate from simple hand-based wrestling and sumo for they were added to by way of a series of skills known as *taozi* (these days referred to as *taolu*). In his book titled *Gen Yu Sheng Ji*,[1] Mr. Cheng Zong You of the Ming Dynasty states: "With regards to Long Fist quanfa (Changquan) there are styles from Taizu (the great Song Emperor) as well as from the Wen Family."

In 1910 a book was written by a Mr. Guo Xi Fen (titled *Chinese Physical Education History*), who stated: "It is absolute and beyond all doubt that the emperor Taizu (Song Taizu) is skillful in the art of attack and defense. For all I know it is possible that Shaolin quanfa has taken on-board the techniques from Taizu and has thus been perfected."

Quanzhou National Art School old address

The full name of Song Taizu was Zhao Kuang Yin — the first emperor of the Song Dynasty, whose ancestral home is Zhuozhou City, Hebei Province. He was crowned in later life and so established the Northern Song Dynasty. In a book speaking of northern style quanfa it states that: "The Shaolin sect is also known by the term *Outer Family* of which Zhao Kuang Yin was the founder. Zhao Kuang Yin kept his extraordinary quanfa skills a very tight secret although one day when he was drunk he let the cat right out of the bag!"[2] The book continues to say that, "Mentioning his skills to a number of officials he soon came to regret this (when he finally sobered up!), and so decided to hide a quanfa manual (that he, himself, had written) within the Shaolin temple." *(Just to clarify this point - here we are talking about the northern Shaolin temple in Henan province and not the southern Shaolin temple in Quanzhou.)* This manual stated, "The highest level of quanfa skill is to use hard strength with direct and straightforward attacks."

Before Zhao Kuang Yin's coronation he held the post of a supreme government official where he was in charge of military affairs. In fear of his own example being followed by those with martial arts skills as well as military powers he summoned one of his government officials (a man named Zhao Pu) in order to work out an effective strategy. Zhao Pu suggested that the emperor take military powers into his own hands in order to avoid any kind of military wars within the country. This was, Zhao Pu said, the only way to ensure a healthy long-term prospect. The emperor took Zhao Pu's advice and so deprived his military officials of their military powers.

Before long, Zhao Kuang Yin began to promote intellectual pursuits more so than the martial arts, emphasizing civil administration at the expense of national defense. This was mentioned in three subsequent books: *Wang Zeng Bi Lu, Su Shui Ji Wen* and *Wen Jian Lu*. From this point onwards it was understandable that Zhao had hidden his secret quanfa manual for he was, at this time, preparing for a forthcoming role within the government.

Although it is possible that Zhao was not the founder/creator of Taizuquan (to be specific here: northern Taizuquan) it was he who hid his manual within the northern Shaolin temple (in Henan) and with his high-standing position as emperor, the discipline that was later to be called Taizuquan (Grand Ancestor Fist) was made to stand out noticeably amongst the numerous quanfa styles that were prevalent at that time.[3]

When Mr. He Liang Chen mentioned the Thirty-six Long Fist of the Grand Ancestor Fist style as well as other quanfa systems he made the comment, "They each had been taught by celestial beings and claimed to be undefeatable in those times. However they lost a great deal in terms of the original format and so had lost a lot of its power(s)." In fact, Grand Ancestor Fist, together with the "Long Sword" skills as passed down by Master Li Liang Qin (also mentioned in Mr. He Liang Chen's book, *Zhen Ji*), was not declining but, in fact, prevailing within Quanzhou City and with no hint of waning.

This finding was based upon two main reasons: the establishment within Quanzhou of the Song Nan Wai Zong Zheng Si (the government that managed the affairs of the descendants from Emperor Zhao Kuang Yin) and the contribution from General Yu Da You, who was the national hero against the Japanese invasion.

Let us now look at the first reason in more depth: According to the book of *Song Shi* ("The History of the Song Dynasty"), the mother of Emperor Zhao Kuang Yin convinced him to elect his younger brother, Zhao Guang Yi, to be his successor rather than his son who was much younger. One of the explanations for this was that Emperor Zhao Kuang Yin and his younger brother, Zhao Guang Yi, worked together in order to overthrow the old dynasty (Houzhou Dynasty, 951–960) and so it would not have been acceptable to his younger brother if Emperor Zhao Kuang Yin had chosen his own son as his successor to the throne instead of him. Therefore, during the Northern

Song Dynasty the first emperor was referred to as "Song Taizu" (Grand Ancestor) whose family name was Zhao and given name was Kuang Yin.

Later on, the royal blood lineage switched to his younger brother Song Taizong (Second Emperor) and then his own descendants. Meanwhile, the descendants from the First Emperor (Song Taizu) retained their royal status but without any rights to the throne. In order to comfort and manage those royals the government established a department (titled, Zong Zheng Si, in the third year of the Huang You period of the Northern Song Dynasty) to be appointed in charge of their royal affairs.

After the second year of the Jing Kang period (under the years when Emperor Song Jin Zong's reigned) the Southern Outer Zong Zheng Si (Imperial Clan Department) was moved to Quanzhou City while Shen, one of the sixth decedents of Song Taizu Zhao Kuang Yin, arrived and settled in Quanzhou. In the book, *Quanzhou Fu Zhi* ("History of Quanzhou City"), it says: "Mu Zong Yuan (name of the royal school) was positioned in the southwest of Xi Kui Fang (another part of Zong Zheng Si), and was built after the arrival of the Southern Outer Zong Zheng Si. In the third year of the Jing Tai period (the Year of Southern Song Dynasty) a magistrate named Ni Si considered the place too small and so moved it to the north-west of Quanzhou and so built a premises called Ju Xian Fang."

Quanzhou City became one of the biggest ports in the world of that time and by the end of the Song Dynasty the number of royal family members from this part exceeded three thousand while their cultural and customary practices and traditions deeply influenced Quanzhou. Mr. He Qiao Yuan (from the Ming Dynasty) wrote a poem which included the lines, "Up until now there have been ten thousands residents including those that are offspring of the dragon."[4]

The culture and customs of those descendants were carried over and passed down so their importance remains in-place even now. One of these customary practices was to launch lanterns shaped like huge turtles[5] while others included playing sumo, learning quanfa, performing Chinese opera and playing traditional Minnan music.

According to the book *Song Tian Yuan Zhao Shi Zu Pu* ("The Pedigree of the Zhao Clan"), all generations of the royal descendants practiced quanfa while some joined the army. Therefore, quanfa was initially passed on only within the confines of the royal tribes as a kind of Zi Sun Quan ("Descendants Fist"). However, Quanzhou Emperor

Fist expanded and was eventually taught to the locals (civilians) and thus developed into a huge sect of martial arts.

The book titled, *Xi Shan Za Zhi*, written by Mr. Cai Yong Jian during the 15th Year of Jia Qing Year of the Qing Dynasty (discovered just a few years ago) recorded some historic facts about the Quanzhou Shaolin temple and its fighting against invasions from other nationalities. In that book he mentions that Mr. Zhao Meng Mo (who was from this part of the royal family and a successful candidate within the highest imperial examinations) together with Mr. Zhao Meng Liang (who left home to become a monk and then became the abbot of the Quanzhou Shaolin temple) became leaders, and went on to organize Chinese troops against the invasion from the Mongolian military.

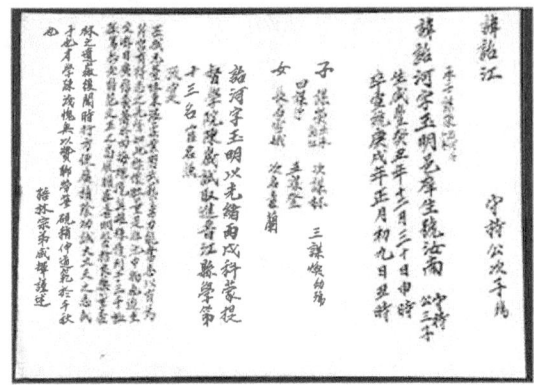

The Cai (Chua) Family Tree showing Cai Yu Ming's (Chua Giok Beng's) details, his achievements and some personal characteristics

At this time there also emerged a military expert from within the Zhao family named Zhao Ben Xue who wrote the book, *Zhao Zhu Bing Fa Shi San Pian* ("The Thirteen Chapters Of Zhao Family Military Strategy") which was not only passing on military techniques from General Yu Da You (the famous general) but also teaching his quanfa art.

In the book of *Jian Jing* ("Sword-Art Manual"), written by general Yu Da You, he recommends strategies such as, "Every punch should put forth effort using one's entire body"[6] and "Go forward with each step while aiming straight ahead and with focus upon every moment," both of which were essential ideas inherited from Taizuquan; where this concept is described as "power, strength and direct attacks."

Now let us look at the other reason: During Mr. Yu Da You's lifetime Quanzhou martial arts reached perfection in both practical combat and theory having rid itself completely of any kind of structured solo practice (forms, taolu, xing) for, at that time, there was a strict focus upon achieving a result as quickly and as swiftly as possible.

Through his book (the aforementioned *Jian Jing*) Mr. Yu Da You took southern martial arts theory to new and incredible heights while in the book titled *Zhen Ji* (a chronicle of troop disposition) and authored by Mr. He Liang Chen), it states within the chapter on practical skills, "In the armed forces, by all means avoid using traditional kung-fu forms (taolu)"; along with, "Upon the crowded battlefield one should advance into the enemy while instantly jabbing and striking with a variety of hand methods with hardly any room to turn one's head."

During his martial arts army training, Mr. Yu Da You strived towards, "maintaining a flexible body using light-power foot methods." Initially, he had learned Taizuquan from his teacher, Mr. Zhao Ben Xue, whose teachings were devoid of all impractical skills. Within his book, *Jian Jing*, he speaks of, Jing Chu Chang Jian ("Jing Chu Long Sword") which he learned in-part from Mr. Li Liang An of Tong'an County in Quanzhou, and in-part from Mr. Ban Bang who was from Liu'an Town in Yongchun County[7] although both are from the lineage of Taizu Zhao Kuang Yin.

In ancient times Fujian province was governed under the state of Chu. Mr. Fu Xuan of the Jin Dynasty said, by way of the article "Duan Bing Pian" ("Short Weaponry"), that "the sword is short weaponry." Mr. Yu Da You therefore addressed the Taizu cudgel as "Jing Chu Long Sword" which made it clear that this method was passed on neither from Hunan province nor Hubei province.

Mr. Jiang De Jing, the secretary of the Grand Council during the Ming Dynasty, recorded through his book, *Ce Hai* ("The Sea of Strategy") that the residents along the Quanzhou-governed coastline practiced Chang Ji ("Long Technique") and so defended against the Japanese invaders. In this book it states: "They were taught the cudgel method through the book of *Jian Jing*." It also states that Fujian soldiers and Fujian ships, addressed in olden days as "changji" (long technique), kept the enemies in certain fear. The regions along the coastal regions such as Shihu, Shenhu, Xiangzhi, Fuquan, Weitou, Dongshi, Shijun (all within Jinjiang City/county); Chongwu (within Hui'an County); Shijing, Yingqian, Lianhe (al within Nan'an City/county); Aotou, Liuwudian, Guan'ao, Shenqian, Lieyu, Jinmen and Shuitou (all

Cai Yu Ming's personal "ying" (stamp) which reads: Yu Ming (Giok Beng)

within Tong'an District, Xianmen City) all produced brave heroes who were far more capable than official soldiers (from Zhejiang Province).

Mr. Huang Jing Fang also said, "Duhu Yu (meaning Mr. Yu Da You)[8] inherited the essence of the ancient and contemporary cudgel methods by training and wrestling with his soldiers. Those that I met were good at cudgel-play and said that they were all taught by their father or their uncles who had, themselves, been taught by Duhu Yu himself." In addition to this, Mr. Yu Da You trained six thousand soldiers from Zhangzhou City. Therefore, Zhang Quan Jun ("Allied Troops from Zhangzhou City and Quanzhou City") fought invincibly and wiped out the Japanese invaders.

Mr. Guo Xi Fen, the author of the book *Chinese Physical Education History*, said with certainty that Mr. Yu Da You had, "trained soldiers in quanfa after the overthrowing of the Ming Dynasty therefore the Shaolin Sect became fully prosperous, the main reason being that it was the result of its promotion by Mr. Yu Da You."

Until this day, then, the Taizuquan cudgel method within the Minnan area is still called Jun Gun ("Army Cudgel"). The movements remain the same as stated within the *Jian Jing* manual which states, "To transform between Yin and Yang both arms must be held straight with the front leg bent and the back leg straight." It then goes on to say that one must, "Slant the body to put forth strength and to step forward with every step."

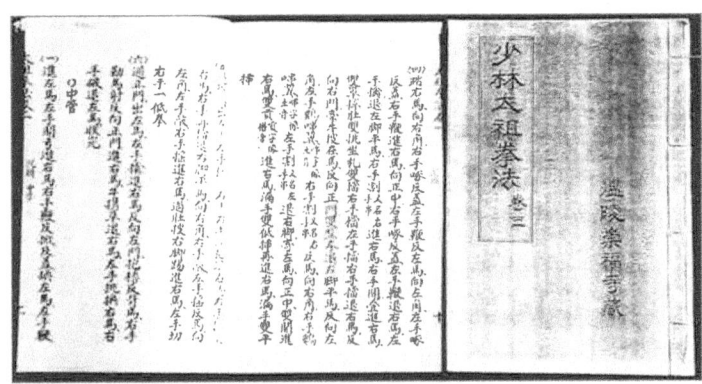

Chongfusi Shaolinsi Taizuquan method (on the right-hand side of this image where it shows the book cover its states: Shaolin Taizuquanfa Volume Three, Wenling Chongfusi Cang (treasured and/or preserved) referring to the enclosed texts)

With hard and fierce attacks and with no impractical movements, this ancient style is thus maintained. The fact that the language in which this manual is written (in the Quanzhou dialect which is called "Hokkien") the terms used for Taizuquan enable those

8

QUANZHOU TAIZUQUAN

that are trained within quanfa to read this ancient book and so put its concepts into practice.⁹

Within the military records (Volume Nine of the book, *History Of The Ming Dynasty*) it states that, "residents from Yongchun County in the Quanzhou area advocated martial arts practice" and that, "The Quanzhou people were skilled in martials arts." Quanzhou city is situated by the sea and was frequented by bandits and was invaded numerous times by the Japanese during the Ming Dynasty. However, the nature of the Quanzhou people was fierce, with martial arts competitions being commonplace amongst the practitioners who were encouraged to train in order to defend their home from invasions from bandits. In this way a variety of martial arts have been passed down from generation to generation through the turbulence of society. This included Taizuquan as well as cudgel-play. It also says, "Unique skills from various families were developed and promoted within Fujian."

The importance of Quanzhou unexpectedly rose in society towards the end of the Ming dynasty and the beginning of the Qing dynasty. General Hong Cheng Chou and Shi Lang, who both surrendered to the Manchu government, as well as General Zheng Cheng Gong and Zheng Jing, who both defended the Manchu government, were born in and grew up within Quanzhou City. The Zheng family stationed troops on the two islands (Xiamen City and Jinmen County) defending against all invaders. Another quote from the *History of The Ming Dynasty* states that, "A great number of young men from Zhangzhou City and Quanzhou City followed them."

Military use of force along the Fujian coastline that lasted twenty-two years resultantly brought to the fore a number of heroes, thus the southern Shaolin martial arts (including Taizuquan and cudgel-play) were afforded even more fame and were credited as bold and powerful and vigorous and sturdy combat-practical disciplines.

When General Zheng Cheng Gong retreated in order to guard Taiwan (province) a number of Triad sects emerged as and when required. Taizuquan, Luohanquan (Monk Fist), Dazunquan (Great Senior Fist), and Xingzhequan Fist (Itinerant Monk Fist), along with other quanfa systems became the main styles of quanfa amongst such secret societies—secret sects such as the famous Hong Men (Red Door) and the Tian Di Hui (The Heaven And Earth Society) to name just two. Thus, for a period of more than one thousand years, Taizuquan became deeply-rooted amongst the local people as a

Martial arts school of Huang Pei Song who achieved first place in the imperial examinations for military personnel

result of domestic battles, fighting against foreigners and political uprisings all of which were *promoted* by the Triads.[10]

In 1993 I visited Dengfeng City (Henan Province) in order to make on-the-spot investigations with regard to (northern) Shaolin temple martial arts. Mr. Chen Si Dong, who was also present and who specializes in Chinese culture and history, introduced Quanzhou Shaolin in a short article that contains about one thousand characters while later on he wrote thirteen articles all in one go and without a break! One of these was titled, "The Ancestry and Pedigree of Quanzhou Shaolin Temple Quanfa." According to his studies and research, the successors from the Ming dynasty (the Wanli period) were as follows: Seng Zhi Ming, Cai Bing Yuan, Cai Yan Geng (from Dongshi town, Jingjiang City in Quanzhou), Feng An (from Nan'an City), Huang Mei, Bai Mei, Feng Dao De, Wu Mei, Miao Xian, Zhi Shan, Liao Yin, and Liao Fan.

After some time the sect was split into two branches. One branch was promoted in Yongchun village and the other in both Nan'an and Jinjiang. Some of the most celebrated successors included Hu Hui Qia, Cai Qian, and Fang Shi Yu from Jingjiang. It is recorded in the book of *Xi Shan Za Zhi* that, "Monks taught martial arts in Southern Quanzhou" and "lived scattered along the coast where they taught in village-based martial arts schools." This book also states that, "the martial arts taught there included Dazuquan, Taizuquan and Houquan" (Monkey Fist).

The *Xi Shan Za Zhi* also states that, "The art of attack and defence within Puli village as well as Shuitou town (of Nan'an County) and the martial performance based on the lion dance in such villages as Guilin, Jingli, Guihu, Shixing, Guochen, Lianhe, Anhai, Shishi, Shenhu, Xiangzhi, Wuxun, Tangdong, Shangbing, Xiabing, Xingcuo, Xianglin and other villages were all practicing the Shaolin martial arts. Mr. Liu Chang Yan (of the Northern Song Dynasty) says in one of his poems that, "The Shaolin practice is everywhere within Southern Quanzhou City."

Nowadays, every original form from Taizuquan is practiced within such places as Tangcheng, Huku, Baipan, Guanshan (all within Yongchun City), Huqiu, Xiping, Jinbang, Xianjing (all withinAnxi County), Sidu and Taoyuan (within Nan'an City), and Shudou, Yanling, Xinbu, Xizhuang, and Bantou (all within Licheng District). Amongst them, Taoyuan Village (within Nan'an County) is especially well-known for its Taizuquan and is a popular career-choice for many of the villagers who can actually sustain a living from teaching this art. One such person was Mr. Fu Chang Hua, who was celebrated in this area during the early years of "The Republic of China" (1912–1949).

Martial arts practice within Quanzhou City had been well-known to both the government and to the public; however, during the Qing Dynasty all the Quanzhou martial arts schools were ordered by the government to close down and all practice of quanfa to cease. Emperor Yong Zheng (of the Qing Dynasty) once declared within his royal decree that, "In the area of Zhangzhou City and Quanzhou City both cultural and martial activities are too active" and so commanded a termination of martial practice. After the "Boxer Rebellion" (Yihetuan) of 1901 where the "Boxers" were defeated, the Qing government strictly forbade martial practice amongst the people.

Mr. Dai Huo Yan's Taizuquan manual

Wuzushenquan (Five Ancestor Wonder Fist) was one of a number of quanfa styles taught to members of the Yihetuan organization. When Manchu troupes invaded Quanzhou city, General Zheng Cheng Gong and his army fought against them vigorously. Eventually the Manchu government succeeded and before long conquered the whole of China and so crowned their leader the emperor of China. Thus the Qing Dynasty was established. However, during their reign there were frequent secret activities going on against the government led by The Triads.

It was the Triads that introduced the anti-Qing slogan, "Fanqing, Fuming" meaning, "Overthrow the Qing and Restore the Ming." Therefore, the quanfa ban was stricter within the Minnan area than elsewhere during those years which led to a very quiet period. During the 1980s I heard from Master Chen Chao Shun, a 96-year-old Taizuquan master, that during the Qing Dynasty, martial arts was practiced in secret

— behind closed doors and at night time and with very little light as they feared being discovered (by the government). In this way, half of the "long weaponry" was lost owing to the confined space in which martial artists could practice (indoors and away from prying eyes and listening ears).

In 1912 the Qing Dynasty finally fell and so gave rise to the Republic of China. At this time, Taizuquan rose and so emerged, over a period of time, a number of influential gongfu (kung-fu) masters. In order to gain contacts for an up-and-coming revolution the Quanzhou-based Tongmenhui (a Chinese revolutionary league) was secretively promoted within various quanfa schools. Amongst these an accomplished master by the name of Fu Wei Bin worked most forcefully and passionately. But the first master to establish a Quanzhou-based quanfa school for the public was a man named Cai Yu Ming (Chua Giok Beng). Master Cai was excellent at martial arts and it was he who took in the first generation of public/citizen quanfa students. At this time Master Cai was addressed respectfully as Minglao meaning "Senior/Elder Ming."

Master Cai opened two martial arts schools in Quanzhou City. One was named the Longhui School (Assembling Dragons) and the other, the Shenggong School (Sacred and Fair). The former comprised of twenty-two students including Li Jiu Shi as well as his son, Li Yao Bao who was also a grandmaster in the art of paper-engraving. When Li Yao Bao was younger he was very strong with his legs and was able to kick and shoot stone beads. Indeed, even as he was approaching the age of ninety he once demonstrated Taizuquan right in front of me! This he had learnt directly from Master Cai Yu Ming, whose style of practice was wholly pure.

Master Cai Yu Ming also trained other celebrated students. The most well-known were Lin Jiu Ru, Wei Wen Bao, You Feng Biao, Jiang Zi Lin, You Jun An, Wong Chao Yan, Yan Jie Yu, Chen Jing Ming, and Shen Yang De. But there were others. The disciples of these Quanzhou quanfa sects not only taught quanfa within the Minnan area but also promoted Taizuquan (or Wuzuquan, Ngo Cho Kun) overseas, taking their art and spreading their art to the Philippines, Singapore and Indonesia.

In the fifth year of the Republic of China (1917), quanfa associations arose including the, Yu Ming Guoshu (Cai Yu Ming National Arts Studies Association), the Ming Qian Guoshu Hui (Ming Qian National Arts Association), the Lu Wan Ding Guoshu Guan, meaning the Lu Wan Ding National Arts School (Lu Wan Ding being a student of Cai Yu Ming), the Minnan Guoshu Study Association, and the Super Star Martial

Arts Physical Education Association. These associations were well-known across Southeast Asia.

Mr. You Feng Biao wrote a book titled, *China Roushu* ("China's Soft Technique") which illustrated various quanfa including Master Cai Yu Ming's martial art. There were also other gongfu masters such as Huang Pei Song, Lin Xian, Zhuang Zhan, Wei Xi Nong, and Liao Dou who also taught many well-known students. Some of these individuals preceded Cai Yu Ming while some came a little later (after Cai). Others were actually Cai's contemporaries.

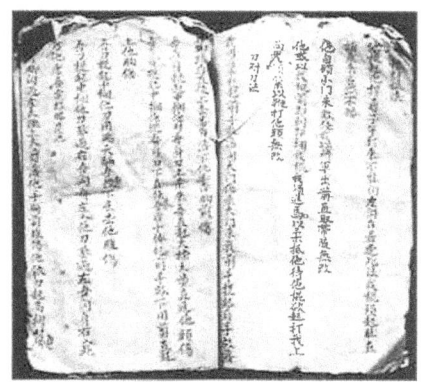

Ancient fist manual (two pages describing technical instruction)

In the sixth year of the Guanxu Period of the Qing Dynasty Master Huang Pei Song came first in the imperial examinations for military personnel and went on to establish a martial arts school which he named, "Zhuangyuan Guan." This was in his hometown where he taught his quanfa skills. His hometown was in Quanzhou — at a location called Dong Shan Pu (East Mountain Port) in Liudu Village, Nan'an County, Quanzhou City.

Master Zhuang Zhan lived within the western quarter of Quanzhou City. His disciple was Lu Yan Qiu who went on to found the Guang Han (Gong Han) Guoshu Guan ("National Art School") in Manila (Philippines). Master Lu Yan Qiu taught Lu Qing Hui and then Lu Si Ming who both went on to become masters in their own right. The three generations of the Lu Family taught, altogether, over ten thousand students during a seven-decade period. When the Japanese troops invaded the Philippines the teachers and students from this school fought vigorously which resulted in a great number of them giving their lives in order to protect their home. This has duly been recorded in a number of history books.

Master Wei Xi Nong taught Wu Dong Liang and Wei Guo Qi (nicknamed Mu Qi) amongst a multitude of others and from cities as well as villages. In fact, many came from afar in order to learn from him! During the 1930s Master Wei Guo Qi traveled southwards to Indonesia taking with him his students Dai Huo Yan and Cai Shui Ying. There they taught martial arts at the Ji'ao She school as well as at the San Sheng Guoshu Guan in Sishui City (in Indonesia) where martial arts are taught even now. Mr. Lin

All female demonstration of Taizuquan

Shao, who was a successful candidate within the highest of all the imperial examinations, wrote two lines to (or about) Master Lin Xian: "In his whole life he never displayed a lack of heroic spirit while everywhere he teaches his unique skills to everybody."

Master Lin Xian, whose quanfa skills were taught to him by his family, passed on his family heritage to his student, Xu Jin Dong (Chee Kim Thong) who then went on to teach quanfa in Malaysia, the United Kingdom, Ireland, and the USA as well as a number of other locations. In this way the arts of Wuzuquan and Taizuquan have been promoted extensively and globally. Needless to say, therefore, that the prospect of Quanzhou *quanguan* (Quanzhou-based quanfa schools) is, "As flowers that blooms everywhere via various sects and various families."

Two events that occurred last century were as follows:

In June 1932, when the 19th Route Army entered Quanzhou City, they together founded the Quanzhou National Art General School Headquarters as well as two more branches of this group. The headmaster of the General School was Master Lü Peng Qi while the instructors were Yao Jin Shi (a student of Master Wei Guo Qi), Lin Guo Zhi (a student of He Chu Xian) and Chen Wei Cheng. The "Head" of the Wenling branch school was my late teacher, Master Dai Huo Yan, while the "Head" of the Fumei branch school was Master Lin Tian En (the son of Master Lin Jiu Ru).

Each sect interacted closely with each other and trained a group of masters that became the hardcore of the quanfa society after the establishment of the PRC (the People's Republic of China) including Master Zhou Zhi Qiang and Master Huang Qing Jiang. There were others. In the meantime, the Fumei branch invited a quanfa master from Xin'an Village (of the Haichang District in Xiamen) to teach Taizuquan to their students while the Wenling branch added the Crane Fist style (hequan) as one more subject for the students to learn.

The other event took place in May 1961. In accordance with the appeal from the National Physical Education Committee that China's traditional martial arts should be preserved and promoted, the Quanzhou government organized and founded the Amateur Martial Arts Studies Group and recommended (and so went on to assign) Master Zhuang Zi Chen as the "Head" of this group while Master Dai Huo Yan was appointed "Deputy Head."

Altogether there were twelve Taizuquan (Wuzuquan) masters amongst the teachers including Chen Chao Shun, Lin Chun Lai and Su Zai Fu. This group accepted members of the general public as students while also sent teachers to train students within the urban and suburban areas as well as in Jinjiang.[11] However, this group was disbanded at the beginning of the Cultural Revolution (in 1966). Up until that point in time this group had trained more than one thousand students and had also made extraordinary contributions to Quanzhou martial arts that were subsequently carried on — in spite of the group's forced closure — thus allowing for future development in years and decades to come.

As I have mentioned earlier, the transmissions of Wuzuquan also include a sect that comprises Buddhist monks. When Master Taixu (a monk) visited Quanzhou, he wrote, "Shuangquantie Luohan Shimu Laonong Chan" meaning "Double Fists Iron Arhat Ten Mu Old Farmer Buddhist Monk."[12] Each and every temple in Quanzhou continued martial arts training as a tradition.

China Central TV Station Martial World Assembly/Conference where the first performance is Wuzuquan

During the first year of the Jingyan period (of the Southern Song Dynasty), monks from the Quanzhou Shaolin Temples fought against the Mongolian troops that had journeyed southwards and into the east part of the city. This was a well-known historic event and was recorded in a book where it states that, "A thousand monks defended the Yuan government" (the Yuan government having been established by the Mongolians after they had invaded China). During the Yuan Dynasty there were multitudes of military monks gathering at the

Kaiyuan Temple (in Quanzhou) and this was recorded by Monk She Da Gui by way of his poetry.

In the book, *Fujian General History*, it states that a monk named Seng Ding Yin (from Quanzhou and who lived toward the end of the Ming Dynasty) possessed, "mastery of Shaolinquan and the cudgel method and taught his martial techniques to hundreds of disciples."

Mr. Gan De Yuan of Malaysia stated in a book (authored by someone else and titled, *The Simplified History of Taizuquan*), that the origin of this style of quanfa was practiced by his uncle, Li Jun Ren. Therein it states that during the reign of Emperor Yong Zheng (from the Qing Dynasty) there was a royal descendant from the Ming Dynasty who withdrew from society to live on Fengshan (Phoenix Mountain, which is commonly known as Dongyue Shan, o Dongyue Mountain) which was located outside the east gate of Quanzhou City. Hiding away his family the descendant renounced his given name and assumed the name "Monk Wuxin" (Compassionate Heart) and taught Taizuquan within Dongchansi (East Chan Temple) which is now the present day Quanzhou Shaolin temple.

This so-called "royal descendant from the Ming Dynasty" mentioned within this book must be one of the royal descendants that "escaped to Fujian province to join General Zhong Cheng Gong at the end of the Ming Dynasty" (to directly quote this book). The very fact that this book makes reference to Taizuquan renders this statement even more credulous.

Quanzhou's Chongfusi (Worship Blessings Temple) became world famous as a result of a man who called himself, Monk Miaoyue. A resident of this temple during the 1920s, Monk Miaoyue was highly skilled in Tieshazhang (Iron Sand Palm).[13] Monk Miaoyue was also an expert in two Taizuquan forms (one being sanzhan or sam chien; "three battles"). Famous for his powerful fists which he sent out with a powerful and forceful sound, Monk Miaoyue's physical strength knew no equal! Monk Miaoyue had been taught his Taizuquan skills by Monk Zhishen and Monk Yanghua. Monk Miaoyue later passed on to Monk Yuan Zhen, and then Monk Chang Kai and Monk Chang Qing.

She Chang Kai[14] (Monk Chang Kai) was once appointed "Head" of the Singapore Buddhism General Association as well as the "Head" of the National Arts General Association. He was also an honorable "Buddhist Fist Doctor. He was an honoured and well-respected figure within the fields of Buddhist meditation, quanfa, and traditional Chinese medicine.

Within Chongfu Temple there are preserved three volumes of Taizuquan which serve as manuals. During the Culture Revolution (1966–1976) Chongfu Temple was transformed into a factory resulting in the dismissal of the monks—so the monks and their quanfa "grew old and withered." At the end of the 1970s I was invited by Monk She Chang Qing (Monk Chang Qing) to train the monks at the temple who fell ill at the time, which then lasted for the next three years.

In 1990 International Wuzuquan Fellowship General Assembly/conference founded in Quanzhou

There we trained regularly and consistently, regardless of the weather, until the time came when I had to stop teaching owing to my obligations as a government employee. Currently, of the monks I had taught, these include the present abbot, She Chang Ding (from the Quanzhou Shaolin Temple, as well as other senior martial monks from Chongfu Temple (in Quanzhou), Nantai Yan (southern platform cliff), Bailudong (White Deer Cave) from Xiamen City, Chongfu Temple (in the Philippines), and Xingyuansi (Character and Will Temple) which is also in the Philippines. But there were, of course, more! Even though Taizuquan has suffered over the decades and generations it is no longer floundering but, on the contrary, it is flourishing!

Taizuquan has developed over centuries while its history and its origins have also been preserved (survived through documentation and oral transmission). Chinese martial arts philosophy maintains that, "One thousand types of quanfa follow the same theory" and "One thousand sects follow the same path," both of which suggests a containment and an harmonious blending within the martial arts world.

Quanzhou Taizuquan has absorbed the nutrition from Dazuquan, Luohanquan, Xingzhequan, Baihequan and more, while elements (forms) from other disciplines (quanfa) have been added and adapted to fit into the framework of Taizuquan.

For such a long time now Taizuquan has maintained the dominant position amid the Quanzhou City martial arts society and thus has influenced other quanfa styles within this area. This is reflected through the fact that the sanzhan (sam chien) concept has become the very core of other southern shaolin-derived fist manuals where essential theories run very much parallel.

Another quanfa manual I have encountered during the course of my research is a six-volume work focusing upon Yongchun White Crane written, edited and published by Master Su Ying Han—one of the representatives specializing in Yongchun Baihequan.

Within this work Master Su states that there are, "multitudes of methods that have evolved up until now and since the days of Master Gui Gu Zi, Luohanquan, and Taizuquan." Master Su continues, "and it was his fist art that made Emperor Song Taizu a hero of distinction in battles and then emperor of the country." Regarding hand-to-hand combat Song Taizu says that one's "head should be held as if wearing a millstone, the shoulders should be as if lifting a thousand *jin*15 and the hands as if hitting stone walls." In defining wuzuquan (Five Ancestor Fist), firstly there is the Damo (Bodhidharma) which teaches the "fa" (method) then secondly there is the Taizu which teaches "shi" (forms). Thirdly, there is the "Xingzhe" (the itinerant monk) which teaches the "tao" (the Way) and fourthly there is the Luohan (the monk or arhat) which teaches "xing" (shape/shapes).

Comparing the techniques between Baihequan and Taizuquan, and quoting the "ershisishi" (twenty-four forms) from Taizuquan, it is not completely impossible to assume that Baihequan might have come from Taizuquan, which sounds more believable than the fairy tale which says how Fangzhonggong (father of Fang Qi Niang, the founder of Baihequan) asked the celestial crane to teach his daughter.

Another book I have encountered is *Fujian Shaolinquan* where the author speaks of a style of Taizuquan called "hequan" within hequan (crane fist) sects.

In 1979 I visited Yongchun County (governed by Quanzhou City) where I initiated and founded a wushu association. In the meantime I involved myself in attempts to smooth out contradictions between the original Baihequan (White Crane Fist) and hard-style Taizuquan.

As these two sects were both considered "Crane Sect" kungfu styles, differentiations had to be made in order to remove any current confusion (of that time) and avoid any future confusion and so it was then that disagreements in opinion surfaced for, very clearly, reflections of and from Taizuquan were apparent in all shapes and characteristics.

Influences from Taizuquan have also been recognized within Japanese *kongshoudao* (karate-do). The word *kongshou* (empty hand) was originally from Quanzhou where the term was *kongshouquan* (empty hand fist).

During the Ming Dynasty the government established a building called "Laiyuanyi" (meaning "*coming from far away*-post" or "a post built to accommodate those from overseas") in Quanzhou City which was also referred to as Liuqiuguan (liuqiu stadium).[16] This was used to accommodate messengers and business travelers.

In 1393 Fujian province sent thirty-six families[17] to the Liugiu islands in order to spread their trades and teach their skills to the Liugui people. Therefore and inevitably Quanzhou quanfa was introduced to the Liugiu people that, again inevitably, provided the stimulus, formula and template for both Okinawan karate and, later, Japanese karate.

In 1990 I visited Japan where I led a delegation of Quanzhou quanfaren (kung-fu practitioners). During our visit a performance was arranged where we saw demonstrated both Chinese and Okinawan martial arts by more than four hundred skilled and senior practitioners. Here, then, did we observe the Goju-ryu style of karate-do and the Uechi-ryu style of karate-do style (in Chinese: Shangdiliu, translator's note) where, by way of their demonstrations, it was clear that their own sanzhan exercise as well as their own horse stance had been handed down from Taizuquan or Baihequan.

As a result of our visit to Okinawa a karate group called Zhengdaoguan and another karate group called Gangbohui visited Quanzhou upon numerous occasions for they were convinced that the origin of their style was from within Quanzhou City. In an article written by Mr. Yong Chuan Xing Shen, the Head of Chongshengdao (Okinawa) Kongshoudao (Karate) Ancient Martial Union, Mr. Yong Chuan Xing Shen states that kongshoudao (karate) and Quanzhou nanquan (southern fist/nanquanfa) are from the same origin.

In 1989 Master Lu Qing Hui, the Head of the Kong Han National Art School in the Philippines,[18] proposed that an International Southern Shaolin Wuzuquan Fellowship Association be established. At that time I was visiting the Philippines with the Quanzhou Wushu Delegation during which I attended the Southeast Asia Southern Shaolin Fist performance which was hosted by the Kong Han National Art School. Together with the help of a number of celebrated wushu masters and grandmasters including Master Xu Jin Dong (Chee Kim Thong) from Kuala Lumpur who was the grandmaster of the Xu Jin Dong Athletic Association (jianshenshe), Master Ye Qing Hai (Yap Qing Hai) of the Malaysia Wushu General Association, Master Chen Jia Hong of the Philippines' Mingqian National Art School, Master Xu Nai Jing from the Singapore Star Wushu Institute, and Master Lu Shao Zhun from Indonesia's Lu Shao Zhun National Art School, we were able to establish such an Association that was Master Lu's dream!

The following year (1990), representatives from six countries arrived in Quanzhou and so the International Southern Shaolin Wuzuquan Fellowship Association was officially established. Ever since that year there has been an annual meeting held in Quanzhou where exchanges and communications amidst various quanfa schools has been the main agenda.

The suggested Chairmen for those meeting have been Master Lu Qing Hui, Grandmaster Ye Qing Hai, Grandmaster Xu Jin Dong, Li Zhi Yuan, Han Jin Yuan, and myself. Besides the earlier-mentioned countries, individuals from more and more nations have come to join our association over the past twenty years and more. These nations include the UK, the USA, Iceland, Ireland, Finland, Austria, France, Switzerland, Italy, Sweden, Norway, Canada, Burma, Russia, Egypt, Iraq, Germany, Japan, South Africa and New Zealand. The total number of participating geographical regions soon exceeded thirty including areas more "local" to Quanzhou such as Hong Kong, Macau and Taiwan. Those attending these regular meetings were mainly from the Wuzuquan school as well as the successors of Taizuquan. With practitioners of all skin-tones, pigmentations and native tongues sharing the same stage as they practiced their common ground — Quanzhou quanfa — everyone very soon realized that such classical and traditional martial arts as Quanzhou Wuzuquan and Quanzhou Taizuquan had, indeed, become an international concern — with a genuine and sincere appreciation from all corners of, and directions within, the globe. By seeing individuals from all races perform quanfa it is all-too-clear to see Quanzhou quanfa has become an international fist-art!

CHAPTER 2

THE SYSTEM OF TAIZUQUAN

As Quanzhou Taizuquan underwent development and refinement it experienced hardship along the way (what with Quanzhou's political climate of that time); but as a result of this came a positive outcome for it gradually forged into its own complete and unique quanfa system. Possessing all the key elements of a genuine style of martial arts Taizuquan, like other quanfa systems, utilized the concept of *siji* (four attacks) as its core. This comprised of strikes, kicks, throws and capture skills specializing in *duanda* (short strikes). Taizuquan was fast and fierce yet very much controlled and full of masculine beauty. Its foot techniques were low, heavy and concise while its use of weaponry embraced both long and short weapons where its purpose was chiefly aimed at battlefield-combat situations. Long weapons were used for short-range combat purposes while the short weapons were employed for long-range combat situations with direct attack and defense strategies devoid of all impracticalities and cosmetic postures.

Double Thrust

Within Taijiquan (tai chi) there is a strategy called *tuishou* ("pushing hands") whereas within Taizuquan there is a technique called *juji* which is a "lifting" technique. Northern-style Chinese martial arts say that kung-fu training is to, "build up tendons, bones and skin for outside and to build up breathing for inside," while Quanzhou Taizuquan (which is a southern-style Chinese martial art) can be both hardness and softness (to strengthen both outside and inside) with unique ways employed for both toughening exercise (*yinggong*) and internal exercise (*neigong*).

Let us now look at five key sections of Quanzhou Taizuquan training, namely: The Empty Fist, Weaponry, Paired-Practice, Lifting techniques, and then the External and Internal exercises.

SECTION 1: EMPTY FIST (KONG QUAN)

The empty hand forms are called *kongquan* ("empty fist"). The Quanzhou Taizuquan kongquan forms total at around one hundred while an exact figure is beyond calculation. But this is the count from across a number of Taizuquan sects. The basic kongquan forms are called Mianqianquan ("Front Facing Fist") and this refers to the basic forms that are shared by, and therefore common to, all the various Taizuquan sects. Of these there are no more than ten.[1]

Sitting Joint

In the past, martial arts schools have often offered four months of training in order to reach the first level, and then the students would be eligible to graduate. During this four-month training period the students would have been taught five or six forms such as the primary form called Sanzhan, then the "Twenty Punches" form (Ershiquan)', the Dazhan (Large Battle) form, the Dajiao (the "Striking and Wrestling" form), the Shizi (Character Ten) form,[2] the Shuangsui ("Double Pacifying") form, and the Zhantou ("Head Battle") form. This meant that by now the student would have learnt enough forms to have built-up a fair degree of physical strength whist also coming to understand martial virtues.

If a student had no interest in continuing to the second level the teacher would focus upon those that did and so would teach them some of the more complicated forms and even, perhaps, some weaponry such as the broadsword or the cudgel. This was called fangquantao ("to let go of the fist"). At the same time the students would be introduced to some *duilian* (paired practice or "two-man" forms).

Many of these quanguan ("fist schools") were where the teachers actually lived (effectively, their homes) and were thus called nianguan ("annual school"). Here, students were trained more systematically and exclusively.

Over the years I have collected a great number of quanfa instruction manuals including one book called, *Nan Taizu Quanpu* ("Southern Taizu Fist Instruction Book") which teaches fifty-three forms. Another book, titled *Shaolin Taizu Quanfa* ("Shaolin

Taizu Fist Method"), is preserved within Chongfusi (Chongfu Temple) in Quanzhou and this manual teaches fifty-four forms. Yet another publication, *Taizu Nanquan Jishou Taolu* ("Taizu Southern Fist Hand Technique Forms"), written by a Master Su Zai Fu, teaches one hundred and one forms.

In 1968 my late teacher, Master Dai Huo Yan, handed me his manuscript titled, *Taizu Quanpu* ("Taizu Fist Instruction Book") which was

Swallow

prefaced jointly by masters Li Tai Zhou and Fu Jin Xing and attributed by Master She Rui Yao. This book teaches sixty-seven forms.

For the most part these forms (taolu) share the same name and the same content and this only goes to illustrate the extreme stability of Quanzhou Taizuquan throughout the decades, if not centuries. My late teacher, Master Dai Huo Yan, also highlighted nineteen of the sixty-seven taolu from the book which, I was informed later by my late teacher, were taught to him by the late Master Wei Guo Qi towards the end of the Qing Dynasty and during the early years of the Republic of China (1912–1949). These are all recorded without any degree of change at all! These nineteen forms are as follows:

- Sanzhan (Three Battles)
- Ershiquan (Twenty Punches)
- Dataozhan (Large Form/Frame Battle)
- Shizi (Character Ten)
- Dajiao (Four Corners)
- Duizhuang (Paired Practice atop Stumps
- Shuangsui Toujie (Head Joint)
- Sijie (Four Joints)
- Disha (Underground Beings)
- Zhantou (Occupying Head)
- Liancheng (Connected Cities)

- Niebu (Opposite Steps)
- Qingfeng (Refreshing Breeze)
- Qianzida (One Thousand Character Strike)
- Sanjiaoyao (Three Corner Shaking)
- Bagua (Eight Diagrams)
- Simen Tiaoqie (Four Doors, Raising and Chopping)
- Baihe Luodi (White Crane Falls to the Ground)

One century later and these forms are still popular and taught everywhere throughout Quanzhou.

The forms within Quanzhou Taizuquan are formed by way of *jishou* (technical/skilled hand techniques), which are both short in delivery and highly practical. Generally speaking, one form will include twenty to thirty jishou (hand techniques or hand movements) although some forms — medium-length forms — will contain fifty to sixty or even seventy to eighty jishou. Large-size forms will include up to or beyond one hundred jishou. But this is unusual yet there is one form — called doudi — that has over one hundred and forty jishou ("technical hands").

Spit

Taizuquan emphasizes force and skill while values hardness over a short-distance and close-quarter strikes. Along with this goes essential intensity and ferocity by way of the hands and the voice — that is to say, a shout that is not dissimilar to the *kiai* (spirit shout) of karate. There is a saying in Quanzhou that describes this: "The fist comes with wind and laugher but without rolling" (*quantou daifeng wugunxiao*). Here the hand and foot techniques are all centered round attack or defense with the strength coming from heavy and ruthless power! Only short taolu can ensure that strength be exerted in totality which is why long forms are, indeed, rare within Taizuquan.

Jishou (technical hands) includes shouji (hand techniques) and jiaoji (foot techniques). Shouji includes single-hand long techniques, double-handed long techniques, single-hand short techniques and double-handed short techniques. These involve attacks, defenses and "dissolves" combined with strikes. Jishou operate within strict boundaries of movement which can be categorized into five essential areas of attack and defense: the upper, middle and lower boundaries and then areas to the left and the areas to the right. The upper boundary is the eyebrows while the lower boundary is the private parts; the left and right boundaries are the shoulders and cartilage areas while the middle boundary is the arms. While guarding one's middle boundary the arms are bent at the elbows while the upper limb joints (the shoulders, elbows and wrists) are sunk.

As short-hand, close-quarter techniques exert crisp strength, longer range hand techniques involve twisting and spiraling actions.[3] While the front hand is used to attack (in much the same way as one would use a halberd) the other hand, being behind, is there to protect (as one would with a shield). The interaction between the hard and the soft and the swallowing and the spitting is managed and controlled through the waist and shoulders, the dissolving and the expanding.

The use of the hand (that is to say, hands)[4] takes on many formats called "methods." These include the piercing method, capturing method, picking method, opening method, closing method, chopping method, cutting method, peeling method, blocking method, holding method, supporting method, eating method, holding method, dashing method, casting method, joint method, lopping method, bouncing method, scratching method, perching method, clicking method, thrusting method, rubbing method, shearing method, breaking method, whipping method, carrying method, poking method, shaking method, lifting method, stroking method, mining method, freeing method, locking method, scooping method, grasping method, binding method, wrapping method, holding method, clawing method, pressing method, snapping method and leaning method. Other "methods" do exist! Each of these methods involve different techniques. In summary, then, I estimate there are no less than four hundred techniques within Quanzhou Taizuquan. There are less foot techniques within shouji.

Taizuquan considers "a starting foot with a half empty side." The foot techniques include sweeping, tripping, kicking, shooting, stamping, bending, and shoveling as well as knee method, bending method, and falling-upon-the-ground method. The Starting

Foot often employs the half-moon kick (*banyueti*) which is also known as, "bad horse, one step kick." This technique can prove severely damaging to the opponent.

Taolu are organized using the hand method as one's center in accordance with the demands of attack and defense and forward actions and backward actions as well as switching and rearranging jishou. The most outstanding characteristics is that jishou does not need transitional movement because one technique follows another as if they are a series of links in a chain, unlike the long-fist method. Connecting the six gates — between top and bottom, left and right, front and back — is effected within the area a bull needs in order to lie down! Unlike some quanfa systems — where one is required to remember the zhaoshi (named movement) and so years are vital in order to learn the essence — Quanzhou Taizuquan can be learnt in a relatively short(er) length of time.

The large number of Taizuquan xing (forms) has made it virtually impossible for anyone to practice all of them — even for the professional practitioner. Yet some masters (grandmasters, especially) practice just one or two taolu (forms) such has their level of comprehension taken them down (along) that path!

If one trains in taolu and takes them to a very high level during the course of one's life then one's strength and technique will be well above average. If one is to train widely in various taolu then although he becomes more understanding and knowledgeable (and this is not to be criticized), they become too much of a mouthful and so they become "too much making it impossible to chew" which is like "walking rigidly which makes it impossible to have good steps." Rather than practicing one thousand zhaoshi (taolu) and thus becoming a master of none of them, one would do better by training just the one zhaoshi thus taking that one form to the level of perfection.

I was once told by my late father that Master Huang Yang Xing (who was small and thin and weighed no more than fifty kilograms) only trained his sanzhan but he practiced this every day. One day, when he was attending a banquet, the host urged him to sit at the banquet table. He was modest and refused and so, instead, sat upon a bench. Along came several men to move him but all failed to do so. Rather, he sat himself still and stable which rendered himself immovable which dumbfounded everyone! So, sanzhan was his chosen form while the well-known monk, Miaoyue, was expert in Taizuquan's shizi form.

My own late teacher, Master Lin Qi Yan, was an expert in the "White Ape Emerging from the Cave" form while the monk, She Chang Qing, is expert in the form called "Six Steps Seated Lotus." Master Wu Xu Xiao is expert in the "Triangular (Three Corner) Shaking" form just as Zhang Tie Long is expert in "Shuang Sui," Lin Qing Tan is expert in "Twin Birds Tumbling to the Ground," Wu Jing is expert in Qing Feng ("Refreshing Breeze") and Lin Chun Lai is expert in the "Five Stomach Occupying Head" form. They have all become famous for achieving mastery in their own right having mastered one form.

Taizuguan

SECTION 2: WEAPONRY (JIASI)

Jiasi (also referred to as *qixie*), is the common name for weaponry within Quanzhou quanfa circles. The single weapons of Quanzhou Taizuquan include the cudgel, spear, sword, knife, rake and spade. Other lesser-known single weapons include the zhanmadao (horse-cutting sword), the razor clam shell, the iron ruler, the bill-hook, the guandao (crescent knife), the fangtianji (an ancient bronze weapon which is a combination of the spear and the so-called axe-dagger), the kaishanfu (mountain-splitting axe), the sanjiegun (three-sectioned cudgel) and the teng-paidao (shield-knife). Amongst the double weapons within Quanzhou Taizuquan are the shuangdao (double blade), the shuangjian (double sword), the shuangbian (double whip), the shuangjian (double truncheon),[5] the liugong-guai (cudgel), the yuefu (moon axe) and the shuangbishou (double daggers). There are also some double weapons created from everyday practical life including the shoulder pole, the bench, the hoe and the umbrella.

Taizuguan

The Quangun (fist cudgel) is the origin of all Chinese martial arts. The variety of weapons employed within Taizuquan is based upon Quangun. Therefore one must

Taizuqiang (spear)

Shuangjian (double truncheon)

first learn the fist art then the cudgel method and then — and only then — other weapons. The weapons style methodology is the same as for the empty fist, particular in respect of "hard strength and straightforward attack" devoid of impractical and complicated postures. When it comes to the use of the body, the waist and the horse stance there is very little difference between the empty fist Taizu practice and the weapons practice of Taizuquan except for the more frequent use of *buding, buba ma* (neither the "T-shape horse" nor the "8-shape horse") and the *gongjianma* ("bow and arrow horse") as well as the "sideways facing enemy" stance.

As it is with Taizuquan's empty fist, so it is with regards to its weaponry — both require every movement to be forceful and loud and with the hands co-operating with and coordinating with the feet — fierceful and solid. The taolu for both short weapons and long weapons are short except for the cudgel. In general there are no more than two or three taolu per weapon, four or five at the very most. However, the taolu are short while each weapon has its own uniqueness and characteristic techniques. This, together with courage, wisdom and swiftness is enough to triumph over the enemy! For example, the bill-hook with its method of shooting, pecking, hooking and cutting; the broad blade with its chopping, splitting, lopping, blocking and slitting; the spear with its method jabbing, blocking, stirring and brushing; and the whip-truncheon with its splitting, sweeping, seizing, cutting, wringing and slapping. These weapons may not possess a huge array of movements but they are all practical. By way of solo practice and paired practice one can become skilled enough to be fast, fierce and unpredictable.

Mr. Ling Yang Zao of the Ming dynasty states in his book, *Li Shao Bian*, that individuals from Zhangzhou City and Quanzhou City are well-trained in the spear and in the cane-shield and sword (where the cane-shield and sword hail from a military background). Mr. Lin Xing Zhu, who was born in Quanzhou city during the Qing dynasty, once led three thousand soldiers with cane-shield weaponry and so (thus) defeated the Russian Czar troops. This skill is preserved within Taizuquan and requires one to be equipped with the cane-shield held in the left hand and a sword in the right. Each movement is designed for out-and-out warfare. The cane shield, like a proper shield, can be used to cover or to crash so one can stand, roll and dive with it in hand while fighting the enemy with the sword — picking, chopping, piercing and slicing at lightning speed.

The most well-known weapons of Quanzhou Taizuquan are the cudgel and the rake both of which exert "hard strength and straightforward attack." The cudgel evolved from the *shu*, an ancient weaponry made from bamboo. In the book, *Zhou Li*, it states that the shu is just like a stick and it is made from a hard and durable wood while in the book, *She Ming, She Bing*, it states that the shu is approximately four meters long, is without a blade, and was originally used in carriage battles. In Quanzhou, the cudgel is also called the *chui*, meaning a mallet. Taizuquan still preserves the four-meter cudgel method. Master Cai Xian Qin of the Huanghan National art school, is highly-skilled in the use of this weapon. At the age of eighty he could still "send strength through to reach the end of the cudgel."

Taizujian (sword)

Taizu Single Blade

The most commonly seen cudgels include the *qimei* (meaning "level with one's eyebrows"), the *jiuchi* (a cudgel of some nine *chi* in length), the *qichi* (measuring seven chi) and the *shuangtou* cudgel (shuangtou meaning "double heads"). In his book, *Jian Jing* ("Sword Manual") Master Yu Da You states, "If one is a master of the cudgel he will be good in the use of other weapons for they all originate from the cudgel." In 1534, Master Yu Da You ventured southwards to the Quanzhou Shaolin Temple where he watched the monks performing the cudgel method. He then made the comment, "This temple is well-versed in and well-known for its sword method which is a result that the truth is lost after the message being passed among people." Then he chose two monks amongst the monks who followed him and so joined the ranks. The temple taught the Yugong Cudgel method which had not changed since it had been recorded in the book of Jianjing and was also the same as the Taizugun (the Taizu staff or pole) method which is still popular today in Quanzhou City. One of the maxims of the Yugong Cudgel was (is), "With each step forward goes a direct attack." Master Yu Da You summarized the cudgel method by way of this rhyme:

> *Ying and Yang is to be transformed; both hands are to be straight.*
> *Front foot is to be bent; the back foot is to be straight.*
> *With every strike and every tear, exert strength throughout the entire body.*
> *Every step is to be forward, never encounter an opponent.*

Another rhyme states:

> *Hard strength is to be exerted before the force from the enemy,*
> *Soft strength is to be exerted after the force from the enemy,*
> *One is to wait calmly when the enemy is busy*
> *And perceive the enemy's method and know how to deal with the attack.*

Master Yu Da You has collected and edited one hundred and seventy techniques from the Cudgel Method including attacking, defending, blocking and dissolving. These are the true tactics from Master Yu Da You which he had amassed during his decades of military experience which includes troop-training and the use of military force.

These tactics were praised by another Chinese national hero — a master named Qi Ji Guang who commented upon them saying that they were, "the most wondrous secrets of all time," while Master He Liang Chen said, "The secrets of the cudgel are recorded in detail within the book, *Jiang Jing*." Mr. Wu Shu Zhi, the author *Shoubilu* ("The Book of Arms") pointed out that, "The cudgel method includes the basic movement 'strike and tear' where the strike is to touch the floor and the tear is to go over the head." Appearing somewhat trite and insignificant — as if farmers were simply attending to their field — it was through long-term training that mastery of the cudgel and the correct use of "strike and tear" proved supreme over and above all other shaolin skills.

Liugong Guai (old man Liu's crutch)

The Quanzhou Taizuquan cudgel method contains more than a dozen forms which, accumulatively, involve the highest number of techniques within all the weaponry handed down from ancient times. These movements include picking, arrowing, blocking, rolling, hanging, knocking, shaving, shearing, driving, piercing and tearing although this list is no exhaustive. The method and the method stated within the book, *Jian Jing*, descend from one continuous line. The military tactics proposed within this book include: "assuming advantage over the intention of the opponent", "making use of the strength of the opponent" and "the work of a high order is to fall upon, while the work of low order is to rise above." Additionally, "make a sound and then step forward, and step forward and then make a sound," "catch up with continuous footsteps" and "straight rising, straight falling, and facing the opponent." Even today practitioners still follow these tactics and see them as standard rules.

Tiger Fork

During his visit to my home, Master He Shan Fa of Tainan (a city in south Taiwan) demonstrated the Taizuquan cudgel which had been introduced from Quanzhou City to Taiwan during Emperor Qianlong's reign during the Qing Dynasty. Later on and at our request he sent me a video-tape which featured the "three steps pressing method," the "closing gate blocking method" and the "seven steps batting method" as well as others. Those forms are all very short while the techniques are similar to those recorded within the book, *Jian Ying*.

The rake also has its own characteristics while its method of usage is similar to that of the cudgel. Master Chen Zong in his book, *Shaolin Cudgel Method Ancestries*, states that, "Each weapon has its own wonderful use however each body and foot method is not beyond the method from that of the cudgel." Therefore a master of cudgel is also able to handle a rake although the rake does include techniques that are unique unto itself. Master Yu Da You promoted the rake as an important weapon of military combat and recorded in his book, *Jian Jing*, instructions as to how to use the rake by way of the rhyme:

> **The rear hand performs the work while the whole body exerts strength.**
> **During movement the top end of the rake is stabilized**
> **although one strike is not enough for one must also strike, shear and dig.**

The essence of the rake is no different from that of the cudgel; the most basic foot method is, "small, straight, equal, small tilting, big tilting and pressing."

In short, the most important aspect to keep in-mind when training with weapons is that each and every solid step has to work in conjunction with each and every hand motion

Fork versus stick

Single blade versus spear

and each and every foot movement. But one also has to work with softness as well as with hardness while understanding that one should meet strong attacks with a side-stepping strategy. Understand the substantial by first knowing the insubstantial. Enter wherever you see space and The Void. Subdue movement with stillness, assertively defend while waiting for the opportune time to instigate an attack. In order to defend effectively and attack (or counter-attack) effectively one must seize the right moment after the opponent has sent out his strength and before he has sent out his next bout of strength. In this way one must send forth one's own strength, sending it into the opponent before he has time to reach you with his skill. When equipped with long weapons one's front hand must be 50% yin and one's back hand 50% yang. One's legs and waist must "sink" as strength is mustered within the entire body so that it is "connected."

Taizuquan's long weapons are held at one's left side (of the body) with the right hand in front with the hand upside down clamped inwardly. This is not the way of the northern shaolin styles which employs a very different strategy all of its own.

SECTION 3: DUIDA AND JUJI

(Paired Practice and Lifting Method)

All taolu within Taizuquan can also be practiced in pairs usually by way of *duitao* (paired taolu) which we Quanzhou people call *duida* — a paired practice where the focus is upon simulated combat developing one's fighting spirit through attacks and strikes.

Taizuquan organizes taolu according to six "gates" — front, back, left, right, top and bottom. Each step is combined with one technique. The dissolving technique has summarized secret tricks as "straight dissolving against the horizontal attack, horizontal dissolving against straight attack, separate dissolving against combined attack, and single dissolving against double attack." Then there are captures dissolving struggles, double captures dissolving double vertical fist, rubbing dissolving whipping, openings dissolving triangular tiger, and more. These tricks have since become routines. Therefore as long as upper and lower techniques cooperate well, paired striking/practicing within one taolu can be completed.

The most well-known forms within Quanzhou Taizuquan are the "Three Battles," "Twenty Punches," "Hitting the Corners," "Character Ten," and "Double Peace," all of which can be performed and practiced in a complete set. Of those handed down by way of ancient fist manuals, with the exception of the "Six Gates Eight Method," which records pair practicing techniques as upper techniques and lower techniques, the rest have not recorded the empty fist pair practicing taolu.

The weapons forms are especially designed for paired practice. For example, the blade and stick versus the spear, Green Dragon broadsword versus spear, Tiger Fork versus Vine Shield Blade, the Crown Princess Hand Double Blade versus Cudgel, the Long Stick versus Long Stick, and the Horse-Cutting Sword versus the Mountain Trident. There is also an empty-hand versus blade form as well as a one-against-two form such as the mountain fork versus the seven chi cudgel and chopping horse blade. Such forms are normally short and intense with vivid attack and defense which are beautiful to watch, are full of strength, and very powerful.

Fist training must involve paired practice so that one can understand the meaning of the technical hand relating to attack and defense. At the same time, fighting each other can test the body method, teach the importance of eye-contact, train the waist, increase one's strength and so gain power and develop one's horse. He who trains by way of paired practice develops fast reactions and maximizes endurance.

There is a unique concept within Taizuquan called lifting (juji) although it is also referred to as combat technique (geji). It is a two-man exercise and is divided into two parts: long lifting and short lifting. When it comes to long lifting, both contenders first stabilize themselves into a horse stance then they both lift up their right arm and seize each other by the wrist and simultaneously exert strength. Whosoever pulls down the

Coil Five Branches

arm of the opponent wins. The short lift, meanwhile, is a contest where both sides seize the joint at the philtrum and lean upon each other which uses a sealing, sawing and sinking motion and whoever seizes and immobilizes the opponent wins. This form of lifting tests not only strength from one's feet and the horse stance, but also the hands. But much more than this, this is about spitting, swallowing, floating and sinking and the transformation between yin and yang and the conversion from hardness to softness. It is also a wonderful exercise for the legs, waist, knees, crotch, head, heart, eyes; Indeed, the entire body. In some ways, lifting is about *dingbu* ("stabilizing steps") and tuishou (the "pushing hands" practice of Taijiquan), and so involves blocking and pressing, bringing forward and following through, converting between the empty and the solid, and also listening to strength and sensing strength. The difference is that the former carries both softness and hardness while the latter carries only looseness and softness.

In the past, when it has come to the fist techniques within competition, it was often called "lifting one technique," which was quite civilized. One documented event in particular was a lifting contest between Master Lin Jiu Ru and Master Cai Yu Ming (Chua Giok Beng). In in the book, *Wuzuquan Narration Summary* by Lu Wen Jun, it states that Lin repeatedly exerted strength but always failed, for each time Master Cai would dissolve Lin's strength and so defeated him through *baojie* (an "exposed joint") which is also known as "floating." As a result, Lin deeply admired Cai and so became Cai's student.

Lifting Technique

During the 1960s I observed Master Lin Chao Shun competing in a lifting exchange with another strong quanfa master. Master Lin exerted sinking and rubbing strength which not only led to his opponent losing his root but also broke his alignment and so he stood no chance in lifting or recovering from his over use of strength. At this time Master Lin was in his nineties and looked as if he could be blown over like a feather in the wind. However, when it came to this contest his entire body acted as an iron pillar filled with superhuman strength. If I had not seen this for myself I probably would not have believed it!

Lifting Technique

Quanzhou Taizuquan possesses other kinds of paired-practice exercises that simulate fighting. One example is "coiling" (*panji*). This involves poking, opening, closing, clus-

Lifting Technique

tering and capturing skills combined with a Changing Horse, a Returning Gate and a continuous exertion.

This represents the major hand techniques within Quanzhou Taizuquan. Both sides are required to generate strength by way of the breath while pitting hardness against hardness. The well-trained practitioner is able to exert power while continuing the exchange repeatedly thus amassing hundreds of movements without a pause. Frequent practice of these techniques will not only harden the skin and bones of the arms but also strengthen the body, waist, foot and horse.

Another example is "capturing and struggling." This can be practiced either from the horse stance or by sitting on a bench. In either case both practitioner dissolve punches by way of captures, hanging, holding, swallowing and spitting repeatedly. Yet another example is the practice of the fundamental form called Sanzhan ("three battles") which involves double thrusts and the sinking joint as well as swallowing and spitting all of which is soft strength although on can interplay between soft and hard. The sinking can combined with floating just as swallowing can be combined with spitting so that a greater depth of meaning can be extracted as one swallows and stretches one's waist and shoulders so as to maximize both speed and strength.

Capture and Release

Capture and Release

Nowadays, those who train fist techniques seldom choose to learn the lifting and the coiling. They don't understand that these two aspects of traditional training are the result of hundreds of years of experience and experimentation from past, if not countess, generations. These days, quanfa is often a matter of solo practice without the use of a partner whereas the lifting and the coiling takes one's training to newer and higher levels by way of receiving and reacting and through the perception and understanding of rooting and the various mutations of strength together with the enjoyment of the wonder and beauty of swallowing, spitting, floating and sinking together with the dissolving and the dodging while strengthening one's basics. From ancient times to the modern day there is no-one more skillful in combat and self-defense than he who trains by way of paired practice.

SECTION 4: NEI GONG, WAI GONG, AND CHUAN CHEN

(Training the Inside, Outside, and Cluster Formation)

Taizuquan is hard, vigorous and fast. However it is a prejudiced union if one only considers Taizuquan as a "hard" yang-based discipline while ignoring the vital aspect of softness (its yin-ness) and its inner meaning. Caring only for what we call the "outer family fist" (*waijiaquan*) while ignoring one's inner training (neigong) this can only lead to imbalanced training. In point of fact, Taizuquan proposes that hardness and softness support each other through the understanding and application of both the inner and the outer. Based upon closed-quarter combat, the hand techniques of Taizuquan require sinking the shoulders and seizing the joint while one's actual range of movement remains small. So, range of movement and economy of movement are two vital aspects of Taizuquan.

Stamping on the "center of the palace" (*zhong gong*), and pressing and leaning within a short distance one blocks hard and strikes hard. At the same time, however, there exists a great deal of hand techniques involving arcs and circles especially when it comes to swallowing, spitting, sinking and floating. Indeed, exerting strength and transforming one's breath, as well as "dissolving and dodging steps." All this reveals the essential soft side to Taizuquan.

Since the majority of Taizuquan's outer characteristics will be viewed as mere hardness the technical gate is required to be tight and intense while both fists and feet must be powerful using endurable receiving versus striking. While the outside exercises mostly focus upon the fingers, fists, palms, arms and feet — for example, training in *tieshazhang* ("iron grit/sand palm" training),[6] *yingzhuagong* ("eagle claw training"), *tiebigong* ("iron arm training"), *tietuigong* ("iron leg training"), *yizhichan* ("one finger meditation"), *erzhichan* ("two fingers meditation"). The most commonly practiced include *zhuajiuwong* ("seizing/catching/lifting the wine jar"), *chashadou* ("thrust sand

and beams"), *timuchong* ("kicking wood pile/poles/stumps"), *dashadai* ("strike sand bags"), *Juqiyongshi* ("lifting the qiyong stone"), beating the forearms and shank with bundled bamboo chop sticks, picking and attacking wood poles and the corner of a wall. Training methods do differ although they do follow the same rule which is processed in an orderly way, gradually and step-by-step. Among them is an exercise called *paoshisuo* ("throwing the stone padlock") which includes techniques such as holding, lifting, supporting, turning, throwing, pressing and carrying. Long-term training of this nature will build up strength in the fingers and the wrists, the waist and the horse, the breath and the dantian and, indeed, the entire body not forgetting the mind. If such training is neglected, ignored and abandoned (and this is, sadly, the current trend) then not only does the art, itself, suffer but so does our nation's very own culture!

One of the most characteristic features of Taizuquan is the combination between fist techniques and strength training. By training both the inner and outer one will acquire everything one will ever need; it just needs to be practiced and maintained. The initial fist training is sanzhan, an exercise centered round inhaling and exhaling. Thousands of fist application methods stem from sanzhan. This is why it is called "the mother of the fist" (*quanmu*). There is a saying: "Training begins with sanzhan and training ends with one's final breath." More than a decade ago I asked Master Xu Jin Dong and Master Ye Qing Hai to write a book focusing upon Taizuquan's neigong training method. These two old friends considered sanzhan to be "an inner fist practice that students have to train continuously in order to reach as high a level as is possible." Sanzhan involves qigong (breathing work/breath training) and neigong together with mind-training/mind-work. Wuzuquan includes a variation upon the sanzhan theme that shares great similarities with the Quanzhou Taizuquan sanzhan form. The type of sanzhan that Master Xu and Master Ye recommended is called "straight horse battle" which belongs to the Quanzhou Taizuquan sect.

Training one's sanzhan is not to train strength without skill. One must strive to achieve the state of "training intention without strength and training strength without intention." The essence of the fist art is the essence of sanzhan which is the swallowing, spitting, floating and sinking while paying strict attention to storing the qi and sending the qi.

Floating: Cultivate a lion's roar by breathing long and slow from the dantian while the throat remains loose and the crown suspended and the teeth (s)lightly clenched.

Sinking: With both elbow joints parallel, transfer the breath from the dantian to the middle dantian (the sternum).

Swallowing: Pulling both palms to the upper ribcage, move the breath to the danzhongxue acupoint.

Spitting: Send out both palms whist returning the breath to the middle dantian while spitting out the breath with the sound of the lion's roar.

In sanzhan training it is required to promote a "shaking body and shaking shoulders" while "lifting the intestines and expanding the belly with the inner breath" in order to promote strength from the waist and strength from the shoulders with the intention of promoting the pulse so that the internal organs will be lifted up and sunken down with the inner strength.

After a great deal of sanzhan training (years, in fact) one will be able to train one's sanzhan while combining and balancing hardness with softness while switching freely between the two. As yin and yang work and interact together with the five elements, each supports the other and are thus inter-supportive; the vigor of one's breath together with the power of one's strength work with and thus harmonize with the "soft outside" and the "hard inside" so that "heavy hands" strength allows *jing* ("energy and vitality") to be sent out with unbeatable swiftness.

Master Xu and Master Ye once led a delegation from West Malaysia to Quanzhou in order to attend the annual International Wuzuquan Fellowship Conference. At this time, I and a number of others took tea at the Overseas Chinese Hotel and it was then that I inquired about the neigong method. Master Ye invited me to attack Master Xu. At the time, Master Xu was in his seventies. At first I politely refused, but then Master Xu unexpectedly reassured me saying, "Don't worry. Just hit my head as hard as you can." I attempted a strike upon his crown but upon striking him it felt as if his head was lifted up with an immense strength supported from beneath. Master Xu then extended one foot and asked me to stamp on it. As I did so it felt as if it was made of iron! This demonstrated his extremely and extraordinary high level of neigong, the likes of which is very rarely seen. Master Xu said there is no need to look elsewhere for neigong training for it is all there within the Taizu/Wuzu sanzhan form.

泉州太祖拳

CHAPTER THREE

TAIZU TRAINING THEORY

Taizuquan is hard as well as soft although its hardness is its main visual characteristic. Taizuquan involves kicking, striking and throwing as well as capturing. With close-quarter battle being its essential performance strategy, Taizuquan also involves hand tactics, foot tactics as well as "earth" tactics although the hands are its main focus. While Taizuquan advances and withdraws it also dissolves as well as dodges. Using a hard bow stance and a hard horse stance Taizuquan employs direct attacks and invasive advances as its main strategy. While its fist performance is fierce and vigorous, Taizuquan is as swift as a swimming dragon while it scatters like a sinking fish.

My late master, Dai Huo Yan, was the first student of Master Wei Guo Qi who was a well-known Taizuquan master in Quanzhou during the end of Qing Dynasty and the beginning of the ROC (Republic of China). Master Dai travelled abroad and it was his skill in nanquanfa (the southern fist method) that established his fame amidst foreign nations. In 1960 he returned to China from Indonesia where he had established the Sishuixie Wushuguan. It was at this time that I became one of his students and so followed him around for almost ten years. In 1968 Master Dai fell ill and handed to me a book (actually, a manual) titled, *Taizuquan Pu*, which included sixty-seven Taizu forms. In the meantime, Master Dai summonsed me to his sickbed where he taught me quanfa by way of verbal teachings and so entrusted me to put in order an article titled, "A Gathering of the Main Points of Taizuquanfa" (*Taizuquanfa Cuo Yao*), which included a very brief introduction to theory and characteristics. Below is what I recall from those bedside teachings:

Taizuquan, as a school of training derived from the Shaolin sect, was handed down from Song Taizu Zhao Kuang Yin. It is said within the quanfa manual that, "Taizuquan utilizes thirty-six movements and even with a single horse (stance) one can be unequalled and unrivaled. The range of movement is short and swift, intense and fierce. Advancing and withdrawing, Taizuquan involves softness on the inside and shows hardness on the outside. With a straight and centered body, each and every punch is therefore strong and powerful. With a concave chest and a rounded back the shoulders must be relaxed and the arms bent at the elbows. With the spine held straight and the chin tucked in, the eyes must be staring beyond the horizon while the teeth are clenched in order to empty the throat. One's spirit must be focused from the inside while overwhelming power must be shown on the outside. One must neither puff out one's chest and stomach nor bend his head or lower his waist. When stepping out always firm one's lower plate/gate (*xiapan*). The width of one's stance must equate roughly to one shoulder width while the weight ratio front foot to rear foot should be 70:30. One should walk like a dragon and step like a tiger! One must tighten each horse with each and every stance and posture while withdrawing the hip joint and thrusting the waist. Take note that the hands, eyes, feet and body must all arrive at the same time.

Whether you are walking then horse or stamping the horse, one's steps should be just like the wind. When thrusting from the legs be low and sink and when jumping from the knees one must glue to the ground upon landing. One's horse must sit firmly while supporting the eight areas and sides. One's movements must conform to the standard from beginning to end. The hands are like two wheels with the waist acting as the axis. The upper gate extends as far upwards as the height of the eyebrows and the lower gate extending as far down as the pubis. The left and right range is to protect the shoulders and ribs while "holding the center" is to withdraw the elbows and sink the joints. Sending out the hands with strength through to the fingertips one should pursue flexibility together with straightness. While one technique is performed out, yin and yang is involved within. Swallowing, spitting, sinking and floating and the interchange between attack and defense involves the use of the shoulders, elbows, wrists and palms. Swallowing and spitting and transferring qi is better from the dantian. If one trains with a pure heart, strength and power arrive smoothly, but if one allows one's qi to float it will bite the chest which will result in plentiful qi held up high while the lower (the dantian) will be insufficient if not empty.

1. The Head Method: The head is the master of the whole body. The upper limbs and every subsidiary channel of the human body through which vital energy, blood and nutriment circulate is under the control of the head. Therefore the head must be straight. By way of one's baihui[1] (the meeting of the one hundred influential points) one's head is held suspended and when both eyes are level one's vitality is also maximized. Whist the eyes home in on the adversary's intention the ears home into the eight directions being pre-warned by way of the slightest of movements.

2. The Body Method: The body is the main part of the whole being. This method is to be flexible so one must draw in the chest, thrust the shoulder blades back and slightly curve the spine. Sinking the shoulders one should relax the joints and control facial expressions. The inner mind is to be relaxed, the out body is to be straight and the gates and joints opened. Move the body to step out, pressing movement after movement. The waist is to be flexible while one is to act as a lady would do being still, and as a running rabbit would be on the move. The movement must not impede the body's status while the body's status must not impede one's movement.

3. The Waist Method: The waist is the axis — as straight as a pine tree and as bendable and flexible as a bow. The stomach is to be firm and the waist is to be loose. With the waist controlling the usage of the four limbs, together this brings out strength from the spine to raise the intestines (and so the dantian) and thus tighten the abdominals.

4. The Cartilage Method: The cartilage is the machine's hinge upon which dodging and expanding relies and depends. One's crossing the cartilage is all down to precise measurement. Tightened cartilage renders oneself unmovable even under a strong force. The cartilage moves slightly but sends out at high speed. By dissolving and dodging one may advance through the smallest gap. One is to move one's body in accordance with the striking horse and the stamping "living gate" (*shengmen*) — with every tightened step showing power while moving.

5. The Hand Method: The front hand aims at the opponent as if it were a spear while the rear hand defends and protects as if it were a shield. The front hand sends out while the rear hand is held back and in reserve, yet both hands support each other. The sending out hand is as if it were an arrow piercing through leather while the reserve hand acts as if it were restraining nine bulls. It is important to have sufficient strength in order to perform long techniques thus revealing and effecting flexibility through straightness. But it is also important for short techniques to embrace the Eight Diagrams so that one may bend having first extended. The long is to defend the short while the short is to rescue the long. No punch is empty and no hand is to return before having achieved a result. Yin and Yang is to be converted as one follows the other. While swallowing and spitting may be visual, sinking and floating is to be concealed.

6. The Foot Method: The fist coordinates with the foot just as a room needs pillars in order to be a room! If one wishes his lower gate to be light while solid he must sink his lower spine (the sacrum), restrain the opening, close the anus, hold the knees and testicles inwards, tighten the calves, glue and claw the toes into the floor and root the feet into the ground as soon as they land. One must interchange advancing and retreating — while advancing one's steps must be like the wind, and like nails as one retreats. One must be like a fox when jumping and landing, and as a dragon while rolling upon the ground. If one's feet are not firm the fists will be thrown into complete disorder and if one's steps are not fast his fist will be far too slow. When the hand is to advance 30% the foot should advance 70%. Nine turnings should not leave the center while one must ensure that both feet stamp upon the center/middle palace. One should lower his footsteps when he is to advance while raising one's footsteps when retreating. Kicks need to be low while no technique should be sent out long-range. The knees need to be employed when one is in close (to the enemy).

7. The Strength Method: How can strength be generated? It is generated from the movement of the waist (*yaoli*). How can it be induced? It is moved by one's qi. When strength is sent out from the waist it must borrow power from the ground while the hands coordinate with the feet, the elbows coordinate with the knees, and the shoulders with the crotch. When the upper region of the body rises, the middle follows and the lower region chases to enable the pathway of one's strength be clear, unobstructed and smooth. Qi is sent forth from the dantian and the swallowing and spitting sent forth from the stomach the purpose of which is, "to increase one's strength by way of the body so that it is strong enough to send off the hat." In other words, "to issue strength from the fingers enough to pierce bones" and "to build strength through the teeth that are strong enough to bite off the tendons." The sudden burst of inner (qi-based and qi-driven) strength allows one to attack the adversary in one given moment. The qi either shakes or bounces so the path of power and strength is clear, crisp and clean. The hard indicates the soft, the solid is seen by way of emptiness and the soft is shown after having receiving the attacker's force. The hard is used before the attacker's force has been exerted. It is important to use strength sparingly and to know how to interchange strength so that it will conform to pace, tempo and rhythm. One must exert strength from beginning to end.

8. The Qi Method: Qi is used to raise and support the body through exerting strength. Qi must first sink into the dantian before being sent throughout the entire body. In this way, tendons and bones will become stronger as a natural result, but only after a long time and a great deal of training. Through a long, slow and deep inhalation one takes in qi, stores it, harnesses it then spits it out as and when needed. If one can first store qi, accumulate it then transport it and send it, one will develop and possess long-lasting if not ever-lasting strength. To raise qi one needs to float, and to support qi one needs to be still. To gather qi one needs to be hard and crisp and to sink qi one needs to swallow and sink. He who maintains these requirements can keep a clear mind, high spirits and undying strength(s). Having completed the very first action of any chosen fist-form, one immediately fills with qi! These are the essential points in training the fist. Now I shall address the essence of *ziwu* ("meridians"), the concept of *ganrou* (on "being hard and soft"), and *yingjie* ("receiving and responding").

1. ZIWU[2] IS ONE OF THE MOST IMPORTANT ASPECTS OF TAIZUQUAN

Ziwu exists within the hands, feet, body, swallowing, spitting, bending forwards, and leaning backwards, opening and turning. Zi and Wu are the two positions within *dizhi* (the twelve earthly branches used cyclically within the Chinese lunar calendar and as ordinal digits; for example, 1, 2 and 3) and so symbolize the correct/standard north and the correct/standard south. One is first to position the line between zi and wu then *mao* (east) and *you* (west) thus establishing the four positions. One must pursue the correct *ziwu* (that is to say, one is to correct and standardize one's body shape via stance and posture). Think, for a moment, how one would be if one was to exert his fist with the head drooping, the waist bent and the foot (horse) loose! In this way his form is already unpleasant and with complete discord. Indeed, how on earth can one obtain and transfer power and strength as and when required? In the olden days, Taizuquan was regarded as "a dragon walking and a tiger stepping" — "with an appearance, an air and an atmosphere of grace just like the emperor" which was, perhaps, based upon the fact that Taizuquan had been created by the Emperor, Zhao Kuang Yin. Thus, Taizuquan is dignified and graceful, elegant and poised, vigorous and imposing (if not intimidating).

When beginning to learn Taizuquan one practices sanzhan thus one begins to straighten and correct one's posture and stance through remolding and reshaping the body. It is said, "One body includes five limbs and should belong and return to an upright and thus correct posture." Through neither inclining nor leaning one achieves the "grave tablet body." With the chest concave and the shoulder blades out, one's shoulders sink while the joints remain connected as one's fist maintains focus and the breath centered. With the foot-horse (re)shaped in the manner of *budingbuba* the 3:7 or 4:6

front-to-rear weight-distribution ratio means that one sits in one's horse as the rear leg/foot sinks and the front leg/foot empties.

Before moving to either to the left or to the right one must first adjust one's body posture through either an advancing horse or a retreating horse, swallowing and spreading (opening and stretching) one's two cartilages while one's hand techniques must be sent out through the right gate. As it is with the cudgel method, every strike and every shearing must be positioned in front of the body — at the middle meridian. If the end of the cudgel is to fall left or right it is regarded as a "losing/failing meridian". All these requirements are not only in accordance with one's physiological composition, but to suit the technical requirements for firm safeguarding while waiting to advance. It is said, "exerting the fist as if walking." Within northern quanfa training there is also a saying, "Wanting to control the powerful opponent, one is to hold his elbows in the middle/center," which proves that countless quanfa all follow the same basic rule. To coin a more Western phrase: "Great minds think alike."

When executing techniques one's body must hide carefully within the Meridian Gate while tightening the Three Gates known as the Upper Gate, the Middle Gate, and the Lower Gate. Initially, one is to first adopt a firm meridian posture so that any postural changes will all be Meridian Gate-based. Coordinating hands and feet in order to establish power and strength through shape one may receive and respond freely and at will. If the opponent is defeated and so retreats but maintains a correct meridian posture with gates closed, one must not follow him or advance towards him.

To sum up, the rule of making the meridian the center is paramount; it is the most important rule in Taizuquan. I have met a great number of experienced senior fist masters - some of them having lived through to the end of Qing Dynasty while others are of the modern day, some in China and others from overseas - and when it comes to talking about quanfa we all agree that the meridian must be the basic rule. When it comes to perform quanfa one must follow the standard posture - firm himself in the horse so that he is to sink and be stable and not to be moved. Based upon this fact we can see that the word "meridian" (ziwu) is truly a life-long exhortation and admonition for those who train in traditional quanfa.

2. UNDERSTANDING HARDNESS AND SOFTNESS

The theory of hardness and softness is well known however the hardness from Taizuquan is neither the kind of hardness as a giant rock pressing the body nor as the steel spear piercing one's throat. Meanwhile, the softness from Taizuquan is not the same kind of softness as found within Taijiquan therefore what is the hardness and softness from Taizuquan? This is a question that one must understand and be clear when it comes to training in Taizuquan.

Every quanfa contains hardness and softness for softness is within hardness and hardness within softness. In point of fact, one dissolves the other. As soon as hardness has dissolved, swallowing and sinking transfers to softness just as when softness is dissolved, spitting and floating transfers to hardness. Thus hardness and softness/softness and hardness support each other. This is the source of and foundation for success and victory.

With sanzhan as the initial training, the swallowing, spitting, sinking and floating teaches this method of interchange between the *gang* and the *rou* — the hardness and the softness. However the hardness and the softness can only be known by way of hand-to-hand combat. The hardness of Taizuquan (this includes the methods of raising, losing, struggling, whipping, breaking, pinning, slicing and cutting) sends out strength and power and so into the opponent. Meanwhile, the softness of Taizuquan includes the capturing, removing, rubbing, leading, pulling and drawing in. While the shoulders, the left and right and the dodging and dissolving, work with the posture in order to borrow strength via stamping, sideways movement, and directional change after strength and power has already been sent out.

The methods of dissolving and transforming are the methods of the softness. If the opponent advances with direct strength one is to dig and carve and strike in order to break and turn so as to dissolve the oncoming attack using the soft strength of the dissolving method.

So where does this lead us?

Taizuquan employs strong tactics for actual combat. It is said, "If there is mercy, one is not to extend one's hands, and if one extends the hands he is not to be merciful." Therefore, in Taizuquan there is no impractical movement. All hand techniques prepare for the opportunity to attack or defend by way of the method of the interchange (between yin and yang). This is why the taolu are vital.

Taizuquan comprises four types of techniques — striking, kicking, throwing and capturing. Each posture and every movement must be black and white although, having said this, solid is not to be solid and void is not to be void for solid combines with void while hard supports soft.

When face-to-face with an opponent one must coordinate hands, feet, body and strength - attacking hard with straight-line advancement one must dodge and counter sideways on. The secret of practical usage lies within the heart as well as hands therefore one must be a master by way of a very clear understanding.

Having studied the quanfa manual and having chosen the most commonly-seen sixty-four methods (including one hundred and twenty seven techniques) I have listed these below together with a brief introduction and illustrations which was, perhaps, based on the fact that Taizuquan had been created by Emperor Zhao Kuang Yin. However the style of Taizuquan is dignified and graceful, elegant and poised, vigorous with an imposing manner, which is a solid fact.

Sanzhan has always been the beginner's starting point for it teaches the novice to maintain a straightened spine and a correctly-molded body shape and posture. It is said, *"The body comprises five limbs (two arms, two legs and the spine) while at no time should one incline or lean. This is called "The Grave Tablet Body."* One's chest must be held-in (swallowed), the shoulder blades thrusting out, the shoulders sunk and the joints connected. The fist should be focused on and should return to the centre, the feet (through one's horse stance) must be shaped as neither a 'T' nor an '8' (buding, buba) while the weight ratio of the front foot to rear foot should either be 3:7 or 4:6 — so the weight and gravity must sit at the back. Prior to moving to either the left or the right one must adjust one's body posture through either the Advancing Horse or the Retreating Horse, or by swallowing and spreading and by opening and stretching the two cartilages. Hand techniques must be sent out through the right gate. With regard to the cudgel method, each strike and every cut must be positioned in the front of the body's middle meridian. If the end of the cudgel is to fall to the left or to the right this is considered a losing or failing meridian.

All of the above requirements are not only in accordance with physiological composition but also to suit the technical requirements for a firm safeguarding and the need to wait in order to advance together with the deliverance of hard attacks and direct advancing. These have become the standard and actually obey the Laws of Nature! It is said, "Exert the fist as if walking."

In northern-style kung-fu (*beiquan*) there is also a saying: "Wanting to control the powerful opponent, one is to hold his elbows in the middle and on the center," which proves that thousands of quanfa all follow the same basic rules while, as they say in the West, "Great minds think alike."

When receiving or performing techniques, one's own body must hide carefully within the Meridian Gate. One must tighten the Three Gates known as the Upper, Middle and Lower Gate. These Three Gates engender one another while harmonizing with the situation in-hand. One is to first hold the meridian firmly and then change position based upon the meridian, itself, while coordinating hands and feet so that one is able to determine shape as well as strength and power. Thus one may receive and respond freely as the need dictates. If the opponent is defeated and so retreats but in his own correct meridian position and with his gates closed, one is not to follow and advance towards him. If one is not in the correct meridian position his mistakes will be evident to the opponent which will thus decide his own failure.

Receiving the opponent by dissolving, the would-be-victim seems to disappear and vanish thus the attacker is "lifted" which results in his strength being destroyed by so-called "soft strength." Within Taizuquan, straight line hand attacks are mostly "hard" while those that move in circles or arcs normally reflect "softness." Stamping in the "middle palace" thus entering and advancing without retreating one remains in control by way of the centre; pushing forward and leaning against and into the attacker with one's entire body-weight and full strength are all ways we can use "hard" strength.

Advancing by way of the side-gate while dodging and dissolving to the left and to the right one may retreat and avoid by way of side-stepping thus foregoing the use of hard strength as one looks for gaps and chinks (that is to say, openings) in the attacker's armour. This is how one can use "soft" strength. The breaking and use of crisp strength can change into permanent strength while loose strength can change into straight strength, horizontal strength and short strength. Thus we can see the interchange between the soft strength and the hard strength.

While a collection of techniques is called "art," turning hard into soft and soft into hard and having both hard and soft supporting each other is called "mastery". If hard strength is not transferred into soft strength when needed it often results in one being controlled by the opponent, and if soft strength is not transferred into hard strength then even with the opportunity of fighting back then without the strength needed it will be very hard to win against a skilled adversary. He who is good at fighting (techniques) must also be good at "following" the opponent then attacking when the opponent is ill-prepared — receiving the opponent's strength early on (before it has time to manifest itself) and dissolving whatever strength the opponent has at its end so that the opponent's power is broken (destroyed) at the beginning of the martial artist's own strength. This is the practical way of using hard and soft strength during combat.

3. COMBAT IS CHAOTIC AND ADHERES TO NO FIXED PATTERN AND NO FIXED STANCE IF ANY AT ALL!

Everything changes in accordance with erratic circumstances. Within the Taizuquan manual it states, "Courage comes first, mastery comes second, familiarity comes third." General Yu Da You taught his soldiers to regard courage as the primary element in military training. When he was a young man he was taught quanfa by Bai Yuan Gong (The White Gorilla) at Qingyuan Mountain (to the north of Quanzhou) where there were giant boulders upon which he leapt and climbed each day in order to train his courage. Upon one of these boulders he wrote two characters: *Lian Dan* ("Train Courage"). He often said that, "Military training should start with training courage and training courage should start with training skills as one's skill should help to boost one's courage." But if one is equipped with mastery skills without adequate courage he might shy away from the opponent being ill-prepared to advance even when faced with good opportunity. Thus he may well be defeated even by those that are not as skilled. Therefore, if one is to be courageous one's heart must be calm and one's eyes sharp. One should have excellent judgement as to circumstance, possess a clear insight, and be familiar with change in the opponent's tactics.

It is said in the book of *Wu-Yue Chun Qiu* ("The History of the Spring and Autumn Period of the Kingdoms of Wu and Yue") that, "Spirit is required for one's inside during hand-to-hand combat so that one may demonstrate confidence and relaxation on the outside."

If one's head is clear and if one has the will and the passion to win, one must be equipped with mastery skills. On the other hand, if one is shown as being short of breath and with a muddled head one must also be both inadequate and shallow in skill. A clear head is essential when it comes to judgement of a situation and circumstance. It is important to master the nature and the interpretation of the fight, for example: what is the distance, what is the direction? Does one attack first or defend first? Is the confrontation one-on-one or against multiple opponents? Is the fight at matter of life or death?

Observing the head and nose of the opponent one is able to judge his next move while observing his body's tendency and shape one is able to judge his restraint and release. For instance, if the opponent is watching me on my left side I should be cautious of his possible attacks from my left; if he is watching me on my right side I should know that his next possible attack must be from my right; if he lifts his shoulders he is clearly about to raise his foot and attempt to kick me.

When engaging in hand-to-hand combat one should always be aware of body movement more so than hand movement unlike combat involving weaponry where one should always be aware of the hand movement rather than the body. Once combat is in progress one should close-in on the Live Gate and so avoid the Death Gate. When attacked by hard strength one should receive it with soft strength while only advancing having first detected an opening on the opponent's side and strike as soon as the opportunity arises. When facing a weaker opponent one should push and press closely and so, without hesitation, exert hard blocking and hard striking.

If the opponent is strong and skilled in upper body movement yet weak in lower body movement he must be broken with the Earth method. One should hold straight the ziwu while maintaining power and preserving strength. Avoid pressing on ahead without due consideration unless one might fail through a premature attack; only attack when the opportunity is ripe. If one is to advance or retreat without correct judgement his front hand and back hand will not be able to work together and help each other as and when required and this is what General Yu Da You declared as "leaping to retreat." It is said that, "Disappearing, vanishing and dissolving one's body is essential to saving one's body." Having come face to face with danger one should know to block the bridge so as to change the danger into a favourable situation. He should also be familiar with the eight-character method as "spreading, turning, dissolving, disappearing, vanishing, dodging, swallowing, spitting, sinking and floating" in order to save situations.

The beauty and wonder of hand-to-hand fighting lies within attacking the opponent using the front hand as a combined spear and battle-axe while, at the same time, protecting oneself using the other hand (held behind the front hand) as a shield. While the foot is to advance following the movement of the hand, the strength is to be sent out from the shoulder-blades, waist and legs, and exerted with each and every technique.

The essence of Taizuquan is summarized as, "safe-guarding and waiting for the opportunity to advance then attack hard with straight-forward advancement." Therefore, one must understand that the hard and soft, the void and solid, the favourable and the contrary engender one another. The oncoming hand can be dealt with using the hard within the soft while the oncoming soft can be dealt with using the soft within the hard. It is essential that one must ensure that the gate is closed, and always pay attention to the lower part of his body such as the feet and horse stance. The upper limbs are to perform swallowing, spitting, sinking or floating so that the five elements are able to engender one another as well as restrain and subdue one another.

During the Ming dynasty it was fashionable to talk about the *Yijing* ("Book of Changes") which, itself, was influential upon the theory of quanfa. For instance, within the Taizu sect theory it is suggested that the punch should not only follow four dimensions but pay particular attention to the Five Elements. The swallowing and spitting of qi was to be in accordance with the eight divinatory trigrams of the *Book of Change*, the feet and the horse stance were to follow the rules of the Nine Palaces, and the body method was to obey the rules of the "middle fixed." The hand method of "lifting" was regarded as a Metal technique, "struggling" as a Wood technique, "digging" as an Earth technique, "capturing" as a Water technique, and "binding" as a Fire technique. Indeed, the Five Elements were to engender and restrain each other.

These clarifications were actually used to explain the basic responding and receiving rules such as "striking the lower after having been attacked from the upper" and "blocking the upper having been attacked from the lower" and, once again, "dissolving horizontally having been attacked from the right". Those that were trained by way of these rules were able to respond effectively in combat.

It is crucial that one be rooted into the ground with each step, that one tightens one's entire body as if it were an iron pillar, that one be familiar with all techniques and all gates, and that one be flexible with one's movements and solid with strength. It has been said that, "one is to attack from the west first if he intends to attack, ultimately, to the east" and that, "Fight initially with the hands then stamp with the foot immediately afterwards." Additionally, "Take advantage of the opponent's movement by borrowing his power then send out power before the opponent has time to launch and effect his own attack."

The trick that is known as, "sending out power after the opponent whist reaching before the opponent" is a secret to success if one is to win over the opponent who moves slower than him by using faster movements. There is a saying, "There are one hundred solutions to one hundred movements/steps however there is no solution to fast movement." To be able to achieve this one must be, "as a maiden when silence and stillness is needed" while one must be, "as an escaping rabbit when speed is of the essence."

What is the meaning of, "taking advantage of the opponent and using his strength"? General Yu Da You used to say (in his book, *Sword Manual*) that, "One is to know where the strength of the opponent lies and avoid that area but, instead, wait for the opportunity to advance between the moment of his opponent's previous strength has passed and the next strength has not yet been sent out and so take advantage of that moment and strike." This is known as taking advantage of the opponent's movement and borrowing both his strength and power. The first-class trick is to fall whist the lower-class trick is to rise. This is truly a clever theory!

The combating method requires that one is not to consider personal emotion at any time during a fight for in an instant there can be a myriad of changes. One must, therefore, be equipped with the knowledge of the Four Elements which includes courage, power (movement/shape), method and strength. Not one of these is/are dispensable! One is not only to understand this through books but also to be able to consider and put this into the right action. A person with noble character should also possess virtues as if they were jade while cherishing skills as precious and priceless as gold. This should be very well-appreciated!

泉州太祖拳

CHAPTER FOUR

THE FRAMEWORK OF QUANZHOU EMPEROR FIST

Quanzhou Emperor Fist is a unique and specific practice drawing upon natural movement illustrated and punctuated by what we call "stickiness" and strength. Specializing in short-range cutting, chopping and thrusting actions, Quanzhou Emperor Fist promotes courage, might and bravery while leaving aside needless and superfluous antics. Concentrating upon detailed positioning of the hands and the feet together with methods of standing and body structure, these are just some of the essentials one has to perfect together with simple and practical body mechanics achieved through strict adherence to rhythm and timing. It is said that one's journey along the Taizuquan path is like one's pathway in life — full of adventure, sometimes dangerous, often rugged and oftentimes hard to fathom.

HAND TECHNIQUES WITHIN TAIZUQUAN

1. Fist Techniques

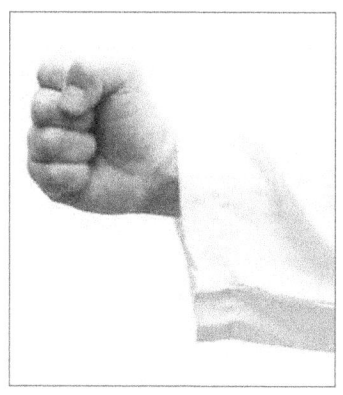

A. Standing Fist (sometimes called Vertical Fist) - liquan and shuquan, respectively

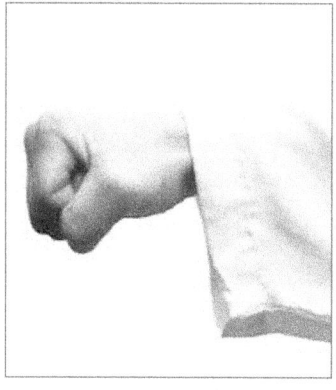

B. Covering Fist (Triangular Fist) - fuquan and sanjiaoquan, respectively

C. Phoenix Eye Fist - fengyanquan

2. Palm Techniques

A. Standing Palm - lizhang

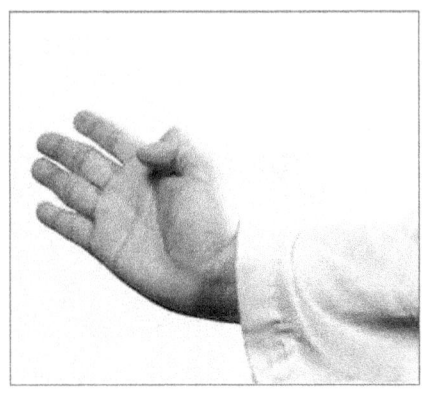

B. Angled Palm/Side Palm - cezhang

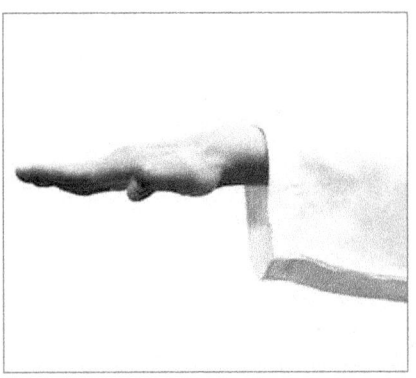

C. Covering Palm (soft palm) - fuzhang, yinzhang, respectively

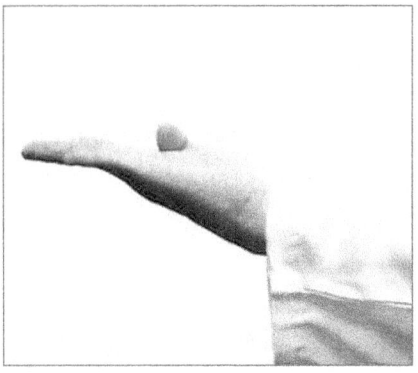

D. Upward-Facing Palm (hard palm) - yangzhang

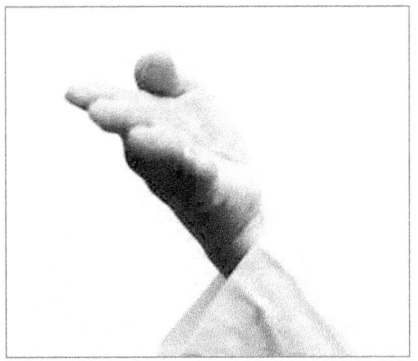

E. Laughing Palm (a poetic way of saying that the palm is like a young person's face that has opened up and lit-up with excitement) - xiaozhang

F. Dog Palm - gouzhang

3. Finger Techniques

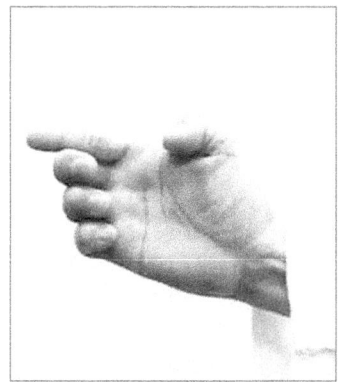

A. Single Finger - danzhi

B. Double Fingers - shuangzhi

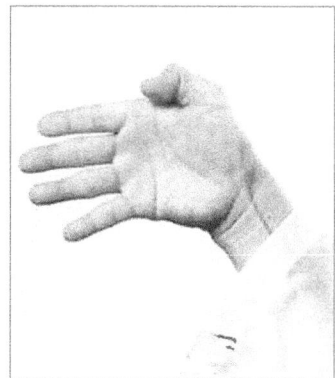

C. Four Fingers - sizhi

4. Claw Techniques

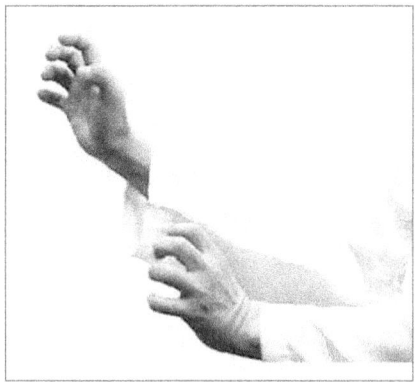

A. Tiger Claws - huzhua

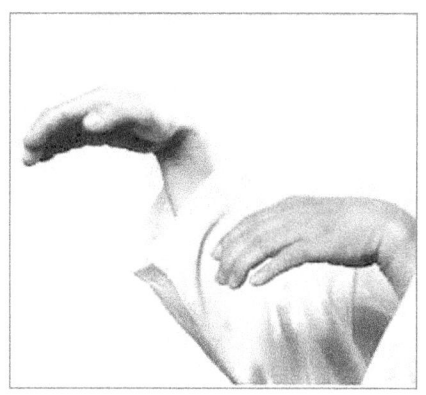

B. Monkey Hands - houshou

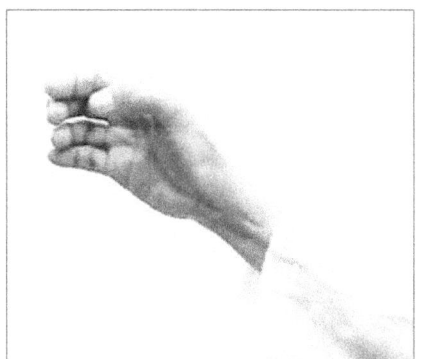

C. Centipede Hand - wugongshou

5. Elbow techniques

A. Level (horizontal) Joint - hengjie

B. Standing Joint - lijie

C. Back Joint - houjie

FOOT POSITIONS (HORSE STANCES) — BUXING (MA)

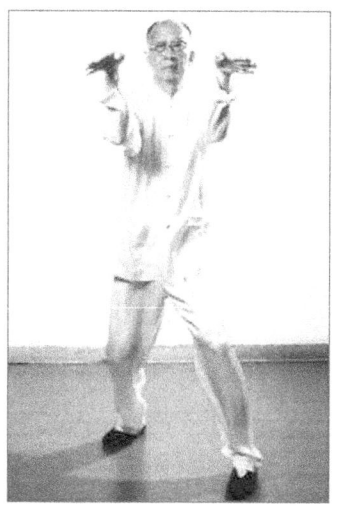

1. Three Wars Horse (Sanzhanma)
Also referred to as the "Chinese character eight horse," this stance goes by a number of other names, including: "one third of a metre horse," "three-seven horse," "four-six horse," and "bu ding bu ba."[1] With all the toes pressing downwards and glued tight into floor and with both knees bent slightly inwards, one's calf-tendons are stretched while the anus is closed and the intestines elevated. Thus, strength begins from the floor and move upwards into the feet and then ascend thought the legs and into the spine, then the torso and to the upper body.

2. Four Level Horse (Sipingma)
Both feet are placed apart and parallel with one's weight centered and with both knees bent slightly inwards. Gravity allows for sinking but the knees are also subtly pulled upwards and outwards.

3. Cross-Step Horse, Empty Horse (Xiema)
In this stance, seventy per cent of the weight is supported by one leg while the other leg is slightly bent at the knee.

4. Bow Horse (Gongjian)
Front bow, back arrow. In this posture, the body needs to be down and the hips need to be "open."

5. Rear Horse
A rear foot-weighted stance with the front foot "empty" (of weight).

6. Character "Ding" Horse (Dingma)
There is a Chinese character meaning "T" shaped which describes a horse stance where the torso (spine) and front leg can be likened to the stem of a "T" while the rear leg and foot can be likened to the top part of a "T" while the overall shape is rather like a triangle.

7. Rising Crane Foot (Qihejiao)
With one leg raised the supporting leg is slightly bent.

8. Cross feet (Jia Jiao)
With one's weight upon the rear foot the front foot is empty of weight as it sits lightly upon the floor, merely grazing it.

9. Sitting Lotus (Seated Guanyin)
With both feet crossed with one sinking downwards, and with one's bottom sitting upon the heel of the other leg.

10. Bend (Qu)
One foot squats, the other foot is in an attitude of kneeling.

11. Double Bend (Pointing at the Ground) Shuangqu (Zhidi)
Both feet bend together with both knees together and parallel, bottom sitting.

STEPPING METHOD

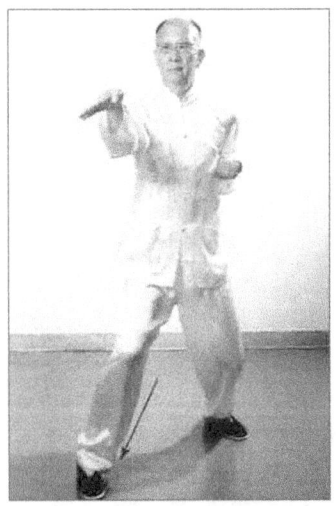

1. Forward-Stepping Horse (Jinma)
In the fist manual, all foot movements of stepping forward are called jinma.

2. Backward-Stepping Horse (Tuima)

All foot movements of stepping backwards are called tuima.

3. Whispering Horse (Qima)

Front foot advances one small step as the rear foot follows, grazing across the ground in another one small step but not crossing in front of the front foot. This is called Whispering Horse.[2]

4. Remaining horse (Liuma)

With the rear foot, step back one small step and have the front foot following also one small step back but still remaining in front of the other foot and so not going behind the other foot. This movement is called Liuma - Remaining Horse or Staying Horse.

5. Stamping/Stomping/Stepping Horse (Diema) or Walking Horse (Zouma)

First forward one small step, again forward one horse, this called Stamping Horse. Three stepping forward horse is called Walking Horse.

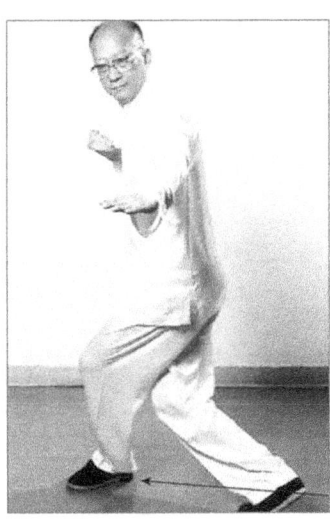

6. Step/Step On/Tread/Pressing opon Horse (Tama)

With both feet crossing over, one foot crosses over and passes the outer side of the other foot.

7. Thrusting Horse (Chama)

With both feet crossing over, one foot crosses over and passes the inner side of the other foot.

8. Three Drops of Gold/Three Taps of Gold (Sandianjin)[3]

By way of two steps and three drops/taps/clicks, one's horse stance changes at the same spot while both feet remain at a Middle Palace (zhong gong) position. This is beneficial for combat in close quarters.

BODY METHOD (SHENFA)

1. Hold the Body Straight (Zhishen) — As Straight As a Tombstone (Mo Pai Shen)

Taizuquan's most basic body shape. Avoid leaning to either side

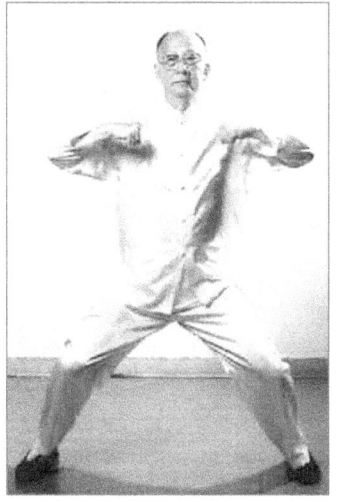

2. Inclining/Slanting Body (Xieshen)

Slanting towards the left and the right, find the upright within the leaning (this is an idiom: xie zhong qu zheng). Stand poised, gaining strength in order to start (xu shi dai fa - another idiom).

3. Body Bending Forward (Kanshen)
"Kan" is from a slang word meaning to bend forward.

4. Disappearing/Dissolving Body (Xiaoshen)
The body turns slightly sideways in order to dissolve an oncoming attack.

5. Dodging Body (Shanshen)
Moving upwards and downwards, to the left and to the right, forward and backwards, dodge so as to avoid the enemy.

6. Twisting/Turning Body (Zhuanshen)

Front and back, left gate and right gate and all four corners, change position in order to be free to advance or retreat.

7. Slanting Body to One Side (Qishen)

Slanting to one side one's centre of gravity shifts left or right.

8. Shaking Body (Yaoshen)

The waist and one's shoulder-blades - one swallowing, the other spitting - draw upon abdominal strength to produce a rapid body shake to stimulate the fist (hands).

9. Handsome Body (Yunshen)

Suck in the ground to draw up and bring out strength. Embrace with stability through one's meridians, immediately and smartly sending out strength and power as if like a dog shaking water out of its coat.

10. Lifting /Holding the Body (Liaoshen)

Swallowing the joints and dissolving the shoulders, one's body should turn sideways thus one faces and so receives the enemy.

11. Falling Body (Daoshen)

Falling to the ground in order to avoid the enemy or to attack the enemy's body.

CHAPTER 5

INTRODUCTION AND ILLUSTRATION OF TAIZUQUAN FORMS

Taizuquan involves both the empty hands and weaponry. In total, there are more than one hundred known forms, while it is generally considered that there are thirty-six weapons forms and twice that number of open-hand forms. Having both kinds of forms is considered complementary for in this way the art can flourish. Some of these forms are considered "classics" having been handed down for hundreds of years while others have been modified and have therefore undergone change by later generations. Most of the ancient and early complex forms have been simplified although they still remain practical and efficient having not lost their essence.

Taizuquan utilizes hardness together with softness and focuses mainly upon short- and medium-length forms that preserve one's qi and develops one's strength. When practicing the forms, one is expected to execute every technique clearly and with a solid feel and in an explosive manner. This is expressed by way of two Chinese idioms: *chuanshan dongbi* (penetrating mountains and piercing walls) and *fawa zhengliang* (dislodging the roof tiles and shaking the beams). Within this book I have selected three of Taizuquan's most well-known, popular, and enjoyable "open-hand" forms: Sanzhan, Shizi, and Zhantou. In order to capture the characteristics of these forms I have included a number of photographs along with the text.

SANZHAN (THREE BATTLES)

Practicing Taizuquan must always start with Sanzhan! In this way, the "three forward and three backward" (that is to say, the sanzhan form) builds up one's strength and one's power while the swallowing, spitting, sinking and floating trains both the outside (through waigong) and the inside (through neigong). But while strength lies within both hardness and softness — with both *in* (yin) and *iang* (yang) working together in an inter-supportive manner — the directions of movement (the "four gates" — north, south, east and west) work together to create a straight, upright and vertical body which gradually, over time, strengthens the meridians.

If one is highly-skilled in Sanzhan one should be skilled in the use of the hands, the waist and the horse stance (in other words, the entire body which is expressed within Wuzuquan as "ngokilat") while one will come to understand that all the forms can be understood by, and interchanged by way of, Sanzhan. Therefore, Sanzhan is considered the *"guanmu"* — the mother of all fist arts and so is a vital exercise to learn for all *beginner practitioners* of any native and indigenous Fujian Fist art.

A GUIDE TO SANZHAN

Inviting Fist (Qing Quan).

Step forward into a right horse stance then sink and sit into the hip-joint before executing a double thrust by way of a swallow action and a spitting action.

Step forward into a right horse stance then sink and sit into the hip-joint before executing a double thrust by way of a swallow action and a spit action.

Step forward into a right horse stance then sink and sit into the hip-joint before executing a double thrust by way of a swallow action and a spit action.

Step backward into a horse stance horse then sink and sit into the hip-joint before executing a double thrust by way of a swallow action and a spit action.

Step backward into a horse stance horse then sink and sit into the hip-joint before executing a double thrust by way of a swallow action and a spit action.

Standing still, execute a double closing action then move forward and perform a double strike action.

Perform a skimming striking action with the right hand then execute a chopping action with the left and then execute a right-handed strike before moving backwards into a hanging horse stance while sinking into a "Child Holds a Tablet" posture.

Finally, withdraw the fists to close the form.

1. Li Zheng (Standing Straight)

Anyone practicing quanfa forms must, from the very beginning, hold the head straight while looking straight. The chin must be tucked in and the neck must also be held straight. The chest must be sucked in slightly so that it is concave, the back must be vertical, the breath even and regulated, and one's attitude must exude might and vigor but not anger or aggression.

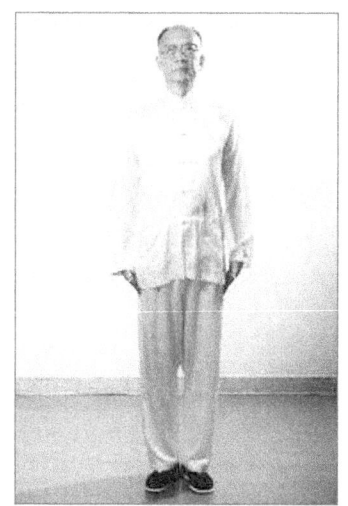

2. Level Horse (Even Horse) - Opening Posture

The right foot steps out and opens into the shape of the level horse stance. Both feet are parallel (*pingxing*) with the feet slightly wider than shoulder-width. Both legs must be bent at the knees. We call this the "sitting horse" (*zuoma*) and both palms must be in front (at dantian level) with the palms facing downwards and the finger pointing inwards. The shoulders must be sunk therefore maintaining a sunken chest.

Please note: One must hold one's body straight. This we call the "gravestone body-shape" (*mupai shenshi*).

3. Left Cross Cartilage[1]

Making one's waist the axis, both palms transform into fists while pressing, twisting and pulling so that they come to rest upon the upper ribs. The body turns slightly to the left while, at the same time, the feet transform into *guo jie ma* (meaning to "cross the cartilage"). Raising one's rectum and anus one must also swallow the cartilage, press the legs together from both sides, and clamp/grip the horse (*jiama*).[2]

Please note: Each movement must be executed with the chin tucked in and the teeth lightly clenched. Crossing the cartilage is especially important within Taizuquan. With each hand method and body posture the body, when turning, must dodge and avoid while such changes must be hidden and concealed. While crossing the cartilage one's strength — from the head, shoulders, body, waist, legs and feet — must send out force-potential as if, all of a sudden, wind and rain descends! That is to say, a storm (*fengyu*).³

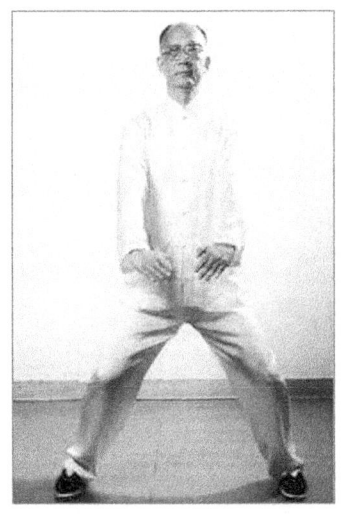

4. Level Horse, Double Thrust
Keeping one's waist as the axis the body turns slightly to the right with the shoulders even and sunken. With both palms facing the floor they thrust downwards simultaneously and come to rest at dantian level with both palms finishing in-line with each other. With both hands pressing from both sides, clamp/grip your horse.

Please note: While thrusting the palms downwards one must not lean forward.

5. Right Cross Cartilage
This is the same as above, except the direction is to the right.

6. Level Horse, Two Brushes Dip into the Ink

Maintaining one's axis via the waist one's body must turn slightly to the left while the cartilage (through the torso and the spine) is held straight and the shoulders even. Standing in pingma both hands transform into fists and point downwards — as if like to two brushes dipping into ink. Held in-line with and in front of the abdomen, press the legs from both sides and clamp/grip the horse (jiama).

Please note: While "dipping into the ink" do not lean forward.

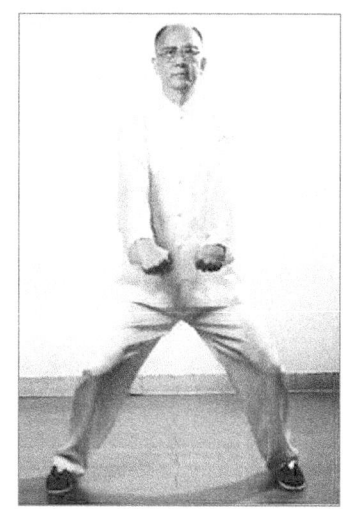

7. Level Horse, Double Capture

Both hands cross over from lower to upper while spreading towards the right and the left then seize (capture). One's palms should face downwards and be held apart at shoulder level.

Please note: Both palms rise and spread out in an arc and must be "like iron on the outside and like wool on the inside."

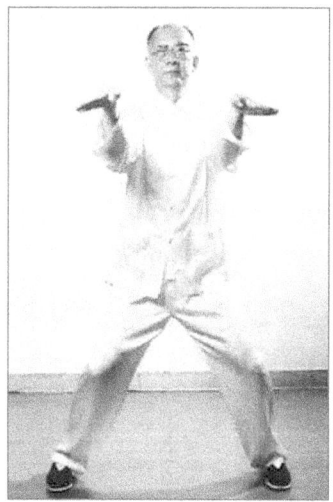

8. Right Cross Cartilage, Double Caress, Swallow In

Both palms transport strength. While outwardly the fists caress and clench, inwardly they wring and twist. The palms are now facing upwards. With the waist as the axis, assume the *gongjian* (bow and arrow)

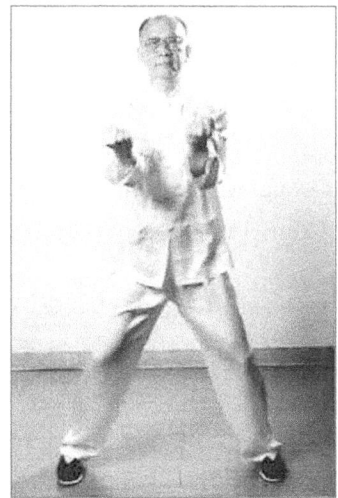 

stance with the right cross cartilage as both fists pull backwards so as to nestle immediately beneath the armpits.

Please note: As the fists caress and so emit strength through the fingers they transform from yin into yang.

9. Level Horse, Spitting Out, Inviting Fist4
Changing into the pingma stance one's left hand opens as the right hand clenches so that both transmit power and ultimately send power and strength outwards. With the right fist (palm upwards) attaching itself to the left palm, both hands reposition in front of the chest. The name of this posture is *Guang Ping Bao Yin* (General Guang Holds The Seal[5]), thus illustrating the Taizuquan salutation (*shili*).

Please note: The body is held straight, the shoulders level and the two joints must connect. As the intestines rise the anus tightens and so the horse firms-up.

10. Double Carry
Remaining in the level horse stance (pingma) one must keep the waist as the axis as one slightly shakes the shoulders and the body. Both fists open as the palms separate sideways and outwards (to the left and to the right) until the palms are shoulder width apart.

Please note: as this is being effected, strength is emitted from the shoulder blades. In Chinese, we express this by way of the saying, *chuanshan dongbi, fawa zhenliang* ("echoes through the mountains, piercing walls, roofing tiles fall to the ground, interior beams shake and crumble").

11. Right Cross Cartilage, Swallowing In

Inhale as both palms swallow to finish beneath the armpits.[6] This is called "floating." The qi arrives at the dantian.

Please note: Do not hunch the shoulders; they must sink.

12. Level Horse, Spitting Out Double Sitting Joints

Turning back in to level horse (stance), both palms transfer/transmit energy and spit out. With the arms bent at the elbows, the palms stand vertically with the distance between both heels of the palms being slightly less than the distance between the two elbows. With the elbows inward, and the forearms parallel with the ground, one spits out (exhales). This is called "sinking"; the qi exits the mouth as if lion is growling (or roaring).

Please note: Holding one's knee cartilage tight, draw upward the coccyx while holding up one's head in order to make the neck strong. Emptying out one's chest one also empties out one's throat. Spit out from yang to yin while turning and sit the joints. With the forearms level and parallel they must imitate the state of flowing water. The palm heels exert strength.

13. Exit the Right Horse with Both Withdrawing

Step forward with the right foot placing forty percent of the weight onto the front foot and sixty percent on back foot. The distance between the feet must be approximately twelve inches. Whist drawing in, swallow the right cartilage and the right shoulder. Generally speaking, one spits while exhaling and one swallows while inhaling. However, one should not force such a practice but, instead, do whatever feels natural and instinctive.

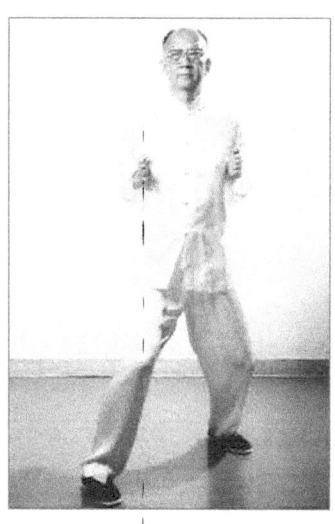

Please note: The upper part of one's front foot is bent while the lower part of the front foot is straight. At the same time, however, the upper part of the rear foot is straight while the lower part of the rear foot is bent. Thrusting from the waist, stimulating the tendons in the hanging foot and hold both legs tight with the toes gripping the floor (which aids one's ability to root).

14. Remaining Horse, Double Thrust

Remain in the horse stance with both hands thrust outwards. The four fingers should be held together and tight while being angled slightly downwards. The height of the arm should be slightly lower than shoulder-level, with both palms parallel and the distance between both palms being the same as the shoulders. Exhale so as to promote power.

Please note: Sanzhan emphasizes swallowing, spitting, floating and sinking. The thrusting out is called "floating." The body and waist must be straight while the shoulders must be level and sinking.

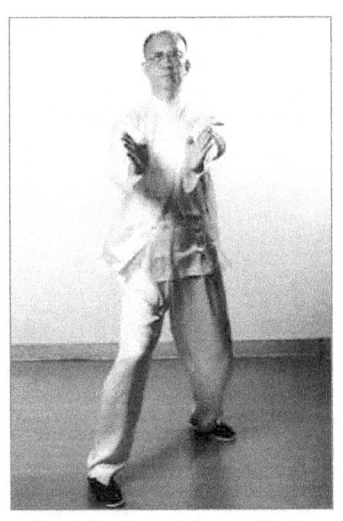

15. Remaining Horse, Sitting Joint

Remain in the horse stance. Ensure that the shoulders are sunk (as are the wrists) and the palms vertical. The elbows are held slightly bent. With power from the toes, one's belly and anus must be elevated and the horse tightened.

Please note: The "sitting joint" is a "sinking" technique while the precise "sitting" point (which is also a strength point) is the heel of the palm. The arms serve as power-transmitting vehicles as one breathes out from and back to one's dantian.

16. Remaining Horse, Swallowing In

Remaining in one's horse as both palms slowly transmit energy and power by swallowing in. The upper arms twist and turn while the vertical palms change into "facing towards the body" palms. As one's body turns to the right one swallows one's right shoulder and right cartilage.

Please note: "Swallowing" is called floating.[7] Inhale with the stomach firm. Strength comes from tightening one's horse.

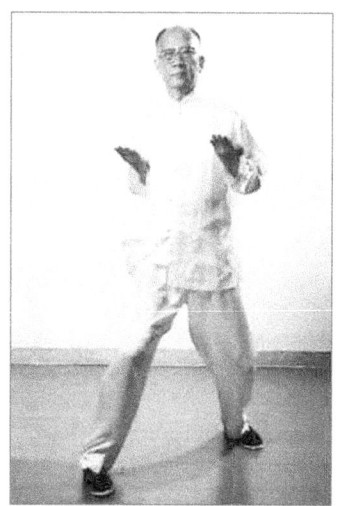

17. Remaining Horse, Spitting Out

Remaining in one's horse as both palms slowly push outwards from beneath the armpits thus transmitting energy through the "spit," slowly twist and turn the upper arms. With the palms facing upwards they transform into vertical palms. The elbows are in, the palms are vertical but facing inwards slightly and slightly angled. The distance between the palms is less than the distance between the elbows. As the left cartilage swallows, the body turns to the left. The shoulders shake and the horse stabilizes.

Please note: "Spitting" is also called "sinking".[8] Exhale and shake the stomach. Both arms must be almost level, but angled slightly downwards - in order to give the impression of water running off the arms. With the palm heels exerting strength, spitting out must have stability and power. This can only be achieved when one's mind is truly focused! When swallowing or spitting one must pay strict attention to the transformation between yin and yang.

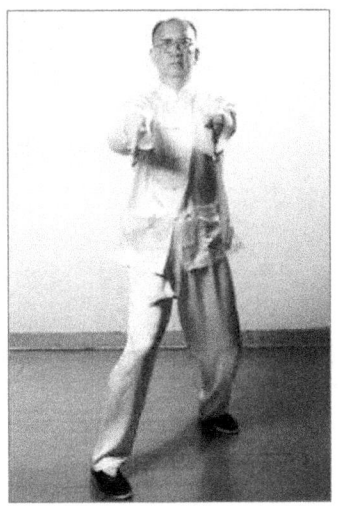

18. Advancing Horse (jingma)
Double withdrawing and double thrusting, the joints sit as one swallows and spits (two steps, the same as before).

The right foot steps forward (about one sole's distance) and the left foot follows. Both hands sit and remain stable.

Repeat, twice (steps 14 -17).

Please note: The above is to practice the Advancing Horse method.

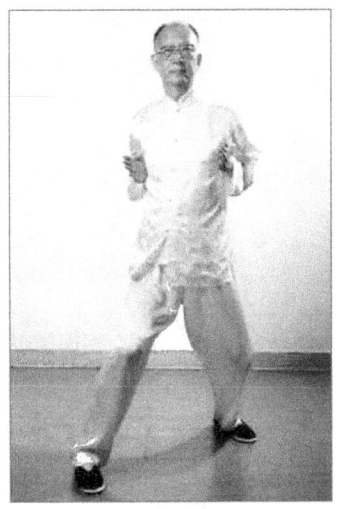

19. Backward Stepping/Withdrawing Horse (tuima), Double Drawing In
The rear foot withdraws first withdraws (one sole's distance) as the front foot then follows (to also withdraw). Both hands withdraw and sit beneath the armpits.

Please note: The following is to practice the Withdrawing Horse method.

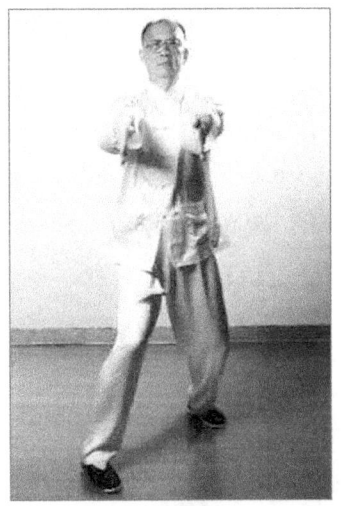

20. Remaining Horse, Double Thrust
As before.

21. Remaining Horse, Sitting joint
As before.

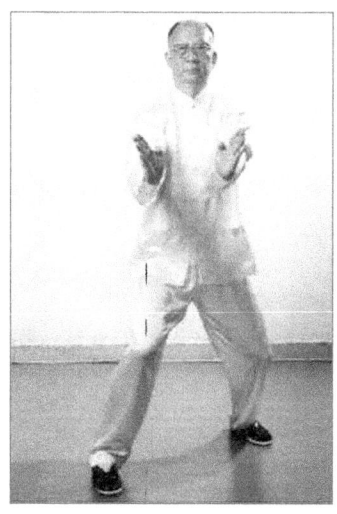

22. Remaining Horse, Swallowing In
As before

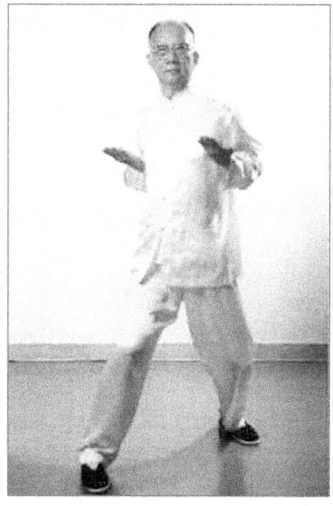

23. Remaining Horse, Spitting Out
As before.

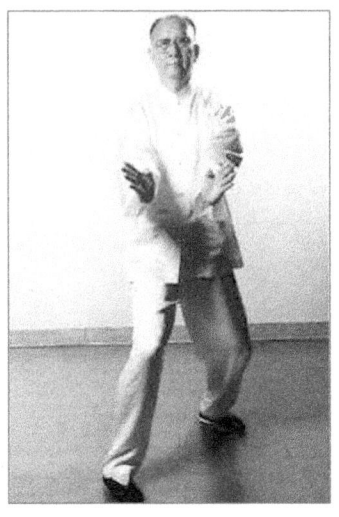

24. Backward-Stepping, Double Drawing In, Double Thrust, Sitting Joint, Swallowing, Spitting

Two Steps, As Before.

Step forwards three steps then backwards three steps and with each step followed by a thrusting action with a Sitting Joint, a Swallow and a Spit. This is Sanzhan.[9]

Please note: The three forward steps and the three backward steps are combined with the swallowing, spitting, floating and sinking with strength involving both a hard and a soft state with yin and yang differentiating and determining. All this is performed within the area required by a lying bull.

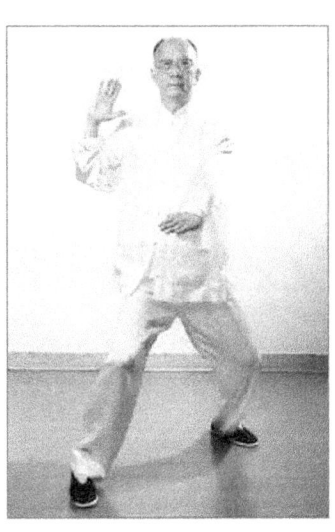

25. Forward Right Horse, Double Closing

The right foot steps forward and the left foot follows. The left hand moves forward using forward strength as the right hand lifts upwards so that it is close to the right ear lobe (into the state of Subduing A Tiger). Immediately, both hands move to the center and attack with the right fist being held at the front and the left fist held close to the "calf of the right hand."

Please note: The two forces must join with both hands striking towards one's center-line and with both fists held in front of the chest.

26. Withdrawing Horse, Hanging Right Foot, Double Opening

With one's left foot, step back one step and withdraw the right foot (as a follow-step) and tap the floor (meaning to assume a hanging stance or empty stance with one's weight upon the rear (left foot) as both hands move from an up to down position as

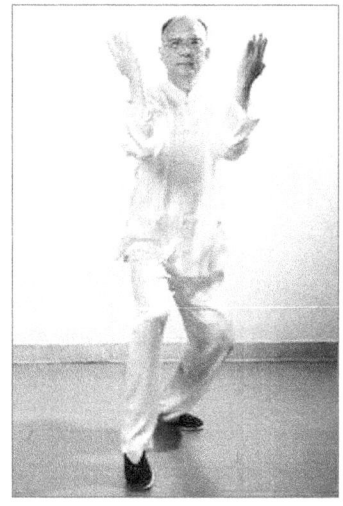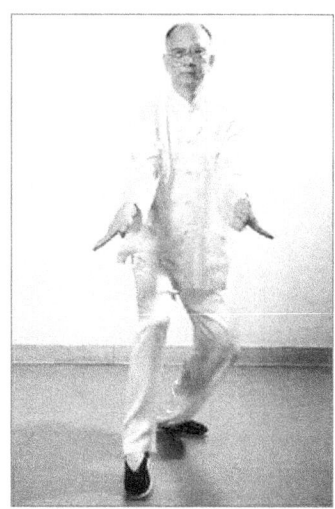

they descend and spread out (separating and "splitting") towards one's left and one's right finishing-up in line with each other (level with each other and opposite each other).

Please note: The separating/splitting/dividing strength with the left hand pointing outwards and downwards to the left while the right hand pointing outwards and downwards to the right must be with both arms slanting downwards so as to imitate the free-flow of water.

27. Forward Right Foot, Striking Joint

With the right foot effecting a large stomp as it steps forward the left foot follows in order to assume the Four Even Horse (*sipingma*). The right hand draws back and lodges beneath the left armpit where it is held reserved thus storing strength.[10] As one's waist

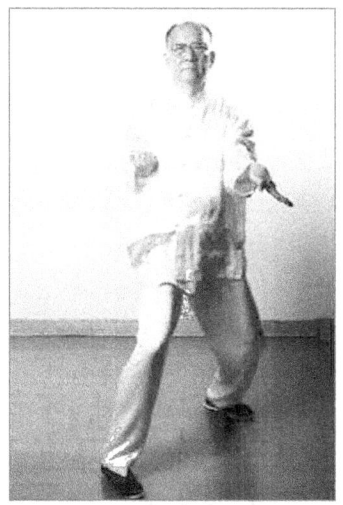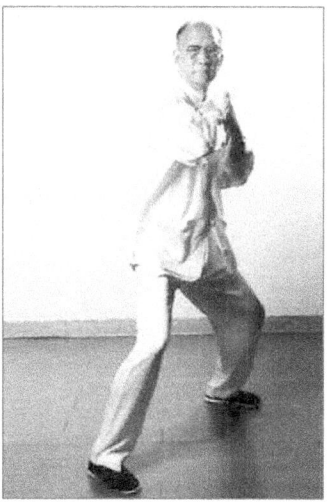

drives the shoulders one bends the arm at the elbow and effects a horizontal strike before one then assumes an Empty Horse. The left hand now protects the right wrist.

Please note: This action employs horizontal strength (force and power). The strike-joint must shake the waist as well as fueling cartilage strength. Strength is driven from the shoulder blades while the tip of the elbow must be lower than the shoulder.

28. Remaining Horse, Right Hand Slicing

From an Empty Horse adopt the Three Battle Horse (sanzhanma) with the right hand twisting palm downwards in a slicing manner. This strike is effected low and is aimed at dantian level. Both shoulders must be level.

Please note: This technique uses a tilting force while the knife-hand strike is to be the focal point of that force.

29. Remaining Horse, Left Hand Driving, Twisting And Slicing (left hand 45 degree)

With one's Horse Stance remaining the same as above, one's left hand must now twist while held tilting backwards. As it twists it must also slice at dantian level. Both shoulders must be held level.

Please note: This technique uses Straight Force (power) while the knife-hand strike is to be the focal point of that force.

30. Remaining Horse, Right Hand Preparing

Withdraw the right hand towards the left shoulder and deliver a downward knife-hand strike. The left hand/arm exerts power to pull back towards the armpit so that both hands effect a freeing-up action.

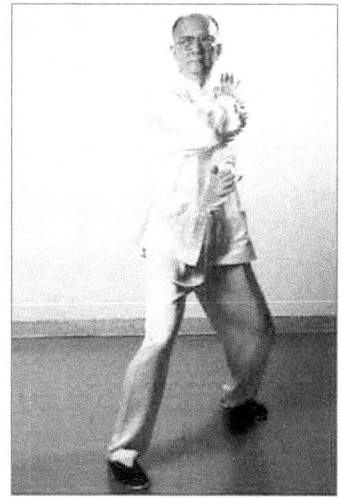 

Please note: This technique uses straight power where both hands must exert opposing yet complementary strengths.

31. Withdrawing Horse, Hanging Horse

With one's left foot supporting one's body (this is where one's centre of gravity is focussed) withdraw the right foot and hold it such that the toes are tapping the floor lightly and gently in an attitude of the Empty Stance. One's left hand is uppermost thus transmitting strength while the left hand and wrist are twisted outwards with the elbow held inwards. The right hand, meanwhile, also transmits with the right hand flexed and twisted backwards as the right shoulder sinks inwards thus both hands assume the "Holding the Tablet" posture.

Please note: Maintain and preserve strength with the yin and yang hands twisted. By way of this posture one defends one's Middle Gate as the left hand is in-line with the left foot and the right foot is in-line with the right hand.

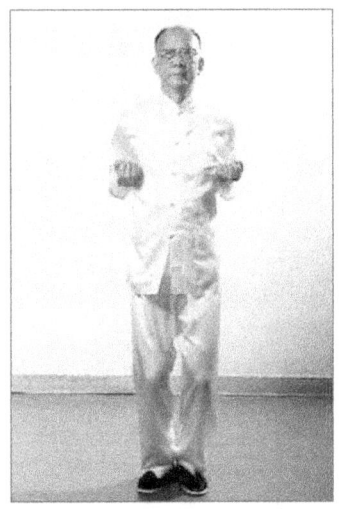 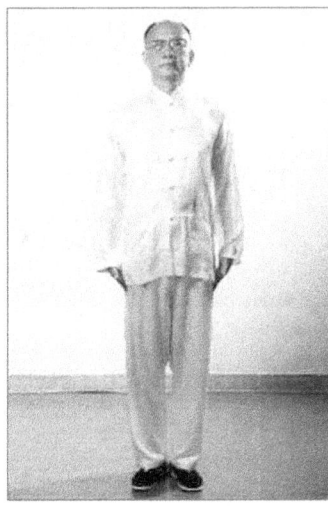

32. Stand Straight with Winding, Coiling, Twisting Hands Withdrawing

With the left hand up and holding firm while the right hand is down (preparing) they cross each other (coiling, winding and twisting back) as the right foot withdraws, thus one stands upright and straight. With both fists holding firm and place immediately beneath the armpits the fists open thus changing into palms then push (rub) down one's sides until they are hanging at one's sides. One has thus returned to one's starting position (posture).

Please note: The coiling hands are achieved by twisting the fists on the double pull-back and the double downward pushing/rubbing action.

SHIZI (CROSS PATTERN)

An alternative name for this taolu is, "Three Battle Shizi" (Sanzhanshizi). Along with "Hitting the Corners" and "Double Tranquility," these three Taizu forms are known collectively as Taizuquan's three essential taolu. This, then, is an essential program for beginners.

While the door and the window must be well-knit, straight-forward actions together with hard strikes and hard blocks is a way to develop fierce forceful fist-momentum. A direct transmission and a transforming of the breath is also used in order to generate power and strength as one sends out the fist, accompanied by loud shouts. Thus, the nature of Taizuquan is well demonstrated by way of these three all-important forms.

A GUIDE TO ZHIZI

Inviting Fist.

Stepping out into a left horse stance, effect a right-handed punch then step forward into a right horse stance and effect a left-handed punch. Adopt a Whispering Horse stance then punch three times before withdrawing into a right Hanging Horse and executing a double break. Advance with a horse-mantis flick/bounce then step into a Whispering Horse stance and strike out at a joint.

Moving into a Stamping Horse stance perform the Child Holding the Tablet technique. Turn towards the Back Gate and into a left horse stance with the left hand capturing. Remaining in a left horse the right hand delivers one punch before advancing into a right horse with the left hand effecting one punch then adopt a Whispering Horse stance and then three consecutive punches.

Withdraw into a right hanging horse and effect a double break then move forwards into a mantis horse and bounce. Effect a Whispering Horse stance followed by a joint strike then adopt a stamping horse and execute the Child Holds the Tablet. Return to a Front Gate posture by way of a left horse and a left hand capture then adopt a remaining horse stance with the right hand effecting a single punch. Use an advancing (right) Horse with the right hand capturing and the left hand effecting a single punch.

By way of an advancing (left) Horse and a left-hand capture technique the right hand performs a single punch. By way of a Remaining Horse with the hand naturally following and raising, the left foot drags and conceals as the left hand chops/cuts while naturally following and raising. With the right foot dragging and concealing, the right hand chops/cuts as the hand naturally follows and raises, then drag the left foot while concealing it as the left hand chops/cuts. Stamp to the corner and cross the left gate with an Even Horse and twist the hand and "double-wipe" (like the action of wiping a brush in an ink-well).

Return to the Front Gate and hang the right foot like a "lion-cub shaking a bell" mirroring the Even Horse with the right rubbing and left shaking. The right hand blocks as you stamp to the corner and across the right gate into an even horse and twist the hand as you double-wipe. Return to the front gate and hang the left foot in the "lion cub shaking a bell" mirroring the Even Horse with the left rubbing and right shaking. The left hand blocks and stamp to the center in a Walking Horse rubbing manner.

Using a Whispering Horse/Mantis Bounce withdraw into a right horse stance with the left hand raising then withdraw into a left horse stance with the right hand dissolving. Adopting a Remaining Horse, hang the right foot along with a Facing the Sun Hand (*Chaoyangshou*) and withdraw the fist.

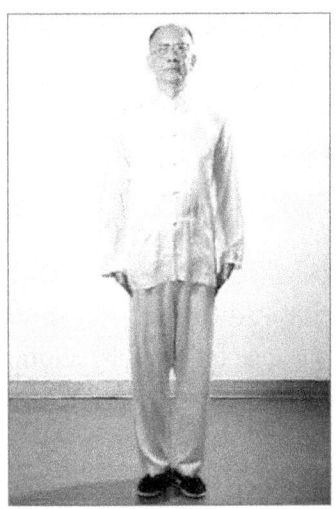

1. Stand straight
Breathe evenly, stand upright, tuck in the chin, look directly forward (horizontally) and sink the shoulders.

2. Inviting Fist
This is performed in the same way as the Inviting Fist of the Sanzhan (Three Battles) form. Each Taizuquan taolu begins with the Inviting Fist which has become the format and standard for this style of quanfa. The Inviting Fist movements and postures include, "double crossing cartilage," "double capture," "holding the inviting fist," "swallowing,"

and "spitting." The ancient version includes "crossing cartilage," "swallowing," and "holding the inviting fist."

3. Crossing Right Cartilage, Right Fist Withdrawing

Cross the cartilage into a triangular body shape/structure with the right fist drawing back so that it is in line with the left nipple.

4. Forward Left Horse, Right Hand Freeing Fist (Coiling)

Stepping forward one step with the left foot into the Three Battle Horse, tighten your horse stance and pass your right hand across your center-line. The five fingers straighten and exert strength with the clench fist as it withdraws and coils back. The fist must twist and turn as it slight sinks. Both shoulders must be level.

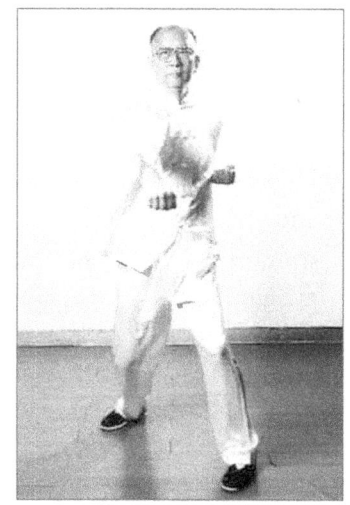
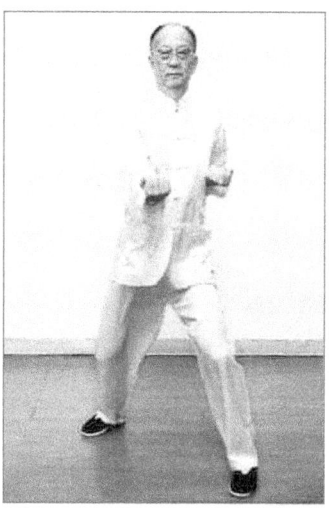

Please note: The exerting fist must be fast and heavy as one generates power though the breath. The shoulders should swallow while one's horse coils and tightens.

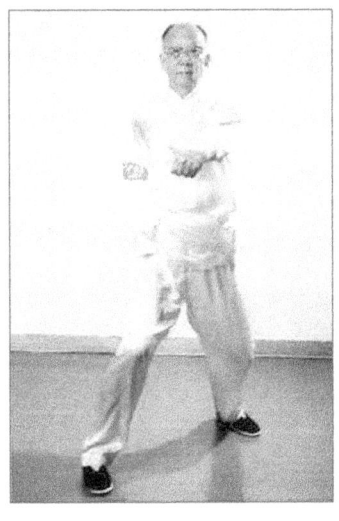
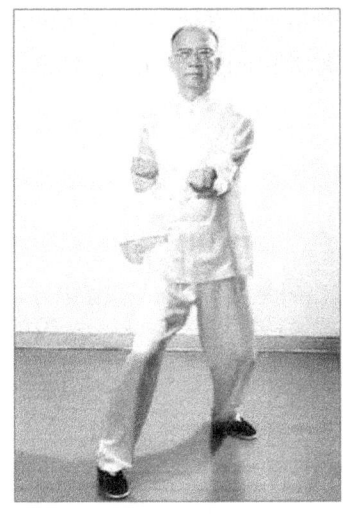

5. Forward Right Horse, Left Hand Freeing Fist (Coiling)

The right fist exerts strength while coiling back. The elbow must be close to the rib-cage and the right foot advances forward one step into the Three Battle Horse. One's Horse must tighten and the left hand must cross one's center-line. The fist must twist and coil and sink slightly. Both shoulders must be level. The coiling method is the same as above.

Please note: Storing strength is like drawing a bow and the punching hand as if shooting an arrow while strength within the punch must exert maximum (100%) power.

6. Whispering Right Horse and Right Struggling (Freeing) Fist

The right foot steps forward one small step ensuring that the space between the two feet is about one foot's length. The left foot follows maintaining the same distance. The right hand crosses one's center-line as with the above technique.

7. Remaining Horse, Struggling Left Fist

Remaining in your current horse stance, your left hand immediately crosses your center-line.

8. Remaining Horse, Struggling Right Fist (Coiling/Twisting/Wringing/Entangling)

Remaining in your current horse your right hand immediately crosses your center-line. Remain in your horse for the next three punches which must be executed all in one breath. After the third punch restrain your horse with the right fist coiling back.

Please note: The three consecutive punches must be continuous and their condition fierce and vigorous. The rhythm and position must remain constant. This is called, "occupy, place and strike."

9. Withdraw the Horse, Hang the Right Foot, Incline the Body, and Double Break Downwards

Withdrawing your left foot your right foot follows and stamps upon the ground so that you end up in a right empty stance. The right hand is poised backwards while

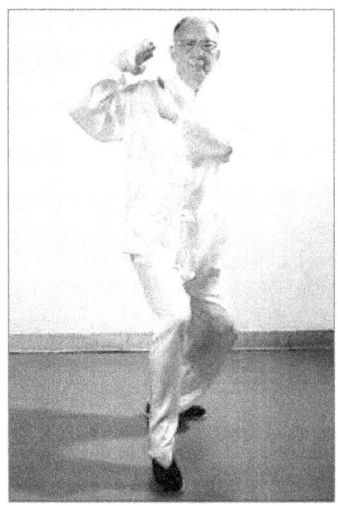 

the left hand protects the shoulder. Holding both palm-blades as your power-point and focal point, both hands break downwards towards the bottom left.

Please note: Inclining and turning your body in order to avoid the oncoming attack, double break in order to defend against the next attack.

10. Whispering Horse, Mantis Bounce

With your right foot forward and with the left foot following, draw back both hands to your left shoulder as you turn your waist and twist to the left. With your right palm facing down but above and your left palm underneath let it spring outwards and forward at a height that is slightly lower than your shoulder. With your body and waist shaking and your back straight allow your hands to spring out as if they were the front feet of a lobster (or dragon-prawns as we call them in China: *longxia*).

Please note: Both arms must be bent not straight (locked). The spine serves as the axis while the cartilage is from opening to closing. Adopt the bow and arrow horse stance in order to maximize the force of the attack. The strength from the waist and shoulder is sent out together - as one - strong and forceful just like a whirlwind.

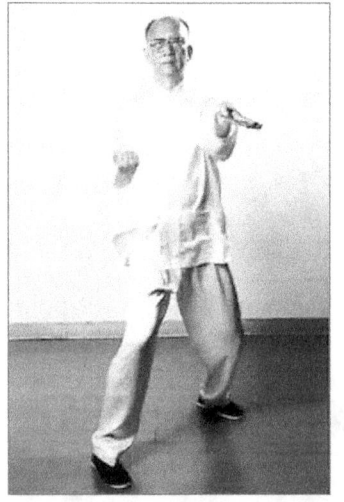

11. Remaining Horse, Left Hand Capture

From the Remaining Horse, hold tight the left hand as it captures in a circular manner from the bottom left. Pausing in-line with the left shoulder, the fingers and palm should tilt outwards and to the left. Strength and power should be exerted strength through both the palm and the wrist.

12. Whispering Horse, Right Hand Striking Joint

Adopting a right horse and with the right arm bent at the elbow, strike horizontally from right to left. The tip of the elbow is forwards and level with the heart while the left hand protects the right wrist.

Please note: The right horse changes into a Middle Gate and trap the forward foot of the opponent while using the waist combined with the joint and strike.

13. Left Stamp Horse

The left hand moves from the top to the right and to the left then open your horse and stamp out into a left horse stance.

Please note: The Stamping Horse first moves forward one small step in order to close in on the enemy thus making it easier to enter and penetrate his gate and so obtain control of his position.

 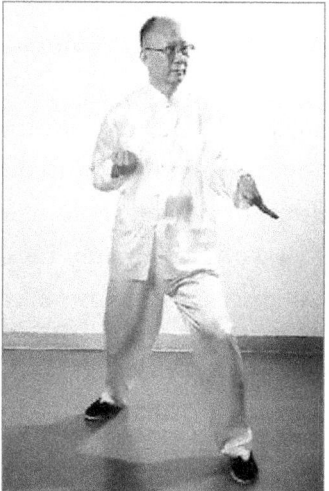

14. Advance Right Horse, Hold the Tablet

Continuing to move up and, at the same time, step out into a right horse stance, the right hand moves from the top and to the left and right holding out. The left hand stretches out in order to defend and protect. Change your stance into a right bow and arrow horse while holding the tablet ensuring that your weight is balanced on the front foot with the rear foot reinforcing the status. Tighten your status and hold both hands into fists as they twists backwards into a Three Battle Horse.

Please note: One's Stamping Horse must be tight and swift while when holding the tablet one must sink and be heavy as well as compact. The right hand "holds" and defends while the left hand is closed. The right hand is spread out and open and so, together with the left hand, splits the oncoming attack. Strength is sent outwards as the hands "enter" the top cavity of the attacker's stomach.

15. Rear-Cross Gate, Stepping Out Into a Left Horse as the Left Hand Captures

As the right foot steps out forward and sideways, next turn left and cross the back gate. The left foot is now in front with the left hand moving from bottom to the right and then capturing to the left.

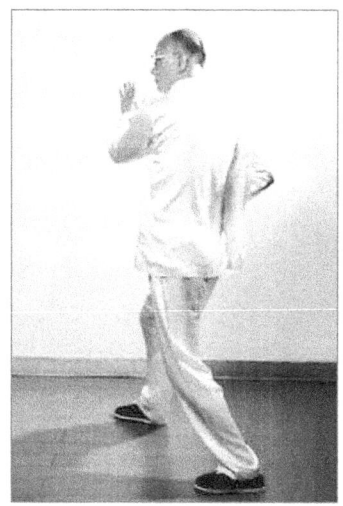 

Please note: Turn the body and capture at the same time while the hands, feet and eyes also arrive at the same time in order to defend a rear attack.

16. Remaining Horse, Right Hand Struggling Fist (Twisting Upwards)

Repeat, as per #5 - #14.

Tighten your horse with your right hand passing your center-line. The fist is held at the same level as your heart. Open your five fingers exerting strength and holding them tight. Twist them

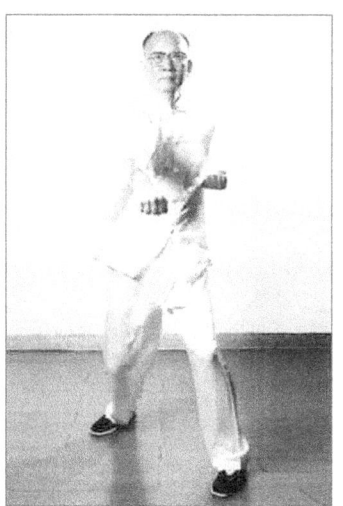 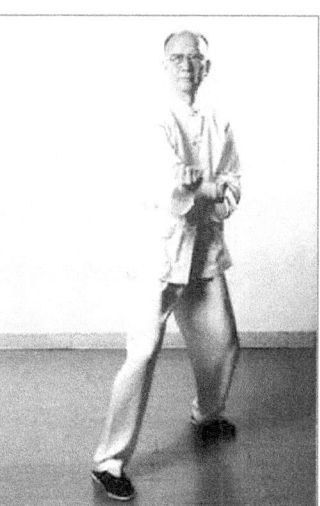

upwards and withdraw the joint. The movement at the Back Gate is the same as the Front Gate movement. Then repeat the action.

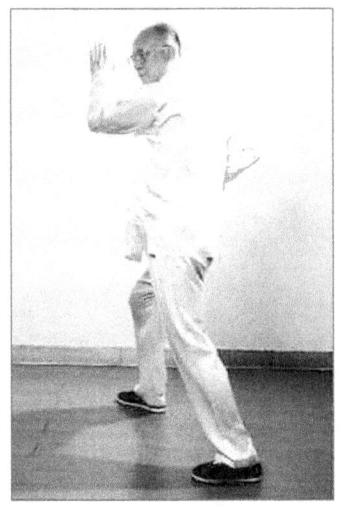 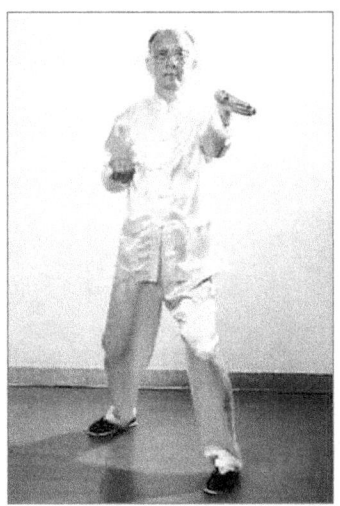

17. Turning Front Gate, Stepping Out Left Horse, Left Hand Capturing

The right foot step across as the body turns to the left in order to complete "Crossing the Gate." At this time the left foot is in front with the left hand passing from left to right in a crescent-shape, arc-like curve, stopping in front of the left shoulder. (Mark, the two lower images are the same as in #15)

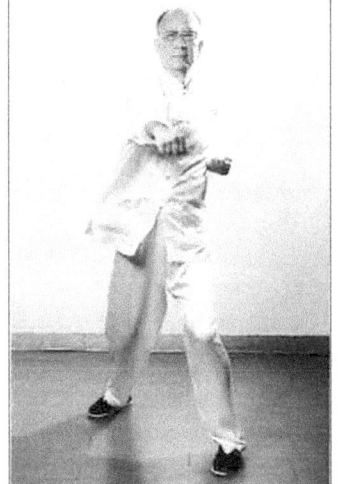

18. Remaining Horse, Right Hand Struggling, One Punch

Remaining in the same stance as the right hand passes across one's center line.

19. Enter Right Horse, Right Hand Capture

Step out with your right foot into a horse stance and immediately effect a right-hand capture from right to left in arc-like and curve-like manner. The stepping and capturing should be done at the same time with hands and feet coordinating.

20. Remaining Horse, Left Hand Struggling, One Punch

Remain in the same horse stance and have your left hand pass your center-line.

21. Enter Left Horse, Left Hand Capture

Step out with your left foot and immediately have your left hand capture. The stepping-out and capturing should be done at the same time with the hands and feet coordinating.

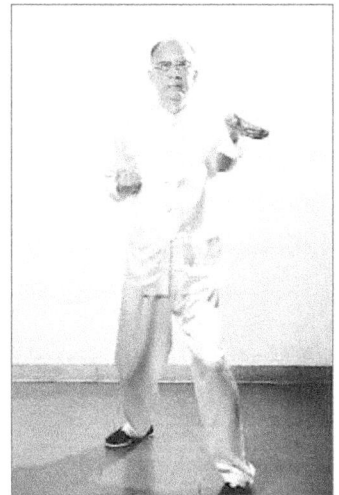

22. Remaining Horse, Right Hand Struggling One Punch

Remain in the same horse stance and have your right hand pass your center-line.

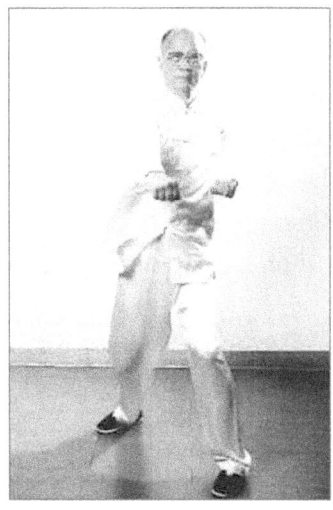

23. Remaining Horse, Right Hand Raising

Remain in the same horse stance and continue with the upper movement. The right hand of the rising fist changes into a palm position while withdrawing and moving slightly downwards as it moves in an arc shape as it lifts outwards and towards the top right. It should be held slightly higher than shoulder level and must exert strength from the waist.

Please note: While raising, swallow the right cartilage. The body returns to the center as the arm rises speedily as the shoulders effect a loud sound.

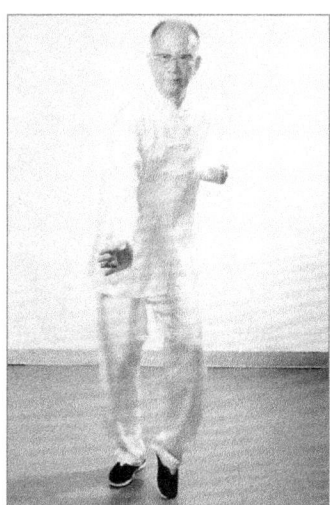 

24. Twisting the Right Hand, Dragging and Concealing the Left Foot

The right hand moves, using firm strength, in an arc shape while moving towards the left and downwards to conceal. Meanwhile, the left foot draws in, in an arc with the little toe (which does not leave the ground) and so, by way of exerting strength, one assumes a right horse stance.[11]

Please note: The twisting hand uses constant force as opposed to any sudden burst of strength. While the dragging foot must exert full but gradual strength, in order to exert strength to its maximum force in accordance with the twisting hand action, support from top to bottom is effected while coordinating left to right.

25. Right Horse, Left Chopping Hand

Remain in the same horse stance while the left hand moves from the left armpit into a side-standing palm-strike (with the palm's center angled slightly upwards). Chop outwards and downwards and towards the front while exerting strength from the palm-blade in-line with the dantian with the fist routed towards the center.

Please note: While chopping, do not loosen the shoulders.

26. Remaining Horse, Left Hand Rising

Remaining in the same horse stance, the left hand rotates and rises outwards from left to right so that it is slightly higher than shoulder level. Strength must be exert from the waist.

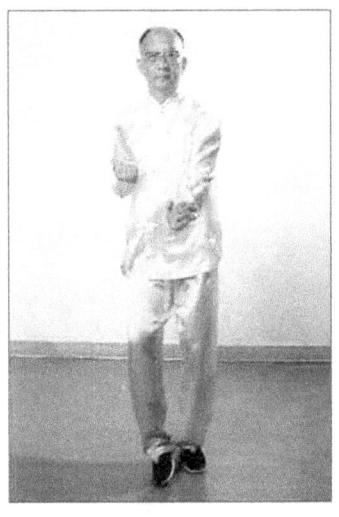 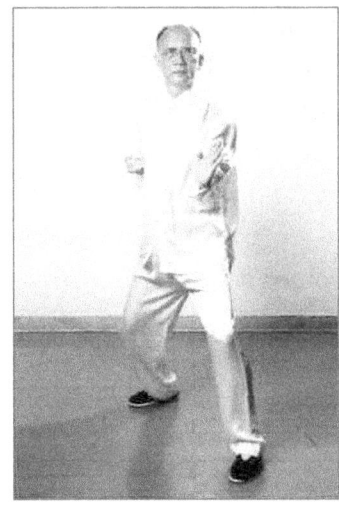

27. Twisting the Left Hand, Concealing and Dragging the Right Foot

The left hand moves from top to bottom drawing an arc in the process. Concealing firm strength the right foot draws inwards in an arc and backwards in order to form a left horse stance while exerting strength.

28. Left Horse, Right Chopping Hand

Remain in the same posture as in #27 as the right hand chops out as in #25; although #25 uses the other hand to chop (or slice).

29. Right Hand Rising

Repeat steps #23, #24 and #25.

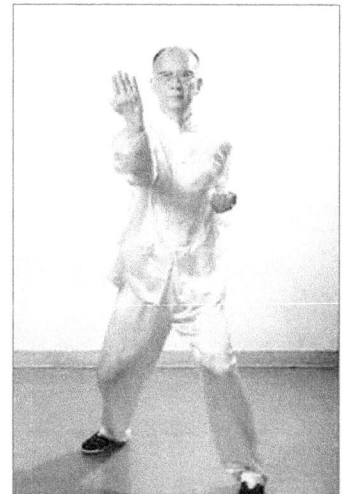
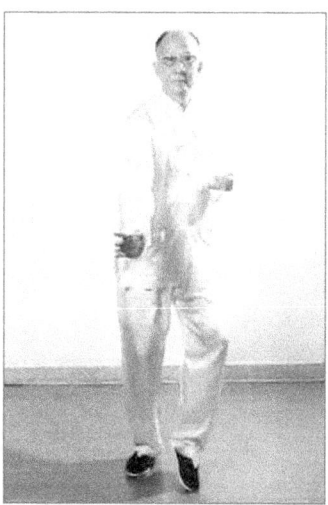

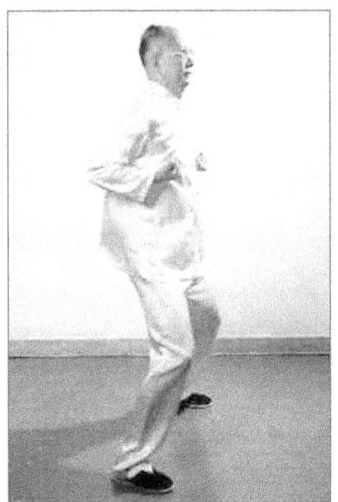 

30. Turning Left, Four Level Horse, Shedding Hand, Double Slam

With your right foot moving out and to the left adopt a level horse stance and cross both hands to shed them out. Hold as fists and place them both under the armpits. Both fists move to the front and fall downwards into a double strike. The body must not lean forwards.

Please note: Adopting the four-level (sitting) horse stance both feet must be parallel and must also sink. Effect a double slam in order to strike the opponent's lower stomach. This way of training - by standing and striking - can also be used as a way of developing "Standing Strength."

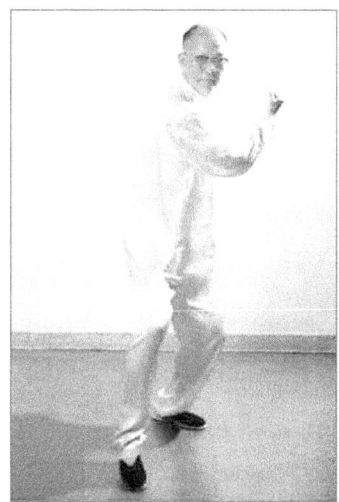 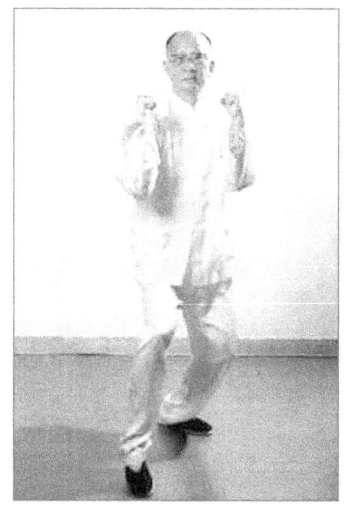

31. Turning to the Front Gate, Hanging the Right Foot, Lion Rings the Bell

Turning your body to the right but still facing the front gate, the tip of the right foot "clicking" the ground[12] so as to adopt a right-footed empty step. Both hands should be held as fists from the lower left with the arm bent at the elbow and so exerting strength as you lift them upwards. Both fists finish close to the shoulders.

Please note: This is an excellent method of dissolving as you bind together the inner joint. Changing from the Double Slam into the Lion Ringing the Bell, one must exert strength from the waist and not simply adopt the correct hand posture. In some other quanfa manuals this technique is called, Double Lifting.

32. Withdraw the Right Foot Into a Level Horse, Cross Cartilage, Right Scratch, Left Shake

Withdraw the right foot into a Four Level Horse and immediately right cross cartilage into an Empty Horse with the right hand scratching and clawing down from top to left and then across to the right. The left hand (palm downwards) should exerting strength from the knife-edge as it is thrown forwards by way of shaking power. The crossing cartilage together with the clawing and shaking must be completed at the same time.

Please note: While crossing the cartilage tighten your horse using the waist in order to draw strength from both cartilage. Turn to the right thus sending out strength swiftly and vigorously. The shaking hand must draw strength from the waist and cartilage as one attacks the opponent's stomach and intestines.

33. Left Cross Cartilage into Right Hand Defending

Left cross cartilage into a left bow and arrow stance with the right hand defending at the same level as the shoulder.

Please note: Whist defending, loosen your shoulder in order to attack from a further (longer range) distance.

34. Turn Right into a Four Level Horse Stance, Shed Hand, Double Spread Evenly to Shake

With both hands crossing over and shedding outwards, put both hands into fists and place under the armpits. Tighten your horse stance both fists falling downwards to strike. Ensure that the body does not lean forward.

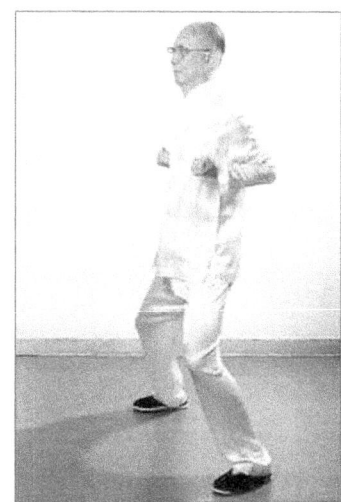 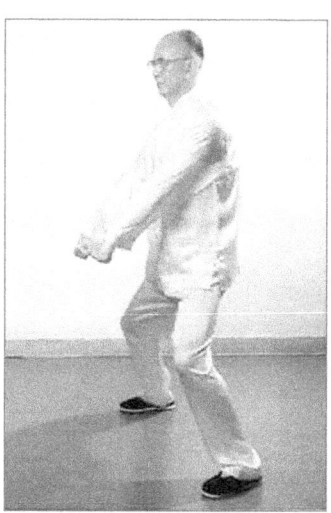

35. Turn to Front Gate with the Left Foot Hanging, Assume a Left-Footed, "Lion Rings The Bell" Posture.

With the body turning to the left but still facing the front gate, the tip of the left foot clicks the ground and with both hands held as fists (from the lower right, upwards) bend the elbow and exert strength and lift up. With both fists close to the shoulders, this technique (in some of the other fist manuals) is called double-lifting.

 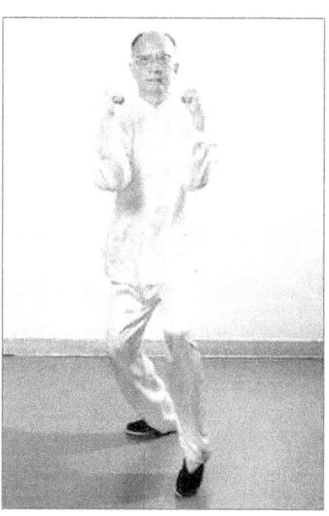

36. Withdraw the Left Foot into a Level Horse Stance, Cross the Cartilage, Left Clawing, Right Shaking

As the left foot clicks the ground withdraw into a four level horse and immediately cross the left cartilage to adopt an empty horse, With the left hand clawing down from top to right and then to the left, the right hand palm exerts strength from its knife edge and shakes out towards the front. Crossing the cartilage and clawing and shaking must be completed at the same time.

Please note: The requirement for crossing the cartilage is the same as in #32 only in the opposite direction.

37. Right Crossing Cartilage, Left Hand Defending

Right cross cartilage into a right bow and arrow horse with the left hand defending at the same level as the shoulder.

Please note: Loosen the shoulders in order to defend.

38. Walking Horse and Rubbing (Mother-In-Law Rubbing)

This movement must be continuous with both feet coordinating with the hands. With the waist as the axis, shake your body to the left and to the right in a similar way that an elderly female performer would do so when stepping in Chinese opera. With the mouth open like lion and the right hand above and the left hand in contact with the belly of right hand, both palms open in the shape of a lion's mouth while both hands twist and tighten as you cross the cartilage while smoothing out and stroking in.

Please note: The "Walking Horse and Rubbing" must demonstrate power and ferocity while also being smooth and relaxed. The rubbing must be firm with the hand, joint, waist and foot exerting combined strength.

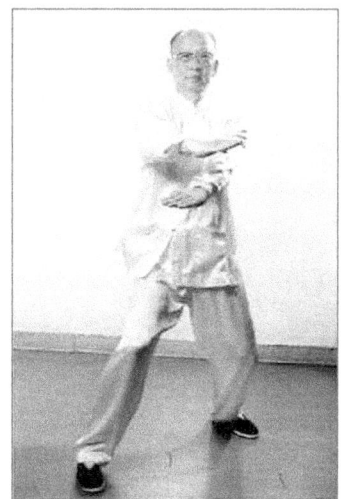

39. Whispering Right Horse, Mantis Shrimp Bouncing

The "Whispering Right Horse" is performed with both hands bending inward as you store strength before bouncing it outwards as in #10.

Please note: Both hands should be slightly bent while bouncing outwards. They must not be too straight while the waist must twist and turn to the right, sending out strength with power. The Whispering Right Horse changes into a Bow and Arrow Horse stance in order to help to maximize power when bouncing outwards.

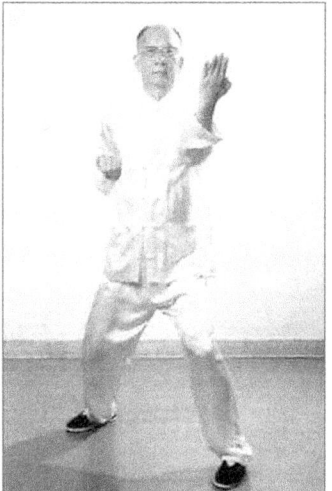

40. Withdrawing Right Horse, Left Hand Rising

The right foot must step backwards one step into a left horse stance with the left hand rising outwards.

41. Withdrawing Left Horse, Right Hand Breaking

Withdraw the left foot one step so as to adopt a right horse with the left hand placed under the left armpit. Send out power directly from under the left arm as the left hand draws back.

Please note: There are three methods of "Breaking": Upper breaking, Level (mid-line) breaking, and Lower breaking. The technique described here is the level breaking method. It can be used in order to attack the opponent's head and face, but it can also dissolve an attack by attacking and can block and attack an oncoming attack when the attack is coming from the upper level.

42. Withdrawing Horse, Hanging Right Foot

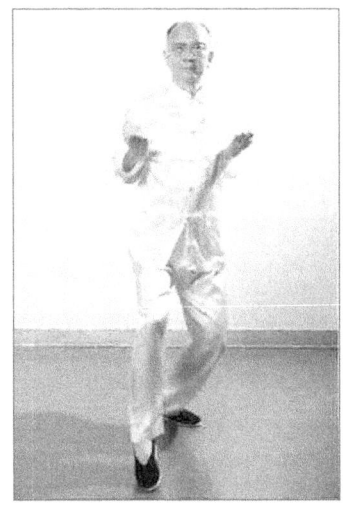

As the rear foot withdraws one small step the front foot follows in the same manner, with the tip of the font foot touching gently upon the ground and hanging there in a right empty stance. The right hand is held higher than the left as it draws in coiling, rotating, winding and spiralling. Each hand is placed under the armpit as strength is exerted and spat out with standing palms. The right hand is in front with the palm facing to the left while the left hand is behind and adhering to the right. With the fingers pointing upwards they adopt the Chaoyang Hands position (Facing the Sun).

Please note: Chaoyang Hands involves one hand being behind the other as together they form the Middle Palace (temple) position and the Eight Diagrams. Attack and defence is based upon opportunities which open up all kinds of combative strategies.

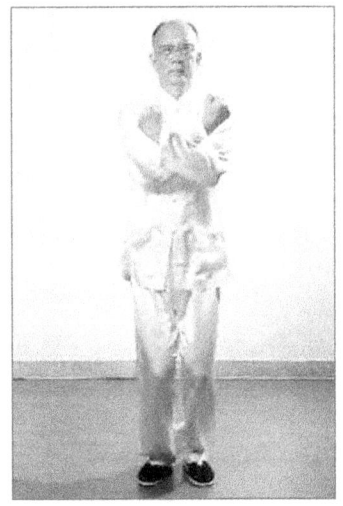  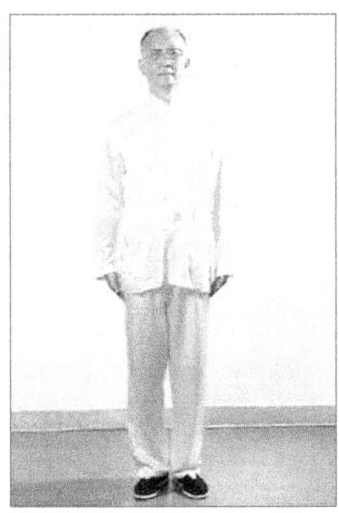

43. Coiling Hand, Withdrawing, and Standing Straight

The right foot withdraws with both feet side by side forming a small character eight. At the same time the right hand is above the left in a coiling and clenching fist, and is then placed under the armpits. Both hands drop downwards and standing up straight as one returns to one's point of origin. This is the end of this fist form.

DANTOU

Dantou is also called *zhentou* or *chentou* in other fist manuals, but within this book I will be using the original name, Dantou. Dantou is known as one of the classic xing of Taizuquan with its strict and intense fist-work, frame and detailed lines. With its variable hand methods and flexible horse (stance), this form is another indication that the absence of impractical movements and non-functional postures is just so typical of Taizuquan.

In order to triumph over the powerful opponent hold your elbows in at your centre with your hands also inside the body (in front of your chest) so they can either release or withdraw, open or close and defend while "waiting" to advance (attack). Whether the launch comes from the upper or lower or from left or right, the body co-ordinates with each and every posture — with one following another with intensity and ferocity. The essential characteristic of Dantou is the three interlocked and interlinked techniques including *bian* ("whip"), *sanjiaohu* ("the three legged tiger") and *shuaidu* ("throwing the stomach").

QUANPU (FIST MANUAL)

Inviting/Enticing Fist (Qingquan).

Stamp your right foot out into a right horse stance and towards the right corner in order to assume the "pluck the phoenix tail" (*fengweicai*) posture. Remain in a horse and perform the "double throwing stomach" (*shuaidu*) technique and then the "double raising," "sitting joint," and "twisting back double defending" movements. The right hand then rises to perform the "triple defending" action.

Withdrawing into a right horse stance with the left hand capturing and the right hand assuming the three legged tiger, withdraw into a left horse with the right hand capturing and the left-handed assuming a three legged tiger. Then, withdrawing into a right horse stance, capture with the left hand then assume a right-handed three legged tiger and twist.

Stamp into a left horse towards the left corner and pluck the phoenix tail then assume the double throwing stomach, the double raising, the sitting joint, the twisting back and the double defending manoeuvres. Then raise the right hand and perform the Triple Defending technique.

Withdrawing the left foot, dodge to the right side and perform a double foot sweep. Withdraw the right foot and dodge to the right side and perform a double foot sweep with the left foot. Then move to your own centre and perform a double foot sweep with your right foot.

Turn to the right corner and step out into a right horse stance with the right hand pecking and the left hand whipping. Change to a left corner horse with the left hand pecking and then a right hand whipping. Now change to a right horse stance and use a right-hand pecking action applied to the centre and then perform a left hand whipping.

Withdraw into a level horse stance and hold your hand close to the shoulder with the right hand performing a slicing joint action. Shedding the left hand and stamping the right foot, double thrust towards the centre and perform the double throwing stomach action followed by a double raising action then the sitting joint action before twisting back in a double defending action.

Withdrawing into a right horse stance, rub the top and then effect a double even strike with the fist. Withdraw into a level horse stance to the left side and perform the Chicken Eating Wings movement then dodge to the right side and perform another Chicken Eating Wings (the state of the wings when a chicken is eating).

Stamp into a left horse double opening posture and then assume a right horse double carrying stance as you perform a double pecking action (meaning to strike with both hands at the space between the enemy's ears).

"Climbing Over the Back Gate," step out into a left horse with the left hand capturing. Stamping out the right foot with the right hand opening, slice with the right foot and withdraw into a level horse with the right hand defending.

Advance into a right horse with the right hand free and defend once again. Stamp into a right corner and step out into a right horse with the right hand capturing. Strike at the opponent between both his ears using a clawing and shaking action. Changing into a left horse with the left hand capturing, strike the opponent between the ears once again with the same clawing and shaking motion as before. Stamp into a right horse to the centre and execute the "Child Holding the Tablet" technique.

"Crossing Over the Front Gate" and step out into a left horse with the left hand capturing. Stamp into a right horse and hold one hand captive. Adopt the Rear Horse Reigning/Shooting posture.

Advance directly stepping out into a right horse and effect a "Cow Uncovering the Grass" (*niu jie cao*) technique. Withdrawing into a right horse with the left hand rising then withdraw into a left horse with the right hand breaking. Remaining in this horse, effect a right foot "Towards the Sun Hand" (*chaoyangshou*) technique.

Withdrawing Fist (shouquan)

1. Inviting Fist (Qing Quan)

As before.

Please note: Sink the shoulders and the elbows, tighten the crotch and knees, and be rooted as you tighten the front gate.

2. Stamping Right Horse Towards the Right Corner and Pluck the Phoenix Tail

The "Right Corner" means the upper right corner at a 45 degree angle. Stepping out with the left foot and into a right horse stance with both palms moving from the lower to the left and to the upper and out in an arc before both hands pluck from the front.

Please note: Stamping into a horse stance, one foot steps out sideways in a fast swift and light manner. Strength is by way of the plucking as the right cartilage swallows and the body sits in order to dissolve the oncoming attack.

3. Double Throwing Stomach

Tighten your horse stance and sink your qi as both hands exert strength from the knife hands as well as from the arms which are held level and in line with each other. Strike the opponent's lower belly (dantian).

Please note: Sinking the qi, the stomach is held firm. Strike out with a loud sound. Both hands follow the movement in order to oppress the oncoming attack.

4. Double Rising

Both hands separate and rise separately. Power is emitted from an outward-bouncing/shaking movement from the lower belly.

Please note: Remaining in your horse stance and borrow strength from the waist with the belly rising and moving outwards. After the front hand, throw the stomach and oppress the oncoming attack then raise one hand and strike the neck and chin of the opponent.

5. Sitting Joint

Bend and sink the joint ensuring that the palm is vertical.

Please note: Raising (floating) the joint, sink the shoulders and thrust out the shoulders blades.

6. Double Defense

Bend the four fingers while standing the palms and sitting the wrists. Exert strength from the palm heels as both hands simultaneously defend towards the front. Ensure they are level with the shoulders and twisted backwards.

Please note: Change from the Three Battle Horse into the Bow and Arrow Horse in order to enhance the power of the movement. Both hands defend and strike the shoulders of the opponent. Slightly loosen the shoulders and sit both wrists.

7. Triple Defense

The right hand rises to defend, then the left hand rises to defend, then the right hand rises to defend once more. These actions are to be done in the Remaining Horse.

Please note: The rhythm, speed and timing must conform and correspond with each other in order to raise one's qi. The strength arrives upon completion of the movement. Exert strength through sitting the wrists as you send out the technique.

8. Withdraw Right Horse, Left Hand Capturing and Seizing

Withdraw the foot into a right horse as the left hand captures.

9. Remaining Horse, Right Hand, Three-Legged Tiger Fist

Bend the left leg at the knee while holding the right leg slightly straighter than the left. Assume a bow and arrow horse stance and hold the right hand towards the front and punch downwards.

Please note: When performing the Three-Legged Tiger Fist one must loosen the shoulders. Follow the movement to bring out the strength.

10. Withdraw Left Horse, Right Hand Capturing

Withdraw the left horse with the right hand capturing.

11. Remaining Horse, Left Hand, Three-Legged Tiger Fist

Bending the right leg at the knee with the left leg slightly straighter than the right, assume a bow and arrow horse with the left hand towards the front and punch downwards.

12. Withdraw Right Horse, Turn to the Left Corner, Left Hand Capturing

The left corner means upper left corner 45 degrees. Withdraw into right horse with the tip of the left foot moving towards the left corner. The body follows and turns, left hand capturing.

Please note: The body needs to turn while withdrawing back into the right horse. This foot method is very simple and swift. Face the enemy as you change position.

13. Right Handed, Three-Legged Tiger Fist

With your left leg bent and the right leg slightly more straight, assume a bow and arrow horse with you right hand first forwards and then downwards as both hands twist backwards.

14. Stamp Left Towards the Left Corner And Pluck the Phoenix Tail

Step out with your right foot one small step to assume a left horse. Both hands change into palms following the step and move from the lower to the right side and then upwards, rolling/sweeping out. Then plucking forward, swallowing the left cartilage.

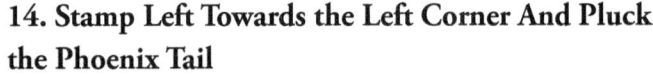

Please note: The Stamping Horse and Plucking must be effected in a gentle swaying motion with both elegance and grace.

116

QUANZHOU TAIZUQUAN

15. Double Throwing Stomach, Double Rising, Sitting Joint

As a double defense technique as well as a twisting back action the right hand rises to effect a triple defense.

Observe the main points as in #3—#7.

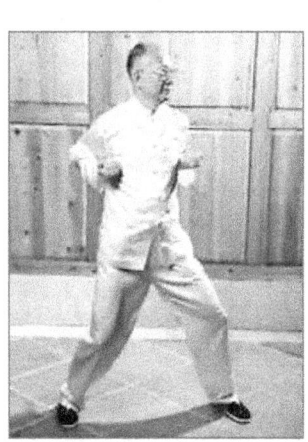

 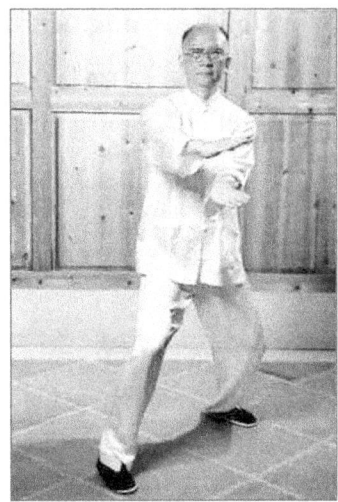

16. Withdrawing the Left Foot, Dodging to the Left Side, Slicing Right Foot, Double Chopping and Sweeping

Withdraw the left foot into a level horse with both hands chopping horizontally from left to right. The right foot moves from right to left in a sweeping manner as you coordinate both upper and lower strength. When the body is in position, pause.

Please note: The double chopping hands and the sweeping legs coordinate strength from both the left and the right and the upper and the lower as one sends out power so that the opponent is felled.

17. The Right Foot Withdraws and Dodges to the Right with the Left Foot Slicing. Effect a Double Chopping and Sweeping Action.

The main points here are as above, but everything is in reverse.

Please note: The horse stance must be wide as you withdraw the right foot - so that the dodging and turning can work better.

18. Right Foot to The Center, Double Chopping and Sweeping

Withdraw the left foot and stamp towards the center. Chop and sweep observing the main points as laid out in #20.

Please note: Advance straight towards the center.

19. Right Foot, Right Corner, Right Hand Pecking

Stamp your right foot towards the right at a 45 degree angle as the right hand exerts strength into the four fingers by way of a pecking motion.

Please note: The forearm coils outwards in an arc as if the capturing hand is receiving an attack. Engage and peck.

20. Following Progressively, Hands Concealing

Move the gravity and sit back in the horse. The right hand moves from an upper position and coils downwards with the fingers pointing upwards and the wrists sinking downwards.

Please note: This range of motion is from eyebrow level to the private parts with the arms cutting an arcing pathway resembling a method of movement indicative of a "lower eight diagram" (*xia bagua*).[13]

21. Remaining Horse, Left Hand Whipping

Shifting one's weight and gravity forward, one's left hand faces directly outwards as it whips straight forwards.

Please note: This whipping motion is one of the most fierce and powerful techniques within Taizuquan. Its fist-shape is crescent-like while the concealed striking outwards and downwards is called, "Pouring Down Upon the Head Whipping" while the strike aimed towards the face and nose is called, "Face-To-Face Whipping." Both techniques must be effected with might and a solid strength.

22. Changing/Switching to the Left Corner with the Left Hand Pecking

Withdraw the right foot and stamp into a left horse. Turn to the upper left into a 45 degree angle. The left hand exerts strength from the four fingers as you peck outwards.

23. Progressive Hand Concealing, Remaining Horse, Right Hand Whipping

The main points here are repeated as in #20- #21 except that here we use the Hanging Hands and the Switching Hands.

24. Switching to the Right Foot with the Right Hand Pecking Towards The Center, the Other Hand Follows Concealed, as You Maintain a Remaining Horse with the Left Hand Whipping

The key points here are the same as in #19 - #21 only the direction is facing towards the center.

25. Withdrawing Level Horse, Left Hand, Shaking Shoulder

Withdrawing from a right horse into a level horse, cross the cartilage, and raise your body with the left hand capturing sideways.

Please note: One must dodge prior to withdrawing into the level horse while shaking the shoulders.

26. Right Hand Cutting Joint

Left cross and dissolve while bending the right hand joint, cutting horizontally with the forearm.

Please note: The left arm draws back with the left shoulder swallowing. The right hand cuts horizontally at the same time crossing the cartilage.

27. Freeing Hand, Stamping Right Foot, Double Thrusting Middle

With the right hand freeing backwards the left hand hangs out in a shape similar to a Bagua palm (baguazhang). Advancing into a right horse facing towards the middle, both hands thrust outwards.

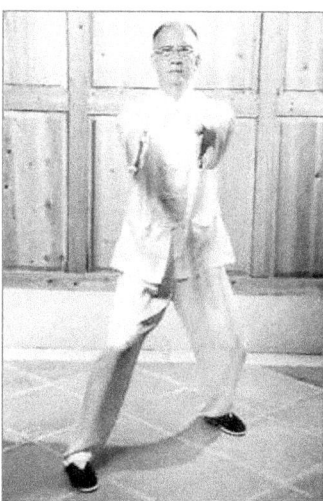

Please note: The double thrusting is performed in the same manner as in the Taizuquan sanzhan form and with both shoulders being level. In other quanfa manuals this movement is expressed as "Right Hand Opening" which we, ourselves, refer to as *diema* or "phoenix tail plucking". In conjunction with a left corner phoenix tail plucking and a right corner phoenix tail plucking, effect three matching movements.

28. Double Throwing Stomach, Double Rising, Sitting Joint, Double Defense

The key points here are the same as described earlier in #3, #4, #5 and #6.

29. Withdrawing Right Horse, Rubbing the Head

Withdrawing the right foot into a "crossing the cartilage" horse with, one's left hand above and the right hand beneath. The rubbing is effected from upper left to lower right.

Please note: Crossing the stomach and rubbing at chest level and abdomen level, one rubs the head in front of the shoulder while receiving an attack from a higher position. Some other fist experts refer to this as, "Crossing Stomach Rubbing."

30. Remaining Horse, Double Level Fist

Following on from this, effect a Double Pouncing Fist striking out towards the Middle Gate slightly lower than the shoulders.

Please note: Aimed at the shoulders and chest area or the head and face area.

31. Withdrawing Even Horse, Left Side Chicken Pecking Wings

Withdrawing your left foot, conceal your left hand as you gather and scoop inwards. Stamping out with your left foot into a level horse/ crossing cartilage stance, effect a right hand cutting joint you're your forearm.

32. Dodging to the Right, Chicken Pecking Wings

Crossing to the right, the left foot withdraws and the right hand conceals and scoops inwards, stamping out with the right foot into a level horse/cross cartilage stance as the hand left effects a "cutting joint" with the forearm.

Please note: The left and right Chicken Pecking Wings is the most characteristic opposing and reversing joint capturing striking method found within Taizuquan. At first, conceal before scooping and then cut the joint. This joint-cutting must bring strength from turning the waist while the concealing and scooping is a shoulder-capture employed to secure the opponent.

33. Advancing Left Horse and Double Opening
Advancing the left foot with both hands opening.

34. Changing Horse, Double Raising
Withdraw the left foot and advance the right with both hands gripping into a fist and strike from upper right downwards.

Please note: To change one's horse one must remain upon the original spot and step back one step with the front foot

then step forward one step with the back foot. This should be done within the range and space of one floor-tile (an area of approximately 18 inches square) and so by way of this Changing Horse method one may execute a complete form! By way of the Double Raising one may not only attack an opponent directly but also dissolve.

35. Whispering Right Horse, Double Pecking

With the right foot advancing one step the left foot follows and both hands peck outwards from the center.

Please note: Both hands are used to great effect with one "revealing" and one "concealing". The left hand performs a rubbing and pecking gesture in order to dissolve an oncoming attack as the right hand (simultaneously) pecks forward in order to attack.

36. Following (Natural) Hand, Pretending To Rub

Remain in the horse stance with both hands changing to a Phoenix-Eye Fist as they scribe an arc and attack from the side.

Please note: The shape of this movement is like rubbing therefore it is called Pretending to Rub. It exerts a short sinking power. This technique is also known by other names due to be having been handed down by different teachers and through different sects. In some quanfa manuals it is called "throwing" while in others it is called "single joining/attending." Others call it "double thrusting."

37. Passing and Crossing the Back Gate, Stepping Out Horse, Left Hand Capturing

Stamping the right foot, turn left and cross the Back Gate into a left horse with the left hand capturing.

38. Stamping Right Foot, Right Hand Opening

Stepping out into a right horse, the right hand opens directly.

39. Slicing Right Foot, Withdrawing Into Level Horse, Right Hand Blocking and Defending

With the left hand freeing and the right hand directly blocking, the right foot hooks and slices from the front backwards as you withdraw into a level horse.

Please note: Using the right heel to trip by trapping the adversary's right foot the defender exerts power in order to make the opponent fall by interruption his balance.

40. Advancing Right Horse, Right Hand Removing Then Returning and Blocking

Advance the right foot with the right hand carving sideways as the hand follows and blocks.

Please note: Removing, entering and swallowing the cartilage, block while loosening both the cartilage and the shoulders.

41. Stamping Right Corner, Right Hand Capturing

Move the right foot out 45 degrees to the upper right-hand side and capture.

Please note: The right hand continuously strikes out with intention that has been developed through repetition from training since ancient times.

42. Right Hand Clawing, Left Hand Shaking

Right crossing cartilage, right hand from capturing hand changing into clawing hand, left hand simultaneously exerting strength and shaking out palm. Both hands one defending one attacking.

Please note: Shaking must bring out strength from waist and cartilage and driving force. "Nine of ten shaking won't work, only the right way bring the force that defend and consolidate oneself," which is the most difficult part to perform.

43. Changing Left Horse, Left Corner, Left Hand Capturing

Moving left foot towards upper left 45 degree angle, left hand capturing

44. Left Hand Clawing, Right Hand Shaking

Crossing the left cartilage, the left hand changes from a Capturing hand into a Clawing hand with the right hand simultaneously exerting strength and shaking out the palm.

45. Treading the Right Horse Towards The Center, Child Holds the Tablet/ Child Holding And Spreading Out (The Hand)
Step out into a left horse by way of one small step with the left hand opening then step out right into a *sipingma* (left) horse with the left hand holding and the right hand spreading as one defend with a combined power.

Please note: The Spreading Out (hand) is used for dissolving the oncoming/incoming attack and then immediately sticks/attaches to the abdomen and anatomy of the opponent. The "holding" is used for blocking the chest and shoulders of the opponent. Both techniques/hands simultaneously exert strength. While performing the Spreading Out and Holding technique one must move closer into right bow and arrow horse stance in order to augment/increase/supplement the power.

46. Turning Over Front Gate, Stepping Out Left Horse, Left Hand Capturing
Stamp the right foot towards the and left turning body, cross the front gate and step out into a left horse with the left hand capturing.

47. Advancing Right Horse, Lifting Body, Holding And Seizing Hand

Advancing right horse with left hand underneath, the right hand is on-top/above with both forearms facing each other. Standing in a Four Even Horse (sipingma) turn your body to the left and sideways together with a holding/seizing hand.

Please note: Facing an attack from the opponent one must lead from the end of the oncoming power, and hold and seize his hand. Sitting in a horse stance, turning the waist and bring the right elbow downward in a pressing manner and aim at the attacker's elbow or shoulder.

48. Reining in the Horse and Shoot

The right foot straightens into back foot leaning horse stance with the right hand peeling/shedding downwards.

Please note: With the left hand as a Withdrawing Fist the right hand sheds out. This peeling can not only attack the chest and abdomen area of the opponent but also dissolve an oncoming kick and three-legged tiger technique.

49. Direct Advancing, Stepping Out, Right Horse, Cow/Oxen Uncovering Glass

Using a Whispering (right) Horse the left foot follows with both hands clenching into fists as the shoulder blades and arms lift as one from the lower left towards the upper right.

Please note: Turning the waist to the right, straighten your horse stance and emit strength from the waist and back. With the right hand lifting out, redirect the oncoming attack as the left hand conceals and performs a Black Tiger Steal the Heart.

50. Withdraw Right Horse, Left Hand Lifting/Raising

Withdraw your right foot into a left horse with the left hand lifting upwards and outwards. The left cartilage must swallow as you tighten and consolidate your horse stance.

51. Withdraw Left Horse, Right Hand Breaking and Dissolving

Withdraw from a left horse into a right horse thus adopting a triangular body posture as the right hand moves to underneath the left armpit then towards the center-line as it breaks and dissolves directly.

Please note: Standing sideways to attack the opponent.

52. Hanging Right Foot Towards/Facing the Sun Hand

The left foot withdraws one small step as the right foot follows and so one assumes a right hanging foot (an empty step or empty stance) with both hands in front of the chest. Opening up and spitting out one exerts strength as the right palm stands in front and the left palm stands behind the front hand as a "towards the sun" hand posture.

Please note: The right hand is held in-line with the right knee and the toes of the right foot while the left hand is held in line with the heart. In this way, both hands guard and defend one's center-line. However, much more than this, this posture actually protects the entire body. By way of this stance one may advance and attack or retreat and defend.

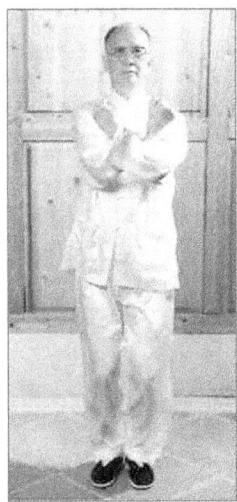 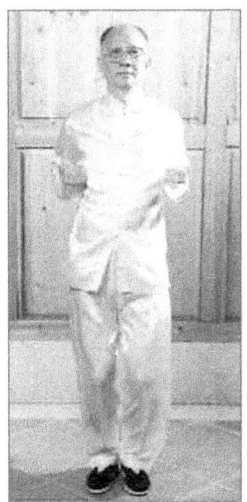 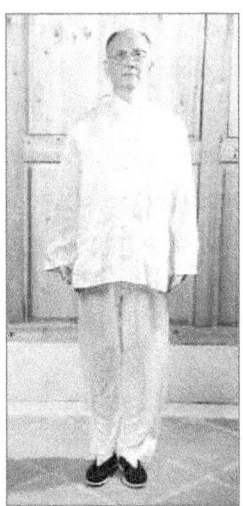

53. Withdrawing and Standing Straight.
Exhaling, withdraw and stand straight to finish.

CHAPTER SIX

ESSENCE OF TAIZUQUAN TECHNICAL HANDS

Taizuquan is ideal for actual combat. It is said that, "If one wishes to be merciful one should not put forward and outward one's hands, and if one is to put forwards and outwards one's hands then this is not the way to be merciful." Therefore, in Taizuquan there is no impractical movement.

All of the hand techniques are for attack or defense and illustrate the method of the interchange between yin and yang. They are organized together with the taolu (forms) but then taken apart in the form of *sanji* (loose techniques).

Taizuquan comprises four types of techniques, namely: striking, kicking, throwing and capturing. Each posture and every movement must be practiced in a fixed and standard way: substantial but not substantial, empty yet not empty, solid combined with empty, hard supporting soft. When face-to-face with the opponent one is to coordinate hands, feet, body and strength. One's attacks must be hard, straight-forward and advancing or, alternatively, dodging in order to aim at the opponent from sideways-on. The secret of practical usage exists within the heart as well as the hands therefore if one is able to master Taizuquan's techniques one must have a crystal-clear understanding. Having studied the Fist Manual I have chosen the most commonly seen sixty-four methods which includes one hundred and twenty seven techniques. These are listed below together with a brief introduction as well as illustrations.

1. Piercing Method

"Piercing-The-Middle" Fist

Taizuquan is very particular on dashing the Middle Fist. Aiming for and piercing the heart requires such power and might as, "shaking the mountain and piercing the walls". Through storing energy and sending out swift fist techniques by way of heavy power and sinking power the twisting and turning of the waist allows the energy pathway of the fist to return to the centre.

Double Pouncing Fist

"Pouncing Fist" means that the palm of the fist-hand is focused downwards. Through sending out both fists simultaneously while ensuring that the width between both fists is slightly less than the width of one's shoulders, this technique must be aimed at both sides of the opponent's chest.

Double Vertical Fists

In this context Vertical Fists means that the fist's center of each hand (fist) is not quite facing each other but they are virtually alongside each other. With the right hand being higher, the fist center is, effectively, towards the left (fist) but the left fist is lower and its fist center is (facing) towards the right. The right fist strikes the opponent's chest while the left strikes the opponent's abdomen thus a combined strength is sent out simultaneously. In this photograph shown here we see the opposite attitude of the same technique — the left fist is high (striking the chest) and the right fist is low (striking the abdomen).

The Three-Legged Tiger Fist

Perform the bow and arrow stance and send out the fist forwards and downwards to strike the opponent's abdomen. This movement represents a three-legged tiger (the two legs and the one forward arm). The punching/striking arm must be executed by way of a twisting and turning motion.

2. Capturing Method

Capturing

This is most important dissolving technique within Taizuquan. Moving the forearm from lower to upper, draw an arc shape to dissolve and capture a direct oncoming attack. Here, one must pick up the joint and sink both shoulders exerting strength through the wrist and through the fingers. Directly dissolving horizontally in addition to the skill and effect of the downwards covering and smothering action, this movement is performed "softly."

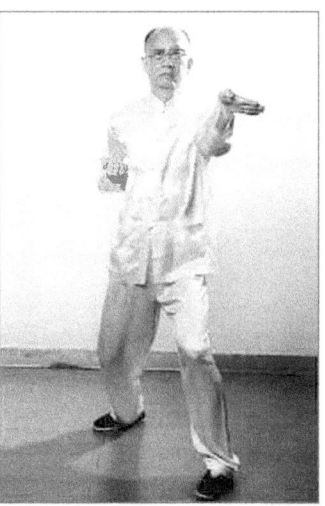

Double Capturing

Both hands simultaneously perform the capturing technique from lower to upper with the hands crossing over and separating. This technique can be used to dissolve attacks such as the Double Pouncing Fist.

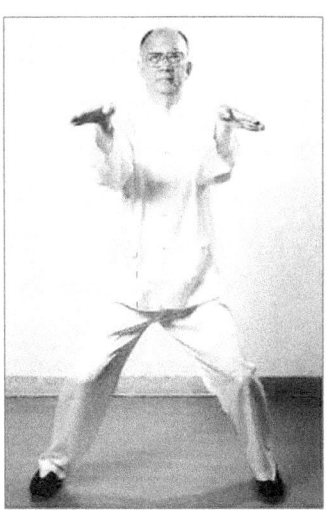

Shaking Shoulders

The same as the Capturing Hand method except that here one must cross the cartilage and turn the body sideways while loosening the shoulders. The Shaking Shoulders is mostly used a) when operating within a confined space (this is expressed by way of our Chinese idiom, *xia lu xiang bi*), and b) when caught off-guard and thus without warning (again, we have an idiom for this which is, *cu bu ji fang*) and so we perform/adopt a dissolving and dodging movement/posture.

3. Raising Method

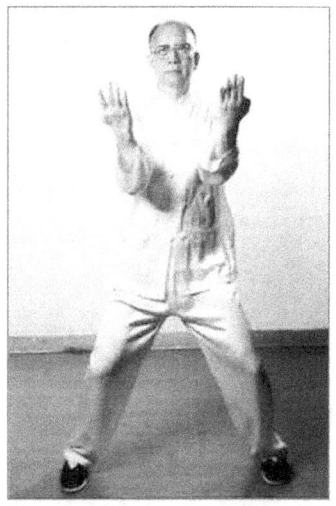

Raising

This is one of most basic dissolving techniques employed within Taizuquan (along with the Capturing Method). Moving from a lower to upper position and towards the side of the body, draw an arc in a somewhat tilting manner and strike while exerting strength from the radius-side of the arms thus redirecting an oncoming attack. The waist must twist and the shoulders must turn. Strength must be crisp and sharp and must effect a loud noise. Potentially, the Raising Method can also be used for attacking - striking sideways at the opponent's rib-cage and neck.

Double Raising

The left hand and right hand simultaneously rise upwards and outwards with both arms exerting power as one guards one's upper diagram (*shanggua*). As a close-quarter combat strategy, borrow and follow the power and posture of both arms as they rise and separate and so strike the opponent's neck. In this technique it is quite difficult to exert strength so Double Raising must be performed together with shaking power from the body which involves pushing both shoulder blades.

Laughing and Raising
Bending (flexing) the wrist with one's palm-center facing inwards, use the forearm as a lever and so exert strength from the bulging area of the wrist thus sending out short power. This technique is used mostly to dissolve and redirect a fist or palm attack during close-quarter combat.

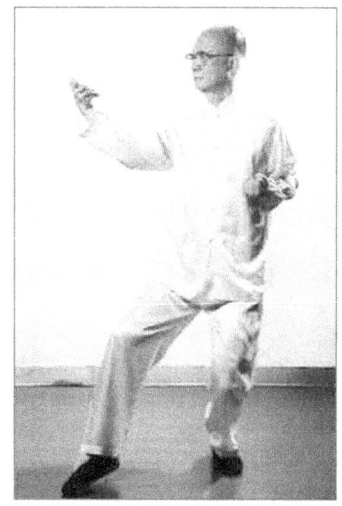

4. Opening Method

Sideways Opening
This is one of the most basic Breaking and Dissolving techniques found within Taizuquan and is performed in the opposite direction to the Capturing Method. The arm draws an arc from upper to lower with the palm hooking sideways thus breaking and dissolving a direct horizontal attack. This Opening Method begins from the between the eyebrows (at the point of the Third Eye) and finishes by the side of the cartilage.

Direct Opening
From a lower, forwards and downwards attitude, strike directly exerting power from the ulna. Facing the oncoming attack from the center (or lower) route, this is often used as an opening/dissolving technique.

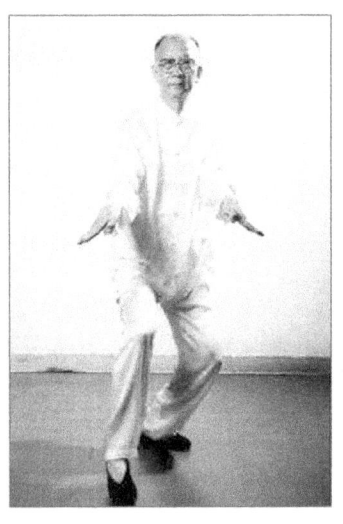

Double Opening

With the left and right hand simultaneously performing a Sideways Opening action, both hands cross in front of the chest before effecting then a Double Opening action downwards by way of an arc. In so doing both palms effect a sideways hooking action. This is used to break and dissolve an oncoming attack with both hands working together in a combined effort thus they "brush away and cross the abdomen." In this way the hands defend and protect one's Middle Gate and center-line.

5. Concealing Method

Concealing

This is another example of the most basic Breaking and Dissolving techniques used within Taizuquan. From upper to lower while exerting strength from the radius side of the arm, the palm must be vertical as it divides and separates an oncoming attack from either a fist or a leg (hand or foot). This technique is a building-block for a throwing and/or capturing maneuver. For example, the raising hand used as a concealing tactic can bind and thus secure and control an attacker's hands behind the attacker's back. Immediately following on from this the defender makes contact with by way of his own shoulders first lifting and then pressing which we call "Wind and Fire Hand" (*fenghuoshou*). This "method" can be used to cut the attack(er) in a scissoring manner as well as throwing the attacker.

Double Concealing

With both the left hand and the right hand moving simultaneously a concealing movement is thus effected and this we call, Double Concealing. It is often used to break and dissolve an oncoming attack by way of visualizing the inner joints of both arms thus one may quickly clamp, control and secure both hands of the opponent using one's waist in a twisting manner and the shoulders in a turning manner.

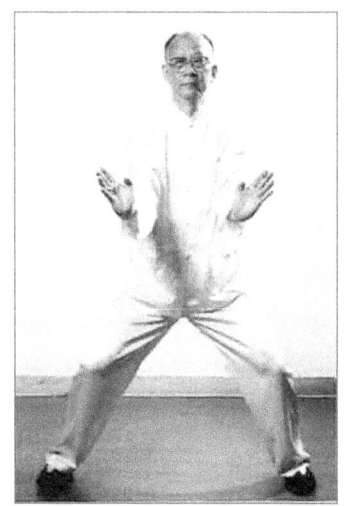

6. Slicing Method

Slicing and Chopping

Send out the palm from the torso exerting strength using the palm-blade (knife-hand) to attack the rib-cage and abdomen.

7. Pinning (Hair-Pin) and Forking Method

Fork and Palm-Blade (Knife-Hand)

Both hands simultaneously move outwards and downwards from the chest, pushing and slicing as they go. With the right hand in front and the left hand behind, both exert strength using the palm-blades. This hand method uses power sent out by way of "winding hands" in order to attack the opponent's abdomen and rib-cage.

8. Peeling Method

Peeling

The right hand is placed just below the right shoulder. By way of a "reserved strength" one swiftly peels ones hand outwards, forwards and downwards and exerting strength using the palm-blade. The Peeling Method is suitable for both attacking and defending.

Pulling on the Horse's Reins and Shooting Method

From a Four Level Horse stance, both hands are held in the posture of Embracing (Holding with Both Hands) A Double-Edged Sword. Immediately crossing the cartilage into an empty horse stance, adopt a right horse thus drawing the bow as the right hand moves downwards in a peeling motion. The left hand, meanwhile, withdraws and is placed beneath the armpit using the strength of and power from the twist. This downward peeling action is used to thwart an oncoming/incoming leg by attacking the opponent's groin, abdomen or rib-cage.

9. Wielding Method

Double Wielding

With the upper hand capturing and the lower hand opening at the same time, this is called Double Wielding and is used in order to separate the oncoming technique such as a Luohan hand attack or a double vertical fist attack.

10. Shielding Method

Child Holding and Shielding Method

With the right hand shielding and dissolving an oncoming technique, immediately enter and attach next to the rib cage/abdomen area of the opponent as the left hand abruptly holds and blocks the opponent thus   causing him to fall. Alternatively, shield from the opponent's kicking leg and hold/blocking his shoulder and upper arm. Both holding and shielding must be done at the same time. The left hand shields then the right hand holds and strikes. Holding and shielding can be done at the same time either with an advancing horse, a withdrawing horse or a Switching Gate. The commonly seen interpretation involves holding and shielding with a Stamping Horse or holding and shielding with a Walking Horse. This is especially powerful if matched with a tripping or/and a cutting action.

11. Blocking/Defending Method

Single Blocking/Defending

Using a Vertical Palm, bend the four fingers as well as the thumb from under the armpit and strike directly forward. Exerting short power from the wrist, the left hand out is called "left hand blocking" while the right hand out is called "right hand blocking."

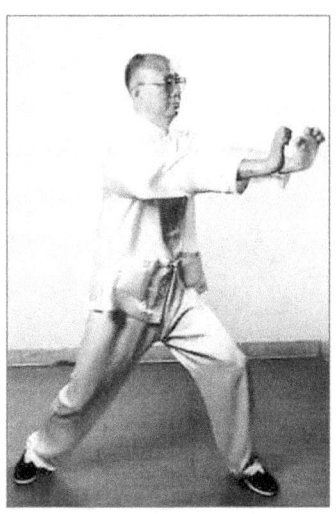

Double Defending
Both hands simultaneously defend outwards as one adopts a bow and arrow stance which assists with the power.

Striking and Brushing the Stomach
Both hands are simultaneously sent outwards from beneath the flank with the hands held as sideways palms where both palm's finish close to each other and approximately one hand's length apart. Thus one blocks forwards, outwards and downwards so attacking one opponent's abdomen and groin.

Strong Man Removes the Attacker's Boots
With the left palm hooking the opponent's ankle, the right hand moves forward to jam the opponent's knee thus causing him to fall. The lower body adopts a Sitting Lotus or a downward "jumping" and bending action.

12. Supporting Method

Supporting and Pecking
With the left hand supporting from beneath by way of the palm or palm blade the right hand flexes into a pecking position thus enabling the palm of the same hand to peck downwards.

Breaking/Dissolving and Supporting
Using the left hand palm heel and palm blade in an upward-supporting manner, use the right hand palm blade in an upward manner moving it towards the left in a lower attitude thus dissolving. This technique together with the supporting and pecking techniques are both fierce and damaging. Visualizing the left hand striking beneath the chin the right hand attacks the carotid artery.

Old Monk Supporting His Alms Bowl
Using your right hand to strike beneath the chin of the opponent, the other hand captures the attacker's forward arm thus securing it. Turning over his body and his back, this puts you into a posture called "Dongbin Carrying the Double-Edged Sword."

13. Clasping (Cradling/Holding) Method

Double Clasping (Fan Zi Carries the Plate)
Both hands from lower to upper clasp upwards. (The distance between both palms at the culmination of this technique is one palm's length). Entering from the Middle Gate, clasp both jaws in a forceful manner.

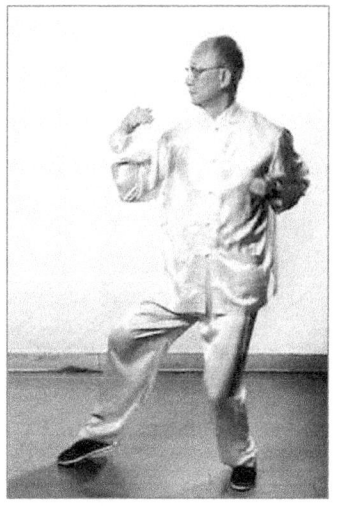

14. The Method of a Chicken Eating Wings

Chicken Eating Wings
This technique is a common capturing method used within Taizuquan where the action/movement is clever, graceful and elegant. With the right hand concealing and immediately twisting upwards then over and downwards thus pressing and clasping the opponent's left wrist, the left arm bends at the elbow as it crosses the cartilage using strength exerted from the crotch, waist and left forearm on the ulna-side which attaches to and cuts the attacker's right arm-joint (elbow).

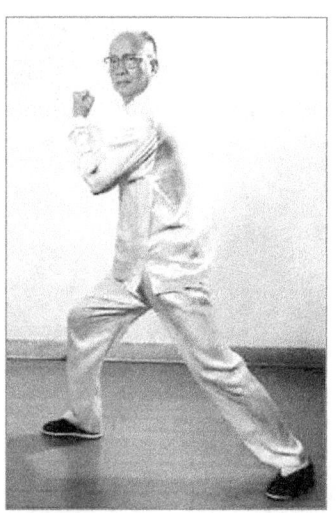

This technique is called "Right Chicken Eating." The "Left Chicken Eating" would thus be effected by way of the reverse (opposite) action/directions.

15. Raising/Lifting Method

Single Raising
With right hand gripping and so clenching into a fist, use the left vertical fist in a lifting manner against the lower (private parts) of the opponent. The power-point used here is the knuckles aimed toward the heart, abdomen or chin. If aiming at the crotch one must squat into a low horse and turn one's body thus this technique becomes a method of hoisting and ultimately/potentially throwing.

Double Raising
As with the Single Raising but here both fists are simultaneously sent out with the targets now being the flanks and the abdomen.

The Father and Son Follow Each Other
With the right hand in front (the father) and the left hand behind (the son) both actions work together. The right hand must first scribe an arc (in order to dissolve an oncoming attack) which then sticks and follows until one is in a position to launch the attack. The upper hand is aimed at throat and jaw while the lower hand is aimed at the heart.

16. Charging Method

This is to make a swift and abrupt linear movement (like a bead on an abacus where the beads are moved sideways).

The upper technique is using to attach and cut as in the method of the Chicken Eating Wings. This can be used by itself in order to dissolve an oncoming technique from the Upper Eight Diagram. The lower technique, meanwhile, exerts power from the radius in order to block an oncoming leg or Three-Legged-Tiger.

17. To Bind Tightly and to Stick (Biao)

Long Binding or Constant Binding
Exerting strength and power from the bulging part of the wrist, the hand strikes outwards from the rib area (lèi jì). This can be used for striking or punching, or for dissolving an oncoming attack.

Double Biao (Double Bind Tightly and Stick)

Both hands move from lower to upper thus drawing an arc until they reach the waist area then bounce off and away from while open up an oncoming double attack from the left and right directions. This must be performed by exerting short power so as to achieve *si liang po qian jin* ("where four taels defeats one thousand catties").[1]

18. Joint Method

Striking With the Elbow Joint (The Horizontal Joint-Strike)

Bending one's arm at the elbow one uses the tip of the elbow in a horizontal fashion in order to strike the opponent. This is a close-quarter battle strategy.

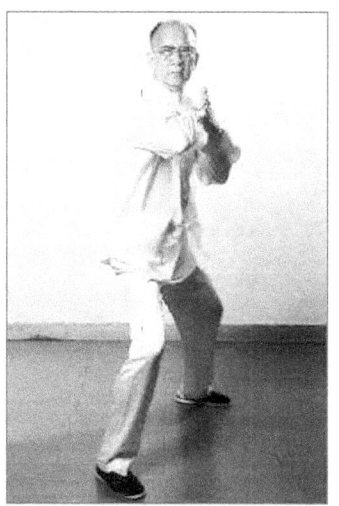

Uncovering/Exposing the Shoulder Blades (Even Joint)

With both hands meeting at chest level, strike out using the tips of the elbows (towards both the left and the right).

Towards the Heaven Joint

Bending the arm at the elbow-joint, use the tip (of the elbow) from lower to upper as you strike out. This technique can be used to break a bear-hug attack from the rear.

Striking Backwards (to the Rear) with the Elbow Joint

Bending the arm at the elbow joint, strike to the rear against the opponent that is stood behind you. Visualizing being bear-hugged by an opponent from the rear, one is to step forward one step and then turn one's body using the elbow to attack by defending, This is an horizontal attack/defense.

19. Capturing Method

Hugging and Capturing Hand

With the left hand receiving the oncoming attack the right hand   simultaneously moves upwards as one twists and turns the waist in order to cross the cartilage. Meanwhile, the right elbow exerts strength in a downward pressing manner in order to cause the opponent to fall.

20. Chopping Method

Carving and Striking

With the left hand moving from the upper and to the right it then carves   downwards so as to thwart the oncoming attack. With the right hand sending out its palm from above the right shoulder it tilts and chops sideways towards the neck, face or the collar bone. This technique is an important method for both dissolving and striking at the same time.

Pi Bian

With the left hand sending out power from above the shoulder it chops vigorously in a tilting manner as a standing palm. This can be used for either dissolving or striking.

Drawing the Bow

With the left hand moving at shoulder-level it peels and slices outwards as the right hand employs twisting power while twisting back. This movement is as if drawing a bow whereby the waist, shoulder and palm simultaneously sends out strength. Here, the forearm must exert a bouncing strength. This technique is aimed towards the head, neck and chest area.

21. Bouncing Method

Prawn/Mantis Bouncing

With the right hand above and positioned palm downwards, the left hand is beneath/underneath/below also with the palm facing downwards with the forward hand bouncing outwards. This must be  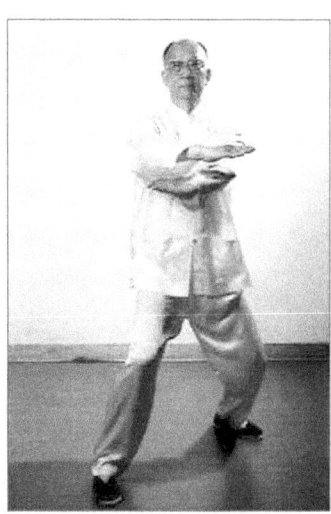 performed alongside crossing the cartilage as one wrings one's waist and twists the shoulders. Exerting strength with both knife hands and both ulna bones, this must not be performed rigidly and directly outwards but with tenacity — as a lobster bouncing out its forearm.

22. Rubbing Method

Rubbing

The same method as the side opening - with the palm towards the side of the ulna bone and hooking inwardly while receiving the attack. Following the power of the opponent, induce his attack towards the lower left or lower right. This technique is for defending one' lower gate from an upper gate attack.

Double Scratching/Rubbing

The same method as double opening, both palms move towards the ulna bone and hook inwardly. While receiving the attack, both hands inducing towards lower left and upper right.

23. Pecking Method

Pecking

Bend towards one side with the palm facing upwards, the four fingers together, and power transferred to the finger tips in a forward pecking, motion — as if a woodpecker is pecking at a tree trunk. This technique is aimed at the face, eyes and chest area.

Double Pecking

With the right hand held above and the left hand beneath, both hands are held bent sideways with both palms standing upright. The four fingers are held together and simultaneously move forwards, pecking outwards. This technique is aimed at the face, eyes, chest and neck, with the left hand slicing in order to rub off/dissolve the oncoming attack.

Slicing and Pecking

With the left hand slicing-off and thus dissolving the oncoming technique, right hand is used in a pecking attitude as it strikes outwards and forwards simultaneously with the left. A "slicing and pecking" technique, this can also be termed "breaking and attacking" (one hand breaking, the other hand attacking).

24. Clicking Method

Phoenix-Eye Clicking

Clench the fist, forefinger extended and using the thumb-nail joint for support this technique can be used either as a forward attack or a sideways block. Aimed towards acu-points this technique can be used as a short strength method aimed at the heart or temple.

25. Thrusting Method

Vertical Thrusting

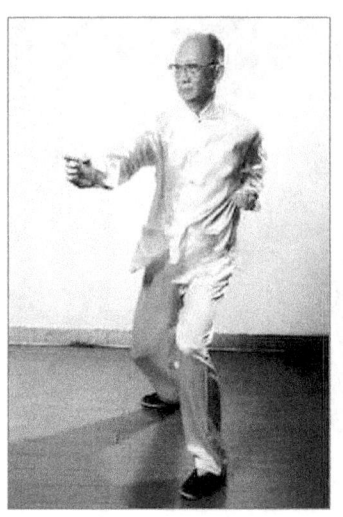

Used as a Standing Fist and thrusting forwards with four fingers together and exerting strength through the fingertips, aim at the chest and neck. Finger thrusting with the palms facing downwards use both forefinger and middle finger in a forward thrust called "twin dragons fighting for the pearl." (Mark - this caption appears to be totally wrong for the photograph!)

Double Vertical Thrusting

Both the left hand and the right hand simultaneously thrust outwards.

Pouncing Thrusting

With the palms facing downwards while thrusting forwards and directly outwards, the fingers are held together with strength exerted to and though the fingertips.

Double Pouncing Thrusting

With both hands and with soft palms, simultaneously thrust outwards.

26. Rubbing Method

Tiger-Cub Opens Its Mouth and Rubs

As the right hand turns into a Capturing Palm from above, the left hand moves from below and attaches to the knife-hand muscle of the right hand with both hands opening and extending, the two hands held at the center

and towards each other in the position of the Tiger Opening Its Mouth. Capturing and securing the oncoming attack, immediately twist backwards and draw in by crossing the cartilage (*guò jiē*). Attack when you see a gap (an opening).

Walking Horse Rubbing (Mother-In-Law Rubbing)

Perform the Tiger-Cub Opening Its Mouth Rubbing while performing the Walking Horse step method (called Walking Horse Rubbing). Walk The Horse with an elegant body form — as if the mother-in-law were walking on-stage at the Chinese opera! This is why it is called "Mother-In-Law Rubbing."

Crossing the Stomach (Rubbing)

This technique is different from the Tiger Cub Opening Mouth Rubbing technique in that the right hand performs a capturing technique while the left the hand attaches to the elbow of the opponent as it borrows and follows the attacker's oncoming power, vigorously rubs inwards and towards the right side in order to make the attacker fall.

Leading the Ox (Rubbing)

One hand uses a Rubbing technique in order to capture and secure the attacker's wrist while the other hand binds, bundles and secures the attacker's elbow as it receives the attack having first dodged it to dissolve then, by way of a Withdrawing Horse, the defender twists his waist and so draws in the attacker — as if leading an ox.

Capturing the Head (Rubbing)

With one hand supporting the chin while the other captures the head, both hands quickly and vigorously interact. Twisting in a circle, this technique is often used as a defense when being held captive from the front by the waist. This is one of the fierce and violent techniques of Taizuquan.

27. Scissors (Cutting) Method

Double Scissor Hand

Using the palms as the power point the right hand is placed alongside the left hand as both combine in order to attack. With the hand binding and securing the attack, the right hand attacks the adversary's elbow in order to block and *attack*.[2]

28. Closing Method

Single Closing

The right hand is held as a clenched fist and shifts to the centre to strike horizontally as either a defence or an attack. Alternatively, the left hand moves to a clenched fist and shifts towards the centre as a horizontal strike in order to defend (or attack by striking) an oncoming attack.

Double Closing
The right hand moves to a clenched fist and shifts towards the centre-line as a horizontal strike while, at the same time, the left hand also clenches to a fist and moves towards the centre-line where it stops next to the edge of the lower forearm of the right arm. The left hand catches and contains the opponent's attacking fist/arm, attacking/striking his joint. This is one of Taizuquan blocks which is also a defense and an attack.

29. Breaking/Dissolving Method

Breaking and Dissolving From a Low Attack
Using one's knife-hand as one's power point and focal point, bend the arm at the elbow and move it downwards in order to dissolve an attack. This technique can be used to block and strike an oncoming arm (fist) or leg (foot).

Dissolving Against a High Attack
The defender's right hand moves from the left armpit and sends out a standing palm strike out towards the attacker's head and face.

Double Dissolving

Both hands withdraw and move towards the right shoulder as one adopts a Sitting (Lower) Horse. Using the knife-palm as the power point, both palms move towards each other —towards lower left and downwards dissolving. This is a Taizu method of dissolving a leg attack with the hands and arms.

30. Whipping Method

Single Whip

Using both the left hand and the right hand, with the top of the hands as the power point and strength point, follow the track of the Exerting Fist parabola and strike vigorously forward and downwards in order to attack the head and face area of the opponent. This technique is often used for attacking and striking an oncoming technique. The position of the whip is focused around the center. The elbow must be bent and must sink while the motion must be vigorous and one's power, great.

Double Whipping

Both hands simultaneously imitate a whipping motion. One hand is used as the main whip whist the other is used as the corresponding whip. The opposite whip attacks the chest (of the opponent) while the main whip is to attack the opponent's head.

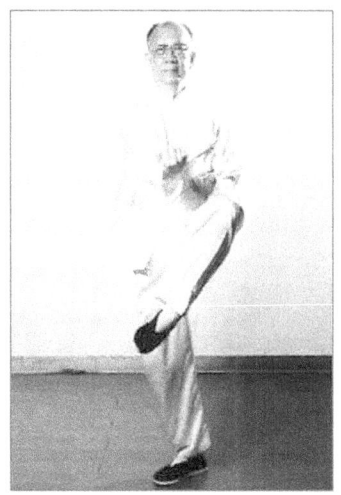

Caressing, Stroking, Whipping

As one hand captures an oncoming attack the other hand must whip (smash!) the attacker's head, face or chest area. This technique deals with an attack from a high-level position and is an extremely fierce dissolving technique while, at the same time, a fierce attack typical of Taizuquan.

Cutting and Whipping

With one hand cutting and dissolving an oncoming attack the other hand whips the opponent's chest, head or face area. This technique is a response to an oncoming attack aimed at one's middle or lower area. The attack and dissolve is a simultaneous "movement."

Opposite Whipping

Also called "The Iron Hammer Sinks to the River-bed," the right hand moves from the left side, through an arcing and curving shape, and is sent out through the fist using the top of the fist in order to effect an attack towards the opponent's head or chest. It should be the opposition direction if using the left hand doing the opposite whipping.

Horizontal Whipping

As the right hand bends at the elbow, hold the fist from left to right using the top of the fist in order to strike horizontally thus attacking the opponent's waist or head. Exert power from the opposite direction if using the technique of left horizontal whipping.

31. Carrying Method

Carrying By Way of the Shoulder

Hold the right hand in a Standing Fist (strike) with the left hand at one's upper- middle-chest. This technique is like the Whipping Method except one pounds and smashes downwards using the bottom of the fist as the power point.

Double Carrying (Coiling the Hair into a Bun)

Both hands should be held as fists which then attack through smashing from the top — forwards and downwards. One fist is in front and the other is behind but very close. The action of "coiling the hair into a bun" involves using both hands first as you coil them and move them past the front of the opponent, in order to dissolve the oncoming attack. This can also be used from a higher position — to block and attack certain techniques.

32. Manipulating and Exacting Method

Double all of the above

Both hands should be held into fists in a forwards and downwards attitude. Twist and wring the fists outwards as you double strike making sure that you also sink the two fists. This is an attack aimed at the opponent's dantian.

33. Shaking Method

Scratching (Rubbing) and Shaking

One hand "rubs" thus ridding oneself of an oncoming attack. One hand slaps vigorously forwards with the knife hand aimed at the opponent's, abdomen, waist or kidney. Changing the knife hand into a claw hand (this is called, "Celestial Being Steals the Peach"), this is aimed at the opponent's private parts. Strength is sent out through the waist while the shaking motion is enhanced by way of crossing the cartilage.

Capturing and Shaking

The difference here between scratching and shaking is that one swaps the scratching technique to a capturing one; the rest remains the same.

Flying and Shaking

Sending out (exploding) power from the waist, the single hand moves from lower to upper right or left as the hands shake outwards. This technique makes use of and takes advantage of the opponent's "openness" as one attacks his chin, neck, chest or ribcage. If one lowers the hand position, this technique can be used to attack the opponent's leg.

Double Shaking

Both hands simultaneously shake outwards and forwards from a low position. One's horse must be low while the hands must be aimed at the attacker's rib cage.

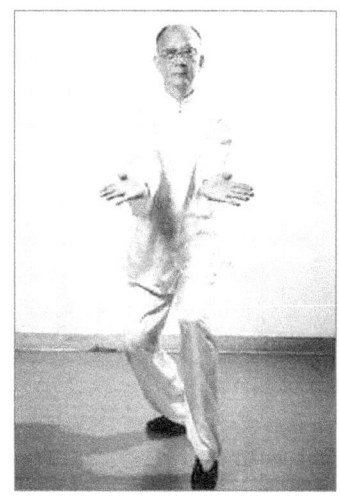

34. Lifting, Uncovering and Revealing Method

Lifting

This is a similar movement to the Raising Method, the only difference here being that one uses the palm instead of the fist. The entire arm picks up the joints and tilts outwards in order to block and strike a direct attack. Owing to the way in which one holds the fist, this technique is more powerful than the Raising Method.

Bull Uncovering the Grass

As the right fist uses the Lifting Method the left hand sticks to the ulna of the right arm and strikes out simultaneously with the right thus not only blocking an oncoming technique but striking it as well. In this way, one hand strikes the opponent's face/chest and the other the opponent's kidney. Tighten your horse while sending out strength and power from the waist.

35. Grabbing Method

Bull Horn Delivery
The right hand forms a fist and moves from the lower towards the upper and so delivers a strike to the opponent's temple.

The Luohan Hand
Both hands form fists with the right on top. Suddenly using the fist to strike upwards and towards the neck (of the opponent) this is effected from a sideways position with the left hand beneath using the top of the fist to strike from left to right at the opponent's waist and kidney. This is called, "Luohan Taming the Tiger."

Double Wind Piercing the Ears
Both hands should be held as fists as they strike horizontally at the opponent's temples.

36. Suspending Method

Double Suspended Entrance
Suppose the opponent attacks directly with both fists. Stamp upon the Middle Palace and advance directly using both hands to suspend and dissolve the oncoming attack. Aim at his center.

Pouncing, Raising, Thrusting, Supporting
Pouncing and Raising is also called Smiling and Laughing. Having dissolved the oncoming attack with one hand immediately thrust at the opponent's eyes, face or neck with the four fingers of the other hand, or attack the hypochondria area of the opponent. This movement is called "Beautiful Lady Looks into the Mirror."

37. Plucking Method

Phoenix Tail Plucking (Treading Horse)

Looking at the Taizuquan form called, "Phoenix Tail Plucking," this is always performed with the Treading Horse - with both hands palms forwards and downwards and pointing outwards. Immediately pluck back in order to dissolve or break an oncoming/incoming attack. This defense must be performed by twisting the waist and swallowing the cartilage, borrowing strength through following the attacker's movement so as to make the opponent stumble.

38. Carrying at the Back Method

Dong Bin (one of the eight celestial beings) Carries the Sword

Capturing the arm of the opponent using the technique known as, "Crossing and Passing, Stomach Rubbing" immediately turn your body and carry the arm of the opponent by the back of the elbow joint on one's shoulder. Bend his waist and bring forwards his shoulder in order to make him fall to the ground.

39. Pushing Method

Shaking Body and Pushing the Shoulder Blades

This technique is the most important shaking and pushing method used within Taizuquan. First adopt a Double Rubbing posture then relax and loosen-up before both hands move into an attitude of double spear hand as they move upwards. Tighten your horse, making your waist the axis, and shake your body swiftly and

vigorously as both shoulders push backwards and forwards. The strength and power of this practice derives from the legs, the cartilage, the shoulder blades and the joints — as if a dog is emerging from a river and shakes off the water droplets. This technique is used most often when one is being violently hugged or forcefully squeezed. It will be even more powerful if performed together with a combination of techniques such as shaking and raising.

Monkey Carries Water on His Shoulders

Crossing both hands, place them upon your shoulders and immediately shake your body and push both shoulder-blades while shaking and pushing out both palms, thrusting to the left and to the right. Visualizing you are being grabbed by an attacker, put both your hands on top of the hands of the opponent and immediately shake and push in order to escape. At the same time aim an attack at the opponent's organs.

Uncovering the Shoulder-Blades and Shaking the Joint

Both arms bend at the elbows and rise until level. Use the tips of your elbows to defend outwards towards both left and right. Both elbows must follow the shoulders, striking horizontally to the rear then pushing forwards. This technique is aimed at defending from the rear and from close attacks whereby one attacks the opponent's chest and torso.

40. Freeing Method

Freeing

Visualizing one hand being captured by an attacker, immediately focus your strength and free yourself by pulling back, placing your free hand - the palm, actually - on top of the opponent's hand thus, and peeling off the opponent's capturing hand with both your hands as they gather up. This is called Freeing.

Free-Hanging Hands

Visualizing one's hand has been captured by the opponent, immediately gather strength and free by pulling back as the other hand crosses through and is placed under the hand of the opponent. With palm facing upwards and forwards, dissolve or break directly.

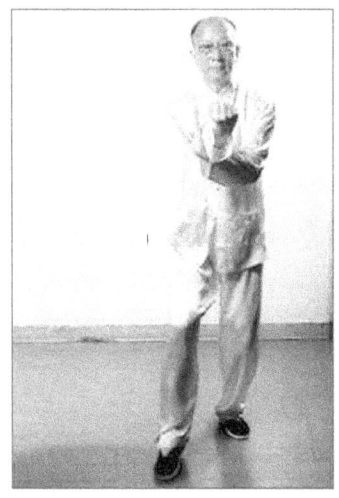

41. Locking Method

Locking the Throat

Clamp the wind pipe of the opponent's throat with your thumb and forefinger and bend your middle finger in order to press against the opponent's larynx.

42. Hugging, Embracing, Wrapping Method

Double Wrapping

Both hands should form the shape of a ring thus wrapping around the body of the opponent. This technique is often used for throwing and should be used in conjunction with other methods such as tripping and twisting. It can also be used for wrapping around both legs of the opponent (and causing him to fall) when the defender is attacked while lying upon the floor.

43. Throwing Method

Throwing the Stomach (Single and Double)

This technique is unique to Taizuquan and comprises two methods: the Single Throwing Stomach Method and the Double Throwing Stomach Method. This method strikes fiercely at the middle part of the opponent's abdomen using the ulna-side of the defender's forearm (that is to say, the knife-hand edge). While training in the use of this method one is to suspend breathing and tighten the waistband (waist-belt) and sink the breath while throwing. This technique also involves the dissolving method of sticking to the movement of the opponent. For instance, one is able to dissolve attacking techniques such as double defences and double fist attacks through lowering both hands and thus bring down the opponent.

44. Binding Method

Binding the Inner/Interior Joint

This is the Middle Gate Entering/Capturing method of Taizuquan. Dissolving the oncoming attack by opening and pushing and then entering into the center of the opponent, the defender captures and secures the opponent's upper arm with both hands in order to control and subdue him.

Binding the Outer/Exterior Joint

This is the Side Gate Entering/Capturing method of Taizuquan. As the defender's left hand dissolves the opponent's right attacking fist he immediately pushes the attacker's threatening arm forward with his right hand crossing and entering from beneath the opponent's armpit, twisting and scooping the attacker's right wrist against the natural movement of the joint. Pressing downward with a sudden and violent force the defender thus controls, subdues, immobilizes and secures the attacker.

45. Covering/Trapping Method

This is similar to the Double Capturing Method but here the hand position is higher. As both hands cross over from lower to upper they also cover and trap downwards which is (used as) a method of dissolving a direct attack.

46. Pressing Method

The Golden Tortoise Opens and Closes Its Shell

Capture and secure the oncoming attack by "welcoming," receiving and drawing it in as one hand applies pressure upon the attacker's elbow-joint or triceps muscle. This is one of the Capturing methods of Taizuquan.

47. Pressing Method

Against The Gold Sitting Joint

Visualizing one's wrist being captured by the opponent one should immediately draw inwards one's captured limb while, at the same time, twisting the opponent's wrist inwards thereby causing him to loosen his grip. One should then reverse the attacker's wrist in order to dissolve and break his manner of gripping. Advancing one's step and turning one's body, one's left hand then captures the opponent's right wrist as one's right hand thrusts and enters from beneath the opponent's armpit against the gold sitting joint. Then apply a downward force against his right shoulder. This is termed "cutting back" (as with scissors) by way of a capturing technique.

48. Tearing, Twisting and Pressing Down Firmly (Method)

Guang Gong Strokes His Beard
Dodging and dissolving an oncoming technique the defender receives the attacker's power and thus causes and encourages the attacker to fall.

49. Bridging, Defending and Combating Method

Bridging, Defending and Combating
With one's forearm one defends against an attacker's oncoming technique in a tilting manner as if being attacked from an upper position. Should one be attacked horizontally — that is to say, directly and by way of one's Middle Gate — the same defense can be used as it can also be used if one is being attacked from a lower position.

Level With the Eyebrow Fist
With one hand directed upward as a defense against an oncoming attack, the other hand should be held as a fist and positioned in front of the chest.

50. Throwing Method

"Carrying the Head" Fist

With the leading hand held as a fist, strike forwards and then downward from the shoulders ensuring that your shoulders are loose and sunken. The forward leg should be bent forward while aimed at the head and chest area of the opponent.

Heaven and Earth Fist

With the upper hand held in a "Carrying the Head" shaped fist[3], the lower hand should be held in a manner of a Lifting Fist while striking the opponent's abdomen. Both fists should be facing each other from an upper and lower position. This is a method of pressing and attacking at close-quarters.

51. Challenging, Holding and Provoking Method

White Monkey Steals the Peach!
Sitting in a low horse stance, attack the lower quarters of the opponent as you hold his lower parts with your four fingers and thumb.

52. Rising, Raising or Pushing Method

A method of inducing and pushing and raising (this is sometimes seen within "fist" manuals as scratching, carving or forcefully rubbing) using a crisp sharp power while shaking the shoulder-blades thereby "sending out late while arriving early"[4] in order to make the opponent fall.

53. Sweeping/Chopping Method

Single Chopping, Splitting Sweep
Using your right hand to "open" and thus draw the bow, make a sweeping action with your right foot and leg. Then, using your left hand to "open" and thus draw the bow, use your left foot and leg to sweep. This is called "Left Chopping, Splitting Sweep."[5] Exerting strength from the both upper and lower, cause the opponent to lose balance and fall.

Double Chopping, Splitting Sweep
If Chopping, Splitting and Sweeping are performed together with a pushing and chopping palm action from the other hand, this is then called "Double Chopping, Splitting Sweep." This is another essential characteristic of Taizuquan. Once again, this technique causes the opponent to fall.

Backwards Opening and Sweeping

This is a method of "reversing" the body and attacking the opponent. Visualizing an attack from the rear, turn your body in order to receive the opponent while simultaneously using one foot to sweep the front foot of the opponent. "Open" (draw) the bow in order to aim at the attacker's head or chest area in order to make him stumble, step back (withdraw) or fall.

54. Tripping Method

Cutting

This a prettier name for "cutting towards the chest." As your right hand captures the lapel of the opponent in order to secure him, advance your right foot so as to trip him as your left hand simultaneously draws the bow so as to make him fall.

Small Gate/Door Cutting

The "small gate" is also called the "right gate." Stamping sideways in order to enter the attacker's right gate, use your right foot in order to trip his right foot as your right hand blocks the attacker's chest and shoulders in order to make him fall.

Striking Joint, Cutting Foot

This technique is the same as the Small Gate Cutting where one also stamps sideways in order to enter the attacker's gate as you use your right foot in order to trip his right foot, the only difference being is that you change the right hand action into a horizontal striking action using your elbow.

55. Shooting Method

Shooting Horse

Step forward into a right horse and advance towards and enter into the opponent's crotch using your foot in a pressing and gluing manner against the front foot of the opponent. As you do this the lower part of your leg must be very close to the lower part of the leg of the opponent. Immediately bend your leg at the knee, pressing forward thus felling the adversary.

56. Treading Method

Anvil Foot

Use your foot in order to tread (actually, stamp) upon the shin-bone of the opponent's front leg.

57. Knee Method

Pressing Against the Genitalia with the Knee

This is one of the close quarter battle "pressing and striking" methods of Taizuquan where one raises the knee and thrusts it into the groin of the opponent after having first seized him with both arms.

58. Jolting Method

Dong Bin was the name of a drunk. He was one of the Eight Immortals (celestial beings) of Chinese mythology. It is also the name of a jolting method - if not *the* jolting method - found within Taizuquan. The most important feature and characteristic of this technique is that one has to raise one's foot and jolt (thrust) it outwards while the other foot is actually airborne! This posture can be likened to the stepping of a drunk — with very slow and jolting (stumbling) steps so as to get close to the opponent and then lean upon him (and thus pressing) with the shoulders.

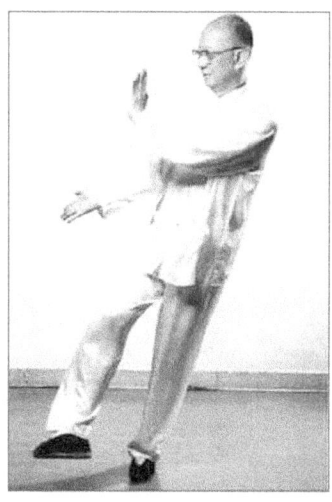

59. Bending Method

Leaping, Jumping, Bending

Here we observe a jumping technique effected while one is in a squatting position. At the same time the other foot is kneeling upon the ground. This method of attack is a standard practice within Quanzhou Taizuquan where, on the one hand, one is avoiding an attack while, on the other hand, one is attacking the adversary's lower extremities.

Pointing Towards the Ground

Standing in an even horse stance where the feet are shoulder-width apart one then kneels down opposite the adversary who has adopted the very same posture. Using both hands so as to hook the opponent's ankles one's also uses one's head in order to press into the groin of the attacker in an attempt to knock him down.

Sitting Lotus

Within the fist manual this posture is referred to as "Guan Yin Sitting upon Her Seat". It is a posture where one's bottom is actually "sitting" (or perched) upon one of the heels. In this way, one of the feet (legs) is used to hide or conceal the other. The Sitting Lotus is a common "Earth" technique found within Taizuquan and is often used as a dodging tactic.

60. Kicking Method

The Half-Moon Kick (Crescent Kick)

Taizuquan places a great deal of emphasis upon the fist whist the foot methods are kept simple and easy. This half-moon kick (*banyueti*) is the most basic and commonly-seen kicking method within Quanzhou Taizuquan.

 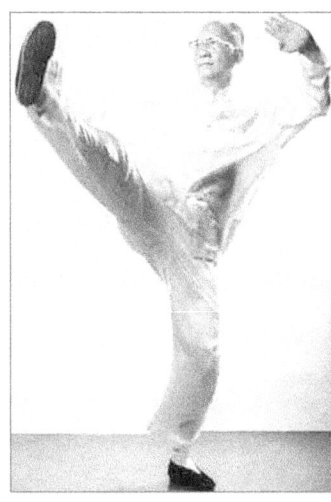

By way of the supporting leg one must effect "springing power" while the kicking leg/foot smashes and destroys. When kicking low to the attacker's abdomen the kick must be heavy while the higher kicks (aimed at the attacker's heart, upper torso or chin) must also demonstrate speed and power derived from the springing power and torque.

61. The Heel Kick Method

Bow Foot

Using the heel as the strength-, focal-, and contact-point one kicks (using the heel of the foot) towards the attacker's front as one infiltrates his Middle Gate. In order to deliver this attack with optimum speed, power and effect one must hold the front leg as if it were a stretched and drawn bow.

62. Stamping Method

Shoveling Leg

As a method for delivering a side-kick using the knife-edge of the foot as the strength-, focal-, and contact-point, one thrusts one's kick into the attacker's waist and abdominal region in a manner akin to shoveling.

63. Jumping/Leaping Method

Jumping

As a method of jumping in order to advance upon the attacker one must be as stable as a mountain prior to moving while effecting an escape (as would a rabbit!) after the event. When jumping in order to enter and land, one uses a fist method or a palm method. In order to avoid a frontal attack one must press against and into the ground with the front foot and jump backwards in a springing manner.

64. Ground Method

Falling Upon the Ground. Catching, Cutting, Trapping and Scissoring Technique

Falling to the ground is a method designed for avoiding an upper level attack whereby the defender counter-attacks the lower section of the adversary. Either bend or fall having pretended to dodge, or leap forward after having discovered the weakness of the opponent. Fall upon ground sideways then trap, wedge and sandwich one of the opponent's legs or feet with both of your own in order to make him fall.

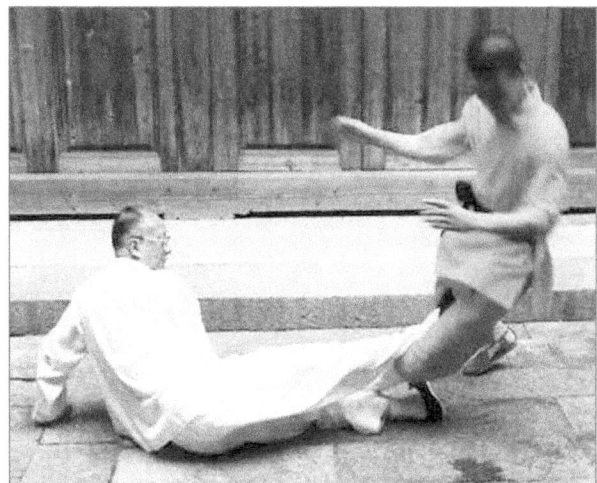

Threading the Needle Upon the Ocean Bed

Having fallen upon the ground, hook, trap and secure the opponent's heel with one of your own feet then kick the opponent's shin with your other foot in order to take him down using the power from both you upper and lower body.

* * *

What I have recorded above over the last thirty-four pages is approximately 70-80 percent of the essential and practical "technical hand" techniques within the Taizu taolu according to the Fist Manual to which I have, herein, made several references. Taizuquan's fist techniques involve either attacking or defending; no movement is wasted or impractical. It is crucial that one should step or stamp sideways in order to dodge or to advance directly. Attacking with hardness while seeking to achieve through softness, combat is effected at a very close range. The movements within Taizuquan remain uncomplicated.

CHAPTER SEVEN

THE BOOK OF DISCUSSIONS ON THE FIST ART

SECTION 1: HOW TO DISTINGUISH WUZUQUAN (WUZUQUAN DISTINCTIONS)

Quanzhou Southern Shaolin Fist has become a very large sect, well-known to the world and with a history that goes back hundreds of years. The book, *Wenlin Jiushi* ("The Ancient Tales Of Wenlin") states that, "The fist-art and weaponry from our city ranks highly across the world"[1] while Emperor Yong Zheng of the Qing dynasty once issued a decree stating, "Within the areas of Quanzhou City and Zhangzhou City civilization is well-developed and martial arts and military power is forever blazing." The fact that martial arts was greatly valued and largely practiced amongst the Quanzhou people was already well-known amidst the government and to shocking effect! At present, the various quanfa to be found within Quanzhou City include a wide range of styles — from southern to northern and from soft to hard. For hundreds of years now the winning fist-types have mainly been from the southern sects that have been taught and promoted amongst the city and the countryside — urban and rural — and with Taizuquan being one of the predominant styles. Now I will present a brief narrative regarding some facts regarding the Quanzhou Taizuquan sect according to my own opinions:

1. Wuzuquan is the General Name for Five Styles of Quanfa

Currently there are two different opinions over the name, Wuzuquan. One considers that Wuzuquan is a new style of quanfa that was created by combining five ancient quanfa. Some disagree and say that Wuzuquan is the general name of *the* five most popular quanfa amongst the Minnan people. This division of opinion is worthy of debate so…which one of them is actually closer to the truth?

A conversation between the author and comrade Xu Cai

Personally, I agree with the latter. The five quanfa are, by definition, Taizuquan, Luohanquan, Dazunquan, Xingzhequan and Baihequan; while all are with similar fist styles and all are with similar hand methods and foot methods (as far as the Quanzhou people are concerned). Owing to the fact that the people of Quanzhou, Xiamen and Zhangzhou are collectively referred tom as "Xiananren" (the lower southern people) the name "Wuzuquan" (Five Ancestor Fist) should be used as a general name for the five quanfa as a collective style of Fujian martial arts. Each of the these five quanfa include both empty hand techniques and weaponry with sanzhan being its opening taolu although some have become rare with the passing of so many years. For example, at the beginning of the Ming dynasty there were masters — including Monk Qiu Leng from the Kaiyuan Temple in Quanzhou, Master Jun Huan (known as Xijiehou[2]), and Master Xu Yun Shi (known from the Northern Gate from latter time) all of whom were well-known for being masters of Luohanquan. Nowadays, although Luohanquan has not completely disappeared but it has become quite rare. Meanwhile, Wuzuquan is defined as being a) one of the five styles that make up Wuzuquan and b) another name for Taizuquan. Still to this day some senior Yongchun Crane Fist masters still insist that their Crane Fist is from Wuzuquan, one such master being Mr. Zheng Wen Cun. This theory has actually come a long way.

A survey carried out by the "Provincial Martial Arts Association" (lead by Lu Xi Rong and You You Bo) revealed that in 1928 Master Pan Xiao De of the Yongchun sect had hand-copied a Baihequan manual that clearly stated Wuzuquan as comprising Taizuquan, Luohanquan, Dazun, Xingzhe and Baihequan, with Baihequan being the youngest of all these five styles of quanfa. Mr. Su Zai Fu (Chairman of the I Cheng Shaolin Martial Arts Association (I Cheng being a district under Quanzhou city) wrote a book called, *Taizuquanpu* ("Fist Manual") which included a similar record. Therein it stated, "First Taizuquan, second Luohanquan, third Dazun, fourth Xingzhe and fifth Baihequan." It also reflected upon the notion that, "One skilled in the twenty-four forms of Taizuquan can be without rival." When we read these two books we observe similarities in that the five aforesaid quanfa first belong to the Five Ancestor Sect (Wuzumen) then later had evolved into five individual sects.

I once visited Master Zhang Ying Qi (a student of Lu Yan Qiu who was a well-known martial arts master from the 1930s) who recalled that, "Master Lu considered the reason behind the name Wuzu (Five Ancestor) was because there was five *zhan* (battles) within it." The five *zhan* were the initial taolu within the five quanfa and included:

1. Zhimazhan (Straight Horse Battle) which came from Taizuquan
2. Luohan sanzhan (Three Battles) from Luohanquan
3. Zuzhan (Ancestor Battle) from Dazun
4. Houzhan (Monkey Battle) from Xingzhe
5. Hezhan (Crane Battle) from Baihequan

In 1961, when the Quanzhou Wushu Association was founded, Master Dai Huo Yan, Master Chen Chao Shun, Master Xu Yun Shi, Master She Rui Jie and Master Wu Jing (there were others) each performed these five "zhan" of the different sects and thus it became clear that when one trains in Wuzuquan one is learning taolu from these five distinct quanfa.

Since these five fist-types have the same common characteristic requirements (chest sunk, shoulders sunk, back straight, joints fastened, fierceful force and defending while waiting to advance…) as well as the trademark horse stance, Bu Ding Bu Ba, all this makes it possible to train in all these five kinds of quanfa.

The famous teacher, Master Cai Yu Ming, trained in Wuzuquan which proves this point. In the book, *China Soft Art Record*, Master Cai is ranked as "being a master of Wuzuquanfa." indicating that Master Cai was skilled in all these five quanfa styles.

Master Gan De Yuan from the Yongchun sect was the teacher of Master Lin Bao Shan and Master Li Zai Luan, who were well-known within the martial arts society of the 1920s. Master Gan wrote an article entitled, "Wuzuquan - The Art and a Brief History," within which he states clearly, "There are five types of quanfa within Wuzuquan namely, Taizuquan, Baihequan, Luohanquan, Dazunquan and Xingzhequan. A student should be recommended the correct quanfa for his or her training which should be in accordance with their physical build."

In Master Gan's view, "Wuzuquan is not only divided by its quanfa but also by way of the individual characteristics while Taizuquan may be characterized by way of its combination of softness and hardness. Similarly, Luohanquan is all about the practitioner's shape and build while Baihequan can be summed-up by its thunder and lighting and its wind and rain while Dazunquan is both temperate and gentle. Xingzhequan is all about the four concepts of swallowing and spitting together with floating and sinking.[3] Even though Master Gan's formulation and statement is worthy of thought and consideration, it also supports the viewpoint that Wuzuquan is the generic term for these five types of quanfa."

2. Current Hypothesis/Theory That Wuzuquan Is Taizuquan

The concept behind this theory is that Wuzuquan is the name of a particular style of quanfa created through combining the essential strong points taken from five styles of quanfa. The reason behind this theory comes from a description of Taizuquan that appears within the book, *Chinese Soft Arts - A Comprehensive Collection* (aka "The Bible of Ngo Cho Kun"), where it states that, "the Crane Wings, Monkey Palms, the Taizu Foot, the Dazun Body and the Luohan Steps" are all characteristics of Taizuquan and yet, in fact, these words are only a rhetoric technique of descriptions in summary of Master Cai Yu Ming's following the proper forms while he performed each of the five fist types. If we really wish to take this further it will be hard to explain the meaning of "Taizu Foot" as well as "Luohan Step." Even if we follow this theory Wuzuquan, as a new form of quanfa combined with the strong features of the five fist styles, will be hard to explain as it has only taken "Monkey Palms" from Xingzhe quan, "Crane Wing"' from White Crane Fist, and "Dazun Body" from Dazunquan. Following along from this theory, if a new style of quanfa has been created based upon five other quanfa there would be six fist types within the Minnan martial arts society. But in truth there are still only five fist types.

When students have come to learn quanfa that are called either Wuzuquan or Taizuquan they are actually taught the same essential taolu, the same basic techniques, the same exercise method and the same training procedures including Sanzhan, Ershiquan, Dajiao, Shizi and Shuangsui which are the five compulsory five taolu.

One is also taught the same hand techniques (for example: capturing, slicing, concealing, opening, whipping, blocking, rubbing and freeing) as well the various horse stances. In such a case the only difference between Wuzuquan and Taizuquan is the individual style of teaching. However the different styles can only represent the differences in sects and not in fist-types. In fact, the sense of Wuzuquan as a new fist type is actually Taizuquan as taught within Quanzhou City and its neighbourhood.

3) The History and Culture of Quanzhou City

The history and culture of Quanzhou City has been deeply influenced by and is therefore closely related to the Central Plain of China, the middle and lower regions of the Yellow River (including Henan province, western Shandong province, southern Shanxi province and Hebei province. In ancient times there have been three periods of large-scale immigration from the Central Plain to the south of China and with each one occurring during the West Jin dynasty (265-316), The Five Dynasties (907-960) and the Northern Song dynasty (960-1127) which brought the civilization/culture from around the Yellow River Basin.

It is said that the embryonic form (that is, the original form) of Taizuquan is from the "thirty-two long fists" that was created by Emperor Zhang Kuang Yin and so therefore it is highly likely that Quanzhou Taizuquan came from the north of China. At the time of the Song dynasty the government established the Southern Outer Department of the Imperial Clan within imperial China with one of the Nine Departments in Quanzhou. The descendants from Emperor Zhao Kuang Yin multiplied in Quanzhou into a large tribe thus Taizuquan was taught at that time as a type of Descendants' Fist (to be passed to the younger generation as a family tradition).

In Quanzhou, amongst the martial tongues, there are traces of languages used amidst China's Central Plain that date back to ancient times. For example, during the "Pian Shen Fang" (sideways defending) movement, the posture known as *chaoyangshou* was also called *zhaoyangshou* while the posture referred to as *chen xiang shi* was also known by the name, *chen jiang shi*. There are other names, terms and words that prove the ancient history of Taizuquan, examples of which include "raising," "opening'" and "bo" which can often be found within the Taizuquan *Fist Manual*. The fact that Taizuquan was

Master Zhou visiting Lu Qing Hui at Lu's old address, Huayuantou

Master Zhou discusses fist art with Xu Jin Dong and Ye Qing Hai

transmitted internally - within Quanzhou City - where it thus became firmly-rooted and so, over time, blossomed has been proven by way of certain historical references and conditions. Let us now look at some of the historical facts that date back to the Ming Dynasty:

Master Li Liang Qin from Quanzhou City acquired fame for his martial weapons art known as "Jing-Chu Long Sword" while the weapons-based arts had already lost their authenticity within the Songshan Shaolin Temple of Henan Province of Northern China.

Master Yu Da You of Quanzhou City wrote the very first martial monograph in Chinese history (called *Jian Jing* - the *Sword Manual*)

Master Zheng Cheng Gong encouraged martial arts training amongst the locals (villagers) and thus organized secret schemes against the Qing government

There was a group of people known as "The Seven Martial Heroes" of Jiangnan (meaning South of the Yangtze River) where one of these heroes was Master Lu Yuan who's teacher was Monk Chao Yuan who had first relocated to Taiwan but then later returned to Quanzhou where he lived and taught a number of students.

Peasant-revolts led to the Quanzhou Shaolin Temple becoming the meeting-place for Northern Shaolin martial arts and Southern Shaolin martial arts which, in turn, led to the promotion of Taizuquan along with an extensive social foundation and powerful traditions.

During a very long process of evolution Taizuquan was adopted by the local people and so it flourished throughout and across the wars and was relied upon by the secret societies (The Triads, no less) and was thus inherited, processed and improved upon by numerous generations while being enriched continuously and was eventually forged into one that is without any impractical movement and possesses vivid regional characteristics and Southern sect styles.

The regions that are influenced by Taizuquan cover far more than just Quanzhou but also include Xiamen and Zhangzhou where they actually flourish more and are practiced more extensively. Taizuquan is also taught in Tangcheng City as well as the Huku and Baipan areas where the forms taught are more rare and revealing given that these areas are more remote and with far less communication with the outside world.

When Master You Yun An, a disciple of Master Cai Yu Ming, promoted martial arts in Shima (within Longhai County), the Taizu master named Xing Yuan from Yongning Town (within Shishi City, Fujian) had already opened a quanfa school there. In 1982 I (the author) went to visit a Mr. Qian Jian Xiang along with a Mr. Su Zai Fu. According to Mr. Su, Taizuquan had already been promoted within Nan'an County (close to half a century earlier in the 1920s) when he, himself, taught Taizuquan there. Owing to the differences between the two interpretations a dispute broke out.

The Taizu tradition of the Chongfu Temple era goes back even further. After the Quanzhou Temple monk, Zhi Can, was tricked and then later killed within the South Military Drill Ground his disciple, Monk Yang Hua, escaped from prison and went to live amidst the Qingyuan Mountian and the Ling Yuan Temple of Jinjiang (in Quanzhou) as well as other places and so continued taking on students and teaching martial arts. Amongst his students were the "Twelve People Association" and this included Master Li Yu from Pu Ming village of the North Gate (Beimen).

After 1899, Monk Miaoyue became a student of Monk Yang Hua. "There was a memorial tablet dedicated to Monk Yang Hua within the Chongfu Temple Ancestry Hall with a special worship memorial for him often held upon special occasions such as when chanting sutras and making offerings." This quote comes from the article: "A falling leaf from the Shaolin Temple mourning the greatly respected master," written by Monk Chang Kai of Singapore.

According to Mr. Gan De Yuan, in a book titled, *The Brief History of Wuzuquan*, Monk Wu Xin already taught Taizuquan at the Dong Chan Temple under Emperor Yong Zheng's reign (1723-1735). Master Li Jun Ren, as Gan's uncle (auntie's husband in this case) was trained by Master Guan Yu Ren. Monk Wu Xin was the grandmaster of Master Guan Yu Ren. Therefore, Master Li Jun Ren had already been trained in Taizuquan for ten years, Crane Fist and Monkey Fist and had combined the strong points from the different sects when Master Cai Yu Ming was a teenager.

When it comes to taolu, technical hands and horse stances there are very few differences between the taolu that have been handed down by Monk Yang Hua from Chongfu Temple and those handed down by Master Wei Guo Qi (who was taught by Master Wei Xi Nong), as well as those handed down by Lin Jiu Ru (who was, himself, taught by Master Cai Yu Ming). The most commonly taught taolu are to be found within all these sects while the most commonly-seen technical hands are of the same names and have the same meanings and content. The keys points are also all very similar with the various sects all being much of a sameness.

Let us look back at the book, *Chinese Soft Art - A Comprehensive Collection*, written by Master You Feng Biao one century ago (in 1917). During his staying and while teaching in Quanzhou City, Master You was one of the disciples of Master Cai Yu Ming. Within the preface of this book Master You wrote: "The commonly seen Wuzuquan has already lost some of its original features that were handed down during the course of a great many years. My teacher and master, Cai Yu Ming, travelled with a bow (weapon) together with a horse for company while also being a master of Wuzuquan." From this we can see that Wuzuquan was handed down over generations and was spread widely and extensively. If Wuzuquan was created by Master Cai Yu Ming it would be no more than ninety years old so how can it be said that this art, "has already lost some of its original features handed down through such long years"? The statement, "being a master of Wuzuquan" doesn't mean "created by himself" and this, here, is all-too-clear. This book was written seven years after the death of Master Cai Yu Ming which should make this viewpoint more convincing than other theories as to — or versions of — the true meaning of Wuzuquan.

These discussions are naturally somewhat limited by my own experiences so perhaps they are not as accurate as one would like. But I have included them here in the hope that, through feedback from you - the reader, my friends and my seniors —I might be better —informed.

Written by Zhou Kun Ming and published by the Fujian Martial Arts Circles, China Martial Arts in 1984.

The author poses with one of his books 'Wuzumen Yanjiu (Studies)

SECTION 2: THE KEY POINTS OF WUZUQUAN

Part 1

The concepts of Wuzuquan — called Taizu, called Guanyin, called Luohan, called Dazun, Xuannü — are five types of fist blending/supporting each other into one sect, therefore it is Wuzu sect. There is also another way of thinking that thinks Wuzu includes Taizu, Luohan, Xingzhe, Dazun and Baihe. Maybe/perhaps Quanzhou has got the profound history of Nanshaolin (South Shaolin), the focused living area of the ancient Heluo people, the fist art is inherited/handed down from the middle part (ancient meaning middle part of China), obtaining the swift and fierce (piaohan) style from the Minnan area, full of muscular and manly quality.

All of the above-mentioned quanfa are performed with small tight horse stances, solid and intense hand-work and hard and fierce fist power emphasizing close-quarter combat and sharing similar fist styles and fist theories such as the lowered shoulders, the knotted joints and the trademark swallowing, spitting, floating and sinking. The locals in Quanzhou city often practise more than one type of quanfa. For example, a practitioner of Taizuquan may also practice Luohanquan, or a student of Baihequan might also practise Dazuquan. In this way one will be equipped with a wider variety of techniques and come to understand subtleties and differences that exist when it comes to hard and soft strength, and speak with more authority when it comes to comparisons and depth.

The reason behind the different concepts of the name Wuzuquan might result from the different oral instructions handed down from each generation of master. Since the five quanfa styles that make up Wuzuquan are so similar and are taught within such a small area as Quanzhou City and are under the influence of each other, they form/represent one big sect called Wuzuquan. In ancient times the Wuzuquan schools within the southern quarter of Quanzhou City presented, respectfully, the ancestral tablets of the five styles — Taizu, Guanyin, Luohan, Dazun, and Xuannu. The tablets of five ancestors were displayed in the centre with the seat of the master placed to the left. When one formally became a student to a master the novice would first pay his respect to the tablets of the five ancestors. This has been a ritual that goes back centuries.

Quanzhou Wushu Delegation visiting the Philippines

Since Wuzuquan involves quanfa from five separate sects it has thus acquired the essential characteristics from each of the five fist types thus the Five Ancestor Fist forms very much enrichen the Wuzuquan style. These forms include empty fist forms and weapons forms. The school to which I belonged taught a great many empty-hand forms and just as many weapons forms. In total there were seventy-two forms including paired practice. Tallying-up the number of forms from all the five sects, the final number would have been virtually countless!

Training in quanfa generally begins with the Samchien form. Wuzuquan starts with wuzhan (Five Battles) which comprises: Sanzhan (Three Battles), Tiandirenzhan (Heaven Earth Man Battles), Lianhuanzhan (Consecutive Battle), Pingmazhan (Level Horse Battle) and Zhigongzhan (Straight Bow Battle). Initial training begins with these Battles as well as training in the Horse Stance, Stamping the Middle Palace, Straightening the Body and the Dantian, and Swallowing and Sitting Breath. Later on the forms would become far more complicated and far longer in terms of their physical size. Progressively, other forms include "Twenty Punches" (Ershiquan) then "Striking The Four Corners" (Simendajiao), "Three Battles Character Ten" (Sanzhanshizi), "Double Peace" (Shuangsui), "Eight Linked/Consecutive Diagrams" (Lianhuanbagua), "One Thousand Small Characters" (Xiaoqianzi), "Connected Cities" (Liancheng), "Two Sections" (Erjie), "Three Sections" (Sanjie), "Four Sections" (Sijie), "Five Sections" (Wujie), "Five Stomach, Sinking Heads" (Wuduchentou), "Double Claws" (Shuangzhua), "Eight Diagram Fist" (Baguaquan), "Heavenly Beings" (Tiangang), "Underworld Beings" (Disha), "Cool Breeze" (Qingfeng), "Bright Moon" (Mingyue), "Four Gates Battling At The Bottom" (Simendoudi) and "Two Lions Showing Their Power" (Shuangshi zhanxiong) to name but a few!

Some of these forms tend to be more difficult to learn and practice than others while each holds its own fascination, attraction and appeal. For instance, a strong student might find Shizi appropriate for their build while someone not so strong might gravitate more towards Chentou (Sinking Head) or Zhigong (Straight Bow). Similarly, a tall student might prefer to work on Shuangsui or one of the "Sections" forms while someone that is short might work on Dajiao (Striking the Corners) or Disha. In this way the various fist arts fit each and every category of practitioner.

Weaponry is performed with the fist-art together with a hard bow and a horse stance with clear striking/attacking actions and uncovering/exposing with power contained within each and every movement. The long weaponry includes the cudgel, staff, spear, the green dragon broadsword, the horse cutting/chopping blade (sword), the cavalry sword, the triple-tipped double-edged blade, the hooked scythe, the mountain-splitting axe, the Buddhist Monk staff, the shoulder pole, the shanba (mountain rake), and the fangtian huaji — a weapon that combines the spear with the battle-axe. In fact, it could be said that the use of weapons covers "the complete eighteen kinds of martial arts" which is a saying we have suggesting that weaponry covers all kinds skills and abilities.

Cudgel-play is the most powerful of all the weaponry and this, of course, includes the Wuchigun,[4] the Qichigun,[5] the liuxinggun (the falling star cudgel), the qimeigun (eye-brow level cudgel), the shuweigun (the rat-tail cudgel), the zhang'ergun[6] and the shuangtougun (the double-headed cudgel). The techniques included herein include splitting, sweeping, cutting, slicing, driving, leaping, knocking, opening, cutting (as if with scissors), clicking, shooting (as if firing an arrow), lifting, raising, placing the flower, pulling the flag, striking with a mallet, turning over the mallet-head, pinching gold, and embracing the heart where power with the cudgel's shaft and tip is trained so that both unite in such a way that can be likened to a dragon swimming the ocean or floating across the heaven. The cleverness of cudgel-play within wuzuquan can largely be credited to skills handed down by Master Yu Da You, a native of Quanzhou City.

Taizuquan's short weaponry includes the single blade, the single whip, the single truncheon, the double-edged sword, the copper pan pipes, the iron ruler and the umbrella as well as the double blades, the double-edged swords, the double truncheons, the double hooks and combined spears and battle-axes, the double whips, the integrated blades, the double crutches,[7] the double daggers and the double shield blades.

Taizuquan's soft weaponry includes the nine-section whip, the three section cudgel and the rope dart while the concealed weaponry of this art includes the dart, the stone and the needle. Each weapon possesses its own traditional and handed-down forms. The inherited forms are traditionally taught in a specific order such as paired-practice including the Five-Chi Cudgel paired-practice, the Seven-Chi paired-practice, the double crutches combat-practice, the eyebrow-level cudgel, the carrying the pole combat, the level-to-eyebrow cudgel, the five-chi cudgel versus the double whips, the shield-blade versus the how, the shield-blade versus the sickle, the horse-chopping sword versus the mountain rake, the mountain rake versus the seven-chi cudgel, the horse-cutting sword, the left crutch right blade versus the copper pan pipes, the seven-chi cudgel, and the double-edged sword versus the double-edged sword, and more.

The Wuzuquan Sect focuses heavily upon actual combat with no impractical movements. Attacking and defending is with clear opening, tearing and dissolving. All its forms can be performed as paired-practice which means that its entire thirty-six empty-fist routines can, in fact, be executed as thirty-six paired practices! And the same can be said for its weapons forms.

When it comes to a wrestling and a trial of strength one needs to enlist the help of "lifting" techniques and "coiling" techniques. Coiling techniques involve picking, seizing, pinching, kneading, polishing, sealing, pressing, holding, clasping, spinning and sinking and use the entire body together with the heart, mind and vision. Solo training works only the fist while paired practice addresses the changes of strength, power, pathways and the indispensable swallowing, spitting, sinking and floating. In this way one is able to strengthen one's basics while improving technique(s). There are also techniques such as the disposition of troops that were originally based upon training military troops. Overtime, however, this evolved specifically into quanfa and so a unique heritage in the form of the Wuzu sect. With forms taking on various shapes and appearances along with various themes — Song Jiang, to name but one (Song Jiang being one of the 108 warriors featured in the literary classic, "The Water Margin") — these forms naturally underwent change(s) together with the inevitable variations upon various themes that are now no longer actually taught within quanfa schools. Resultantly and tragically they have since been lost!

Part 2

Our sect includes martial arts combining both hardness and gentleness while advocating short-range combat instead of long-range fighting. Responding and receiving must be virtually one and the same. Our forms focus upon kicking, striking, throwing and capturing. Founded upon the use of the hand as well as the use of the horse stance, the body and waist coordinate with the swallowing and spitting and the sinking and the floating. The forms, handed down from ancient times, total more than one hundred while the starting position and posture and ending position and posture must be contained within the same specific area. Sending out the fist with fierce strength, a strong shout and obvious power, one must aim at the opponent with his rear hand as it were a spear while concealing his front hand as if it were a shield.

Quanzhou Wushu Delegation visiting Japan

The hand method is divided into short techniques, long techniques, single techniques and double techniques and should include the use of the fingers, the wrists, the palms, the fists, the joints and the shoulder. The basic hand technique include capturing, raising, opening, concealing, stringing, cutting, closing, scratching, plucking, rubbing, bumping, whipping, slicing, chopping, shooting, thrusting, grabbing, blocking, locking, sectioning, floating, flicking, pecking, lifting, splitting, eating, separating, pinning, shaking, breaking, dissolving, chopping, freeing, falling, clawing, provoking, sealing and more with one technique developing and merging into a multitude of techniques.

In detail, fingers, wrists, palms, fists, elbows, and shoulders can all be used in an interactive way. The fingers can click, shoot, press, sweep. The fingers attack whenever the mind indicates and the strength arrives whenever the fingers arrive. The strength is by way of sending out power through the fingertips instead of sudden strength and withdrawing the joint as soon as it clicks when performing the dian xue (clicking xue, an acupuncture point) and fengxue (sealing xue) technique.

The palm method is to send out strength by way of the hand-blade and includes grinding, throwing, breaking, slicing, chopping, flicking, peeling, opening and splitting. The palm is used upwards and downwards and like a fan — opening and closing, blocking and thrusting and touching and feeling with techniques interchanging as and when required. The hand-blade must be vertical while the palm-center must be concave. The palm must be as quick as the wind with power applied at the moment of impact. The wrist sits or blocks while the joint floats, the hand is to send out straight and sit backwards. The shoulders sink and elbows are held level as the left and right

The author with his daughter

sides follow each other. The shoulders must not exert strength. The crisp strength is applied by way of the laying or sinking so the wrist can be flexible instead of being stiff. In this way one's strength will prevail and will not be blocked (by the aggressor).

There are varieties of fist shapes including the phoenix-eye fist, the goose-eye fist, the triangular fist, the vertical (standing) fist and the upward-facing fist as well as methods of combining two single fists into a double fist. Whist sending out the fist - whether it be pecking, seizing, raising, whipping or falling, or be the double vertical fist, the double poking fist or the double even/level fist - the strength is to send power out from the waist and the knees by way of shaking the crotch while the power is sinking and the strength is heavy.

With the fist focusing upon one's center and in-line with the nose which is also in-line with the heart, in this way one is able to gather one's qi. One must also twist and turn with soft joints and limbs as well as with hard fists thus sending out rapidly so as to achieve power and the effect of, "penetrating the mountains and splitting rocks."

The joint techniques are performed by way of short power (over a short distance) to achieve ferocity and strength. These attacks involve horizontal joint strikes, rear stabbing joints, sky-facing joints, double uncovering shoulder blades, and pressing joints. Both attacks and defenses here include clasping the joints, chicken eating wings, cutting and slicing joint actions, and binding inner joints as well as others.

The key points for the elbow method includes lowering the body and the "sitting horse" together with turning the body backwards and achieving power through correct posture. Avoiding the solid and approaching the void one "enters the gate" that leads to the failure of the opponent. One must move the elbows by way of the shoulders while the hand in front should be held relative to and in proportion with the behind hand. Initially soft but later hard, one receives upon one's meridian line (taking care not to lean or tilt) so that strength from the joints can be performed in a heavy manner yet fluid manner while, at the same time, sinking.

The use of the shoulders and the back is also executed by way of close-quarter combat where one can press against the opponent and then strike. There are five methods including stamping, pressing, shaking, pushing and carrying upon one's back which involve postures such as Monkey Fetches The Water, Otter Clothing Power, Shaking The Body and Squeezing the Shoulder Blades, Mi Le (the Bodhisattva or Maitreya "Compassionate" Buddha character with the big belly), and Dong Bin (actually, Lu Dong Bin who was a Tang Dynasty scholar and poet who was later elevated to the status of "immortal") who carries a double-edged sword. There are others. These postures exert power from the shoulders and the back, especially through shaking the body and pushing back the shoulder blades where the latter is one of the most unique skills within Taizuquan. This posture is pretty and preserves power through withdrawing the chest and hunching the back. The shoulder blades first float then thrust. The breath is closed/preserved within the dantian and the crotch is tightened as is the waist which induces power using the waist as the axis. One shakes continuously — like a dog shaking water out of its fur. This movement is extremely swift and whoever is being touched is thus bounced away.

The hand method involves the five elements of Chinese philosophy, namely metal, wood, water, fire and earth. These elements engender and restrain each other. Within the *Fist Manual* it states that, "Coming directly and going horizontally, coming horizontally and going directly, breaking the lower from the upper while dissolving the upper from the lower." This, then, explains the general rule. Wuzuquan techniques are divided into three

Gold Technique

Wood Technique

Earth Technique

Water Technique

Fire Technique

routes: the Upper, Middle and Lower. One is thus prepared for any form of capturing and wrestling one may need. Each hand-to-hand technique practiced during training is done so as if for real! In an instant, anything can change and anything can happen thus one must be sharp-sighted thus foreseeing a striking opportunity before the opponent while adapting to the situation before the opponent acquires the upper hand. Attacking upon the advantage of the situation, entering wherever required and advantageous, one uses the attacker's energy against the attacker and so defeats and wins through his being swift versus the attacker's lacking.

The Wuzuquan sect is all about advancing towards and pushing through while stamping the Middle Palace (Gate) and entering the Front Gate. With hard blocking and hard attacking, one's technique must be heavy and the hands hard yet flexible. The "leaning" techniques and the "lifting" are to be used along with the feet via the horse with power and strength from the physical pathway — foot to fingers where the skill of the hand is just like an arrow — hard, swift and direct. Whoever is good at the Fist Method must be good at the Bridging Hand. What is the Bridging Hand? Bridging refers to the joint. Two joints rely upon each other as if building a bridge. Whoever has crossed my bridge is able to approach me while I am able to approach whoever has not yet crossed the bridge! If the gate of the opponent's is closed I, myself, must build a bridge (if there is not already one) and thus push through the opponent's Middle Gate thus creating a situation where the opponent just has to fail. If I am at the gate that will lead to failure, or should my opponent be too powerful I must block and break the bridge that has already existed and so dissolve it through disappearing and dodging in order to make sure that I am absolutely safe. The power of gongfu is performed depending upon the understanding from the master.

Part 3

The fist art is performed using the horse stance as its foundation. The basic foot method within Wuzuquan is sanzhanma (the three battle horse stance), budingbubama — a horse stance that is neither the character "ding" (a "T"-shape) nor the character "ba" (eight) meaning that the foot formation is between "ding" and "ba" where the front void and the back is solid.

The initial Fist training starts from and with sanzhan, with its three advancing steps and its three retreating steps which thus trains the stamping steps. Therefore, this is called sanzhanma.

One of the sanzhahma is called "sanqima" (the 3:7 horse) where the back foot exerts 70% of the strength while the front foot exerts the remainder. Another is called "siliuma" (the 4:6 horse) in which the strength is divided between 4 or 6 out of 10 on the relative foot, and the latter is a type of foot-horse that helps one to safeguard while waiting for an opportunity. One is called "wuwuma" (the 5:5 horse) where each foot shares half the strength thus containing and concealing inner power ready for an attack and thus, maintaining flexibility so as to change and transform whenever and wherever necessary.

The battle horse (zhanma) method requires that one sits upon the rear foot while "wrapping" the other with both knees facing the tips of the feet. Exerting strength from the front side of the lower part of the leg one lifts the calf tendon with the "yongquan" acupressure pressure-point empty (of weight) and the sole of the foot sticking to the ground. As one steps, one lands into a "sandianjin" (three drops of gold) posture with the shoulders sunk and the abdomen loose. The stomach hangs while the coccyx and sacrum sink. Tightening one's cartilage and lifting one's anus one thus preserves one's qi by way of the central area of the spine. Lowering the body and sinking the breath, stand steadily as if imitating Jin Gang (a guardian deity of Buddhist iconography) with one's power piercing the ground.

Knowing exactly when to be solid and when to be empty, advancing or retreating, move one's feet with strength from the crotch. The rear foot must be heavy (like a tiger squatting) and the front foot light. The rear foot sole must not float but, rather, be heavy and steady, not tilting and not leaning. The opening and closing of the waist and crotch is essential for one's horse while the power of the arms stems from the waist.

Having stamped, lock from the waist and cartilage. Tighten one's foot-strength is as if rooted underground as deep as one metre and execute the sending-out fist as if a giant tree challenges a gale-force wind - with the branches and leaves dancing whist the root is as steady as a mountain. This is the method within Wuzuquan that is called "falling upon the floor and rooting underground.

There are seven or eight out of ten taolu involving the Battle Horse (zhanma) therefore they are all recognized as being very important. As long as one is able to master the Battle Horse, it is not difficult to master other Horse methods such as the Bow Horse, the Character Ding Horse, the Four Level Horse, and the Hanging Foot Horse, as the theories of each would be made clearer to grasp.

The foot-horse works the entire body thus depicting the movement of a lively dragon or a vivid tiger through advancing and retreating as well as rising and falling both vertically and horizontally, moving and shifting, dodging and dissolving. The foot method includes the Advancing Horse, the Retreating Horse, the Remaining Horse, the Changing Horse, the Whispering Horse, the Walking Horse, the Folding Horse, the Squatting Horse and the Collapsing Horse together with the Thrusting Horse as well as the Leaping Foot, the Three Drops Of Gold, the Seven Star Step, the Mandarin Duck Step, the Spiral Step, The Riding/Rippling Wave Step and the Eight Divinatory Trigrams Chain Step. Then there is the Jumping and Bending, the Sitting Lotus, and the Pointing Towards The Earth. Meanwhile, the foot must co-ordinate with the technical hand. The upper divinatory trigram would be empty if the step is unstable and this would lead to instant failure should one's step be inflexible.

The Quanzhou people often say that, "one must also train one's foot if one is to train one's fist" and that, "the foot-horse must be trained to be able to fall." When it comes to judging fist techniques one must first be judged through one's foot-horse. If the foot horse is too long, if the substantial and insubstantial are not clear, and if the foot-horse is too wide one's "gate" is "open" and this is not good.

If one performs with a ferocious fist alongside floating energy and disordered steps, he will be seen to be incompetent. He would, therefore, lose his balance and fall in the hands of one that was more competent. Therefore the "southern (martial arts) people" (the Minnan people) often spend their entire life in an attempts to master one single taolu thus ensuring their horse is stable, their foot (step) is flexible, and their fist-skill very high.

If one is to perform a solid horse, one must train their rising and falling, their opening and closing, and their bundling, joining and pausing while training to be as strong as iron as he/she draws the bow. If one is to perform a lively horse one must clarify between the solid and the void while walking and falling without a sound. One's foot must step out first (before the enemy has time to act) where the heart directs in one's desire to advance. One's foot must withdraw first (before the enemy has time to act) where one's body desires to retreat, moving alongside the change of the technical hands. If the horse is stable but not flexible it will be considered dead. The horse must be alive if one is to pursue stability based upon flexibility. If one is to perform with a strong horse, one must train heaviness before training "light power," kicking the sandbag while stomping and stamping, and raising one's qi in order to train both strength and power. Within the Wuzu sect the fist strikes within the area of a lying ox while one's horse methods change in accordance with the various terms of the taolu. Therefore, utilizing the fist as if walking along a road while utilizing one's footwork within a natural range of motion and movement one takes advantage of one's flexibility to advance and retreat by way of a small but high horse thus overpowering and defeating the low and wide horse. Walking should be energetic thus one retrieves the essence while understanding the purpose of tightening, holding and bundling with steady footwork and focused punches as one advances step-by-step.

This theory is reflected by way of the expression, 'Hurried walking does not promote the best footwork while slow walking does bring out good steps." The gate must be clear and the six gates must be switched back and forth with flexibility. Stamping and advancing through the middle gate/palace while dodging from side to side as the hands and body follow the feet in a coordinated manner will bring forth and send out power, as we say, "of the wind and rain" (again, fengyu).

Friends from around the world visiting Quanzhou Shaolinsi

While some say that Wuzuquan executes fist-work without exploring foot-work, this is simply not true! Wuzuquan utilizes low and heavy stance-work where the number of variations upon the footwork exceeds ten! These include the use of the heel and the toes and the knife-edge and the sole while the feet and legs through the body leap and twist utilizing the bow and arrow (stance)

Friends from the Philippines, Malaysia and Macao attending Wuzuquan Fellowship Conference

not unlike the ways of the northern fist (beitui). The popular wuzu sect foot methods include kicking, bending, slicing and sweeping combined with speed and power and with viciousness and ferocity. The blocking strategies of Wuzuquan include sideways kicking, scratching legs, stamping, chopping, treading and pressing.

While in close contact with the opponent the foot methods includes tripping and binding, pressing against the knees, hooking the knees, thrusting the crotch, and twisting the waist while the foot method executed from the ground includes scissor-cutting, hooking, treading, falling, and rolling. The various techniques include kicking the heart, old tree coiling the root, black dragon coiling around the pillar, deserting the upper and aiming at the lower, rolling as a dog, and coiling as a snake. These are all used in order to bring an opponent down.

The foot method that soars up into the air includes whirlwind/tornado leg, flying kick, flying and scissoring, and long distance high jump. One is to advance closely for attack and retreat for defence, subduing the opponent's fist by way of one's foot. One may also subdue the opponent's foot/leg technique by way of one's own foot or feet. The variations are numerous and cover every scenario.

Wuzuquan is particular upon its use of steady footwork and the controlled application of one's body and body mechanics. There is a saying, "The body is in danger of becoming useless as soon as one droops one's head;" and so in order to defend oneself from possible attack one must sit backwards before lifting up and sending out one's foot. The foot method is more often used when one is in need of dodging or avoiding an opponent thus transforming potential failure into positive success. The kicking method is often aimed at the lower three routes with one's shape being that of a half moon and with the height of the kick being no more than one's belly-button thus one immediately sends forth power as soon as one is close to the enemy. In this way one's power is too sharp to defend against.

Part 4

Each kind of fist practice focuses upon a particular shape, energy and spirit. Each fist must have its form where the most important part of the form is its body method. These movements include standing, squatting, rising, falling, advancing and retreating along with reserving and turning - they all depend upon changes within the body method. The fist performs well if the body is flexible. The fist will be loose and without power if the body is stiff. All fist disciplines follow the same theory and this includes, of course, Wuzuquan.

The wuzuquan body method follows the way of nature. This includes the five forms and the four correct faces together with the, "interfacing of the meridian". The four correct faces refer to the form without titling or wobbling and the form without bending at the waist, without titling the head and without drooping the shoulders. The head must be straight and the neck must be straight, the chest must be sunk and concave and the abdomen must be withdrawn, the buttocks must tightened and the horse must be sitting while the body must sink.

The "interfacing meridian" refers to the baihuixue (an acupoint which is the crown of one's head) facing weilüxue (which is another acupoint) with the fingertips facing the tips of the toes, with the point of the elbow facing the eye of the knee, and with both shoulders being level and in-line. The knees must not be beyond the big toe while the fist must be focused upon one's center-line.

The body form of Wuzuquan interchanges between the "grave stone body form" and the "triangular body form". The grave stone body is level and steady and this is referred to as *si ping ba wen* — the "four level and eight steady" which is another way of saying that one develops all-round awareness while heightening all the senses thus one becomes full of positive energy while making ease of defending one's center-line. While facing the opponent the triangular body form first poses as a defensive shape as it preserves and stores up the necessary power in order to instigate an attack while maintaining flexibility within the body for advancing or retreating. The fist power is able to float and sink while the head becomes the "head of the family" with the joints serving as the meeting-point for energy and blood. If the head is correct, the body is also correct.

As for the "body turning method" one must turn one's head before one's body turns either left or right. In this way one is able to observe from six routes and hear from eight directions (*yan guan liu lu, er ting ba fang*) and so be able to judge a situation as to whether or not the adversary be "the guest or the host," or whether him "being the stronger or weaker" — in other words, the submissive or the commanding, in-charge or obeying.

One is able to lean backwards for an upper attack and bend forward for a lower attack. The eyes must function in accordance with and be rooted within the heart. The eyes must be bright when the heart is calm and at peace. Upon the battlefield one must judge the next movement from the enemy be it moving or still, empty (pretending) or solid (actual). One must wait for an opportunity (*the* opportunity) to attack and win with sharp observations of the enemy's body language although here we are talking about the opponent's body and not his hands!

Should you detect a movement from his shoulder you can tell that a hand movement is going to follow; if the body is rising one can tell that the foot is also going to rise; if the opponent is looking at your right side he is going to attack you at your right and if the opponent is looking at your left side he is going to attack you at your left side. Therefore, it is said that one can foretell the next movement from the opponent from his eyes. If the eyes of the enemy are looking uncertain and are constantly moving one can tell that he is afraid; if the eyes are lacking in focus and so are without spirit one can tell that his skill must be shallow and insufficient. A skilled fist-master often has eyes as sharp and as bright as lightening but with an expression of calm although intimidating — with an inner fierce intention but not showing (and thus not revealing) by way of outer/external expression.

There are not fixed receiving body postures. The body method/shape include vertical structures, sideways structures, tilting, somersaulting, turning, shrinking, squatting, bending (forwards, backwards, and at the knees), jumping, leaping, falling and rolling. A rising body must be horizontal while a falling body must be vertical; advancing steps must be low while retreating steps must be high; withdrawing must be as if taming a cat and letting go must be as if freeing a tiger. One must especially understand the body method of dissolving and dodging. One is to move his body using his steps in order to avoid a sharp frontal attack while one is to follow the oncoming power from the enemy in order to dissolve his power and his strength.

The change of the body and the stepping method must provide the correct opportunities for dissolving and dodging if one is to avoid the solid and receive the void. It is easier to foresee a receiving method if the opponent approaches slowly; if an attacker approaches all of a sudden and with fierce power it is better to dissolve it or dodge it. When an attack is approaching from a close proximity one must immediately change his body-form and dissolve the oncoming power within both seconds and inches.

American friends attending Wuzuquan Fellowship Conference

Due to an earlier failure the opponent must change his form/power and approach to attack. If a failure within an opponent is detected late one is not able to prepare and dissolve the oncoming attack. The wonder of dodging and fighting is based upon following the opponent and staying within range as if in contact but actually not. Dodging, disappearing or quickly entering and thus subduing an opponent one must not employ large visual movements (that is to say, do not "open big" or "close big") but, rather, use waist movement and cartilage movement in order to change one's form while being formless. Therefore, the method of crossing the cartilage has to be in detail. In this method one must exert strength through the center of one's heel while gathering strength from one's waist and spine — with one's veins opening as if bursting and with one's feet following the waist as it rapidly twists and turns as the shoulders are employed with absolute co-operation.

The gravestone body shape quickly transforms into a triangular body shape as if the wind is blowing and shaking a willow tree — being neither stiff nor pausing, be neither dull nor still. Having avoided the oncoming sharp power from an opponent one must quickly occupy the Living Gate then take both the opportunity and the advantage from the disappearance of the enemy's previous power and his forming new strength. Strike before the enemy sends out his technique thus by utilizing minor (conserved) strength one is able to defeat the enemy. There is a saying, "The fist is able to strike a thousand times by way of a natural body method." The changes of the body method is similar to the military method where both exist within one's mind and heart. Only if the body method is natural and flexible will the strength and power be in-range and fluid. One can thus exert a foot technique and a hand technique with full power and perform faultless attacks or defenses. One should think long and hard over the meaning of these words.

Part 5

Wuzuquan is full of and rich in muscular power and energy, and is often looked upon as being a hard-fist "external family sect" style. In fact, even though this fist-method is imposing (as if it were full of male characteristics) at the same time it couples strength with gentleness and so therefore it is a fist-method of great beauty both inside and out as it strengthens branches and puts down a solid root.

Using the sanzhan taolu as an example, all those that are trained in Wuzuquan (no matter where in the world they or their teacher is from) must begin their journey with sanzhan. There is an old saying, "Starting with sanzhan and train sanzhan until you breathe your last." This is because sanzhan is the mother of this quanfa style. Even though it consists only of three advances and three retreats, all the rules of Wuzuquan are based upon and centre round sanzhan.

With one's head held straight and facing directly forward, the neck must be vertical and the chin tucked in. The eyes must be looking straight ahead while one's vision (focus) must be set to infinity. One's torso and dantian must be elevated and the chest concave like the shell of a tortoise. The shoulders must sink and the joints tightly "connected" with the ribs on both sides while thrusting. The lower spine sinking and the meridians returning to the center as one adopts a sitting horse which must be stable. The sinews must be tightened and the intestines lifted. The kneecap must be stretched whilst strength must be exerted by way of the three drops of gold — with the front void and the rear foot solid. One must also be rooted as soon as one lands upon the ground. When changing one's horse stance, one must bring an advancing or retreating horse to a stop while one's technical hands and strength must also come to a halt. While opening and closing, one must follow certain rules and order, and interchange between the yin and the yang; one's qi must reach one's dantian upon inhaling or exhaling and the strength must reach the four limbs as soon as one has exerted strength.

The strength of sanzhan consists of eight kinds: straight and direct, horizontal, hard, soft, long-lasting, crisp, sinking, and flattening. All should be exerted by way of swallowing, spitting, sinking or floating. As soon as this this is understood the hard or soft strength is as if rolling down a rock from a high mountain. If one is trained to swallow, spit, float and sink naturally — thus filling and widening one's dantian and opening and stretching one's two arteries (ren and du) — then not only can one's muscles, bones and skin be strengthened, but one's internal organs can also be strengthened.

Previous chairman of the International Wuzuquan Fellowship General Conference receiving the official seal representing authority of chairmanship

Swallowing, spitting, sinking and floating is a breathing and energy-transferring/exerting method and a method of withdrawing and sending technical hands which includes tilting, straightening, shrinking and stretching the body. When one withdraws one's hand one must inhale through the nose thus inducing the crossing of one's sinews, loosening the upper diaphragm, sinking the qi, and tightening one's stomach. This is all termed "swallowing." In order for "swallowing" to transfer/become/change to "spitting" one must exhale at the same time that one sends out one's technique — first slowly and then faster. In order to "sink" one must "sit one's joint" whilst pressing/exerting strength with one's "baihuixue" (an acupoint located at the crown of one's head) which must be aligned with one's coccyx and with both shoulders locked and fixed. Exerting strength by way of the waist and shoulder blades, tighten the anus and "sink" one's qi as part and parcel of the "sinking" process. In order for the "sinking" to shift naturally to "floating" one must ensure that one's qi is exerted without obstacles and obstruction as ones expands one's chest whilst the center of both palms are facing upwards in order to draw in one's qi — from heaven to earth — thus it is sent mindfully to one's dantian where it is stored and harnessed. Swallowing or spitting resides within the movement of sending and withdrawing by way of the hands while the interchange between floating and sinking also follows the interchange between swallowing and spitting.

When in battle one must float when the opponent sinks and sink when the opponent floats. One must spit when the opponent swallows and swallow when the opponent spits. One must build a bridge when one's situation is favorable, and borrow a bridge when the situation is favorable to one's opponent. Where yin and yang residing within each other and where interchanging follows the movement of the hands, one's qi must flow freely as one exerts strength which arrives at both the center of the heels and the tip of the head. One *must* swallow and spit qi deeply with a natural speed although one *must not* hold one's qi in one's chest or breathe via one's chest for this will float one's qi and scatter it in a disorderly manner. One's body will not be straight if one's foot (step) is not steady, and one's strength will not "arrive" if one's mind is everywhere but in the moment. Therefore one must train one's qi if one wishes to train one's fist. One's strength will be adequate if one's qi is adequate.

The truth of, the key to, and the way of fist-training emphasizes that vitality, energy and spirit should be harmonized. Vitality must focus upon and gather together energy that has to bloom while one's spirit must be calm. When it comes to performing such movements within our Sanzhan form as the double thrusting, the sitting joint, the swallowing and the spitting, one must reserve strength through relaxation and launch strength gradually, exert strength evenly, and gather speed with each step. One's heart must be as the General's, one's eyes must be as flags, and one's will must be able to reach a high very level. But all this is possible only if one constantly trains all three elements. Therefore, if one trains the Wuzuquan sanzhan one must pay particular attention to take heart-health and an elevated spirit while also understanding one's mind. Thus, one's qi should be even, moderate and placid. If one's mind is clear, one's technique can be skillful but, on the other hand, if one is muddle-headed one's technique will be shallow. If one exerts energy (qi) in accordance with his mind one will have plenty of energy, one's blood vessels will not become clogged but, on the contrary, free-flowing, and one's energy will be adequate. So one will be free from a floating body that might be a result of the energy floating upwards. If one's heart is as calm as water and yet casting no reflection one's qi can be harnessed and reserved and can be transferred and transported throughout the entire body along with one's movements as one moves. Training the sanzhan until one's very last breath is one of the most important concepts within Wuzuquan.

Previous chairman of the International Wuzuquan Fellowship General Conference receiving the official seal representing authority of chairmanship

When it comes to debating the "exerting fist" we Quanzhou folk often judge it upon whether or not the practitioner has adequate "water energy" (*qishui*).

Adequate qi and full strength is like flowing water and this is from where the description comes. Wuzuquan is a style of quanfa based upon strength and is well-known to the world as a hard-fist art. The taolu within Wuzuquan as handed down are often short — with the small taolu consisting of ten to twenty techniques whilst the large and longer taolu possess nearer to seventy or eighty techniques. The reason behind this is not that its taolu cannot be long, but the fact that each movement is vigorous and powerful which makes it hard to be part of a long(er) form. Wuzuquan uses Taizuquan as its basic style. The fist manual states that Taizuquan is like "a dragon walking and a tiger stepping." It is as majestic as an emperor — with the fist so powerful that it produces the effect of drilling the walls and piercing the rocks. However, Taizuquan involves more than just hard strength.

The characteristics of Wuzuquan's strength can be summarized in three words: hard, fierce, and tenacious. Its strength is as powerful as if Taishan Mountain is pressing downwards against one's crown, which is the reason it is called hard, its speed is as fast as a tiger crossing a forest which is the reason it is called fierce, and its strength is soft as if drawing a bow which is the reason it is considered tenacious. Its strength is induced and produced when its spirit is in harmony with its qi. Its inner strength is exerted through the mind sending qi through the two arteries known as Ren and Du. The key to exerting strength is by way of one's Dantian — this is most important — and one must lift the intestines and hang one's stomach thus exerting qi from the inside and send strength towards the outside. The second important aspect is the waist and the shoulders. One can only send forth power if one is able to shake the waist and the crotch freely towards the left and the right. After all, how much strength can one send out only through one hand and one leg alone? Only if one can use the waist as the axis and the shoulders for support, induce strength by way of the mind then shake out/send out sudden strength and power can strength be gathered through the entire body. In this way one can become ferocious! One must assume the proper posture prior to sending out one's strength. In order to achieve this one must correct one's horse (stance) ensuring that the waist and knees are both wrapped and closed, and reserve strength in within the dantian and breathe naturally. As soon as one sends out one's strength one must open his previously closed mouth (that is to say, unclench one's teeth) so that energy/qi flow is optimized by way of filling through the arteries Ren and Du where the spine his held slightly bent, the waist sunk and the crotch hung. Opening and closing in this way one's strength is sent out through the breath and by way of one's qi. With then body, hand and strength arriving in coordination with and in harmony with the

Previous chairmen of the International Wuzuquan Fellowship General Conference receiving the official seal representing authority of chairmanship

mind, all four arrive together. As soon as strength and power has been sent out, the body will return to its main position and gather strength through inhaling, and so reserve power in order to safeguard as well as waiting for opportunity to advance (strike).

The power is crisp throughout as the hard blends with and inside the soft whilst the soft blends within the hard. Therefore, one must not use stiff strength or dead strength. One's body posture must be erect while the body must also be triangular in order to harness and store strength and power. One must relax the hand, transform soft strength into hard strength then send it out by way of one's forehead in a natural manner. When speaking of winning or losing, the key factors that are usually taken into account are no more than the greater power overcoming a lesser power, the fast hand defeating the slower hand, therefore the hand must be tight and heavy. In truth however, only when one exerts a crisp and springy power can one send out techniques like a thunder-clap which is so quick that one can barely cover his ears to avoid the hearing and the inevitable damage. Power must be accurate at the point of contact where its force is achieved through flexibility and its whip-like, spring-like delivery.

One can never send out powerful strength through straight chopping or hard charging but must send it through mastery of the technique, looking for the right opportunity and borrowing the right power/depending upon the favorable circumstance. Wuzuquan also pays carefully attention on its being swift and flexible although it is also particular on being hard – hard receiving and hard attacking. Having said this, Wuzuquan places even more value upon defeating powerful attacks using minimal strength. There are certain techniques that will make this happen but these are very difficult to master. These techniques require that one must send out techniques as soon as the opponent does. This ensures that one borrows the right situation and the right strength/power then transfers such strength from soft to hard before the opponent has the opportunity; thus does one transfer the attacker's strength from hard to soft. This type of tactic depends largely upon the techniques therefore one must pay particular attention to studying the techniques. For instance, the shaking technique is commonly commented upon as "nine out of ten people exhaust themselves through shaking," which is a way to humor those that cannot induce/exert strength through their waist and crotch. In order to exert strength through the shaking technique one must depend upon turning back and restoring the waist to its main structure whilst transferring energy/qi and exerting strength which borrows from the left and the right as if a tornado was ripping through threes and sending them skywards! One's waist and sinews must be able to rotate and the shoulders sink whilst the fist also rotates. In this way one's fist is heavy with a piercing and penetrating power. When it comes to dissolving an oncoming attack one must bend the five fingers slightly while dissolving upwards in a sawing manner. Thus one's opponent will stumble, stepping back as soon as he is touched. When it comes to blocking there are also examples within the five coiling techniques (*panwuji*) where one must use sawing, pinching and stamping tactics within movements such as raising, opening, closing and skewering/stringing in order to dissolve the oncoming power from the opponent and rid him of his foot-horse.

A fist without strength merely floats; therefore, one must train/build one's strength from the very outset of one's training. There are many methods used to train one's power and strength. One begins such training with Sanzhan and then moves onto rock padlocks, sandbag-throwing ("throwing dumplings"), carrying rocks loaded onto a pole, bamboo chopsticks, bamboo pipes, all of which are used to train one's finger strength, gripping strength, fist strength, shoulder and arm strength, waist, sinews, and foot-horse whilst also hardening one's skin and muscles whilst increasing one's energy. However, the above methods can only build up silent strength; one must train year after year before one is able to master the methods of exerting various strengths such as hard strength, soft strength, tenacious strength, crisp strength and lasting strength as well as the ability to transfer and transform yin and yang and inhaling and exhaling by way of the mouth.

Previous chairmen of the International Wuzuquan Fellowship General Conference receiving the official seal representing authority of chairmanship

When it comes to training "loose" techniques, one must train hundreds of times in order to explore and understand such mystery, wonder and secret! Coiling techniques and paired-practice are used to build the paired-up students as they learn, together, about right opportunity, the correct range, when to advance, when to retreat, how to release, how to restrain, and the theory of yin and yang. Thus one is able to exert strength as if going through *jiuquzhu* (literally: "nine bend, nine curve pearl" but meaning, here, a kind of pearl with a hole within which there are bends and curves that make threading extremely difficult – Editor's note) and so reaching the entire body. In this way one can exert power and send out strength as often as one needs and as much as one needs. One not only appears relaxed from the outside but able to build-up spirit on and from inside. One can be as quiet as a maiden, as still as a pond, and as fast as an escaping rabbit upon committing to movement while any obstacle there is he is able to conquer.

Recounted Orally by Lu Qing Hui

Written down by Zhou Kun Min

Written in 1994, published in the Philippine newspapers "World Daily," "Business Newspaper," "Worldwide Daily."

SECTION 3: MONK CHANG KAI DISCUSSES NANSHAOLIN TAIZUQUAN

Quanzhou Nanshaolin quanfa has been handed down both within the Buddhism sect and amongst the people that are not of the Minnan area. In Quanzhou the Chongfu Temple is well known as a heritage of the Nanshaolin (southern Shaolin) sect. During the 1920s Monk Miao Yue worked as its abbot and so during his term there a healthy number of monks whose names began with Fu, Yuan and Chang also became known as masters of quanfa.

In 1977, when Monk Yuan Zhen who was then the abbot of Chongfu Temple, passed away, Monk Chang Kai from Singapore (who was one of his disciples) wrote an article titled, "A Falling/Drifting Leaf from Shaolin Mourning His Beloved Shifu." In this article he recounted the origin of the Nanshaolin martial art as well as an excellent description of Taizuquan from the Fujian area.

In his opinion:

"The fist-types that have been handed down within the Fujian area originate from the Shaolin sect. When the Manchu army crossed the border and took charge of China they established a new government known as the Qing government where a great many

Chinese did not want to surrender so they went to Songshan Shaolin Temple and secretly organized to overthrow the Qing government. Later on the Songshan Shaolin Temple was destroyed as was the Quanzhou Shaolin Temple due to its close connection as part of the same sect. Owing to ongoing persecution the multitude of Shaolin disciples scattered across the nation. The Shaolin monk, Yang Hua, was imprisoned by the Qing government as was the governor of Quanzhou (at that time) who was Sun Kai Hua. Later on, Monka Yang Hua escaped using his Kungfu skills then secretly lived on Qingyuan Mountain where he taught Shaolin quanfa."

Monk Miao Yue was one of his students. This is why, "there is an ancestral tablet dedicated to and in remembrance of Monk Yang Hua within Chongfusi (Chong Fu Temple) which is worshipped on certain (special) days, in memory of Monk Yang Hua." Later on the title Shaolin Fist was changed to Taizuquan — in order to adapt to the (then) current and certain circumstances.

Nanshaolin Taizuquan belongs to the hard sect fist-type. It is passionate, fierce, vigorous and powerful — full of muscular and fearless energy. When Monk Chang Kai talks about the characteristics of Taizuquan he states, "There are five methods within Shaolin quanfa: the mind/heart must be clear and pure; the eyes/sight/vision must be bright and sharp; the hands must be quick/fast; the body must sink; and the feet/ stepping must be accurate and precise. One must advance in order to retreat, and one must be still in order to make the next movement. One must be still if the opponent is still; one must moves first if one perceives the opponent about to move. One must attack/strike as soon as one sees a gap (the opportunity) and one must repair and fill the gap as soon as one observes the void. One must able to change and adapt according to the situation and be unpredictable to the opponent.

Monk Yuan Zhen states that for a beginner that has come to learn Shaolin quanfa he must first learn correct postures then train his strength and learn to how to send out that strength. Finally, he must train his speed and timing. When he trains his fist he must take it very serious and be diligent, ensuring that each and every posture is correct, accurate and precise. Monk Yuan Zhen also writes, "This begins by being slow and gradually becoming faster then moving towards urgency and, after that, perfection. When his skill reaches a high level he can then decide upon separation and division, joining and rounding. Having achieved all of this he can then decide whether it arrives or not. He can make it arrive while it does not seem to be there, and he can make it not arrive when it looks as if it is there! If one is able to do this he has reached a level of "the mind arriving ahead of the fist." Having arrived at this level his hand method will always involves both attacking and defence. He can suddenly change from stretching into spreading and can also quickly change from swallowing into spitting. While inhaling he can change from defence into attacking through one advancing step. Being pressed he can change from attack to defence through one retreat — by stepping back one step. The person who exerts his fist should look at ease and maintain an even breath. He should be able to hide his fierce intention beneath a calm exterior."

Which level of Taizuquan training can be considered as to comply with the standard? In Chang Kai's opinion one must send out his fist to the sound of *pengpeng* (editor: a seemingly vague if not antiquated Chinese term used to describe a kind of booming, thumping sound not unlike the sound that wind come sometimes make). While sending out his palm(s) to the sound of *huhu* (editor: another Chinese term referring to the sound of the wind, or the sound of someone's breathing who is sound asleep) where he must reach a level of "pushing the palms with a loud sound and with powerful strength while sending out his leg(s) without a sound, turning and twirling at will and sending out his hand according to where his mind wants it to go." He must *be* as if as a pond of water in autumn when he is still, and he must *do* as if emptying the sea and turning over the river when he is on the move. The fist that he sends out must have the power of piercing through the mountain and drilling through the rock. As soon as his feet are planted into the ground he must be as steady as if it is rooted beneath the ground. When engaging in combat with an opponent he must make sure that his opponent is not able to see through his situation be it solid or void, and the same applies to the defender's means and methods of attack and defence. Thus the attacker retreats and retires in low spirits having been utterly defeated through his own failure.

Monk Chang Kai is a first-place disciple of Monk Yuan Zhen and assumed posts and titles such as the Vice-President of the "World (Buddhism) Sangha Association," the consultant to the "Singapore National Art General Conference" and was honoured and respected in both quanfa circles and medical fields. During the early 1960s he asked both his shifu (Monk Yuanzhen) and Monk (She) Chang Qing to take charge of the surviving manuscript from Monk Miao Yue, and format this into a book of three volumes which was to be called, *Shaolin Taizu Quanfa*.

I heard from Monk Chang Qing that Monk Chang Kai cared deeply for Quanzhou quanfa, and had expressed a will to rebuild the Quanzhou Shaolinsi. However, unexpectedly he fell ill this autumn and passed away in September at the age of seventy-five. In August 1990, when Monk Chang Jue from Taiwan was on his way to Singapore via Quanzhou, my father asked him to pass a message to Monk Chang Kai. In this message my father asked if Monk Chang Kai would attend the, "Quanzhou Nanshaolin Wushu International Academic Seminar." Now they have become separated permanently. Monk Chang Kai is now in a different world — the world of clouds and skies. By chance I read the book titled, *In Permanent Cherish of Memories of Monk Yuan Zhen*. Therefore, I am writing this article in order to grieve for this monk who was a quanfa master.

—Zhou Ruo Heng
(the daughter of Mr. Zhou Kun Min).

Written in 1990 and published in "Wuzumen Studies," Quanzhou Nanshaolin Literature Collections.

泉州太祖拳

POSTSCRIPT

Quanzhou is the origin of the southern Shaolin Temple and Wuzuquan is very popular among the people of this area. My grandfather trained in Taizuquan, my father trained in Taizuquan, and even my uncles and aunties practiced Taizuquan — some more than others. Therefore, I myself came to know about and be in contact with Taizuquan ever since my childhood.

My father was well-known, within our social circle, for his studies of books and his training in the double-edged sword. However, his martial arts training was not only for the purpose of physical strength and well-being but also reflected a life-long purpose and a very real passion for him.

Thinking back to my childhood I remember that I would often follow my father to visit his friends during the summer evenings. Sometimes I would sit by a trench beneath the dim light, and sometimes under the old banyan tree — with its lightly drifting beard and whiskers — while I watched and listened to the conversations going on among the adults. This would often address the happenings within the martial world including how heroic someone had been as well as how outstanding and extraordinary somebody had been in martial arts. I felt both a yearning and a curiosity… until my eyes became tired and I could not stop yawning. Meanwhile, the adults would continue their excited dialogue.

Back then my father was young and strong and would get up early each morning in order to practice quanfa. As there was no courtyard at our old home my father would practice his Straight and Dashing Fist (Zhichongquan) upon the wall. As time went by the lime on the wall first became dark. Then it bulged. Then finally it fell off from the wall which led to an interesting scene (or exchange) amongst my family!

At that time a good number of young people came to train with my father after hearing of my father's reputation. My father taught them either quanfa or weaponry either in the evenings or at the weekends while I played by myself. The place where they had their training was, at the time, a quiet spot and without any electricity. I could, therefore, only see moving shadows, and feel the wind that was brought by their fists beneath the moonlight. Taizuquan was handed from generation to generation under harsh conditions by word of mouth and physical movements. Quanfa training is very hard while Taizuquan, specifically, requires sending forth hard and fierce strength. My father was an extremely strict teacher and would not let pass a single inaccurate or imperfect movement. His students had to practice by imitating the teacher repeatedly whilst dripping with sweat. There was no way that one could stand this kind of loneliness and hardship without true passion from his heart.

Now some of those students are already in their fifties and have become too busy to continue. However, my father has never given up his passion towards Wuzuquan, no matter how many changes there have been during his training. There are always masters among our home visitors including Chinese people from Hong Kong, Xiamen, Taiwan and beyond. Even non-Chinese have assisted by way of interpreters. When speaking of Taizuquan my father can talk non-stop and always with passion. Of course, he himself is no longer practicing or teaching Taizuquan the way he was when he was younger, but he is promoting the art and uncovering resources and editing materials as well as building friendships and fellowships among the people from Wuzu Sect, be it in China or overseas. In the 1980s and the 1990s my father twice led a group of martial artists to the Philippines and Japan and so made the dream of Quanzhou Wushu "going beyond our national gate" come true. Nowadays Quanzhou Taizuquan has become more reputable because of Nanshaolin, while it is also one of the cultural heritages which Quanzhou people are so proud of. Being in this family which is full of the Wushu atmosphere I have been privileged to have a glimpse of Taizuquan, be able to get to know experts within the martial arts circles, and witness the whole process that Quanzhou Wuzuquan has developed — from a local fist-type to become a draw-card for the city — from performing in martial schools to performing at international joint performances.

Quanzhou Taizuquan is another my father's latest book. It has taken him a considerably length of time so I am delighted for my father, that he has finally completed this book. This book not only records the effort that my father has put in Taizuquan over all these years but also reflects the accumulated wisdom from Quanzhou Nanshaolin.

I would like to say to everybody that appreciates this book of my father's thank you so much!

Zhou Ruo Heng
9th September 2007

EPILOGUE

Now that we are at the end of the book it is time for me to answer a recurring question. People are always asking me: How did you come to learn martial arts?

The reason I first began to learn martial arts is that as a youngster I was physically weak and often sick and so could not attend school. My father asked me: "If you are physically weak, how can you benefit society?" Each morning I was woken up very early by my father and told to walk to the back of my house where I was "to eat fresh air." At this time my father began to teach me step-by-step the Sanzhan form as well as "loose techniques" such as capturing, raising, chopping and slicing, in the hope that my body would become stronger.

In 1961, the Quanzhou Wushu Studies/Research Society was opened at the site of an ancestral hall next door to our house so my father enrolled me, with his hard-earned money, together with my second youngest brother. The monthly tuition fee was three Yuan (renminbei) for the two of us. This kind of fee would have been an expense and a luxury for most Chinese at this time; for at this time, China was enduring a three-year period of intense suffering. I recall buying an ink-well for half a yuan (50 fen) which was very expensive for most — so the kung-fu fee was clearly outside of many local people's budget! My brother learned beiquan (northern fist) while I learned nanquan (southern fist), for I was already practicing Sanzhan which was the foundation of nanquan. However, I was not able to adapt to the teaching method of the Research group so I begged my father to find me a teacher who would teach me one-to-one.

I knew that several of my father's best friends were accomplished in nanquan so it was not long before a man named Zhang Ying Qi was teaching me Eershiquan (Li Sip Kun) in the lounge of our one hundred year-old house. At the same time a man named Huang Yu Shui also taught me the Sanzhan Shizi nanquan form while Huang You Quan taught me the San Jiao Yao nanquan form. Zhang was one of best disciples of Master Lu Yan Qiu (Lo Yan Chiu) — the founder of the Guang Han (Kong Han) National Art School — while Huang Yu Shui and Huang You Quan together with my father, were all students from the Yao Jin Shi Zou Kui Guan. All these men possessed outstanding martial arts skills. I was quite amazed, at this time, for when Master Zhang executed a "Middle Fist" technique the house beams felt as if they were shaking! When my classmate from the same year was practicing martial arts I already possessed more skills than him given that I was not only learning martial arts with the Research group but was also receiving private tuition — but not just from one master but from three!

At one point in our group training a master named Dai Huo Yan (who was the head of the Research Society and who everybody called "Yanbo" — a respectful title meaning Uncle Yan), took a group of us to the opening of a brand new martial arts school. There I was invited to perform the Shuangshui. This was sprung upon me without warning! Yanbo saw my performance and was impressed so he beckoned me over to him and invited me to "follow" him. This marked the beginning of a ten-year teache/student relationship where he showed me great and sincere affection throughout. Yanbo passed away in 1970. In 1978 I collected and rearranged the quanfa manuals for which I wrote within the index some of my recollections of the time when I was watching my teacher performing quanfa where he advanced and retreated within the space required by a cow when it lies down. With the power of the wind from the Eight Boundaries while Swallowing, Spitting, Sinking and Floating, Yan Bo was flying like a phoenix and diving like a dragon! When he gave lessons he emphasized correct posture: Posture must look good on the outside and have content within. His advice was always sound and his expression forever calm. As one of his students I was taught one-on-one, year after year. Correcting me in one single technique often took days, if not months, and would sometimes begin in one season and not finish before the end of the next! Co-incidently, my two teachers (Master Dai and Master Yao Jin Shi) were both students under Master Wei Guo Qi, who was a very famous martial art master from the end of the Qing Dynasty and start of Min (Republic of China); therefore, the martial arts I learned from my early learning period was all from the same Wuzuquan sect.

During this period I also learned quanfa from Master Lin Qi Yian. Although Master Lin and Master Dai both taught me Taizuquan, Master Dai taught me the importance of being sturdy, rigorous and cautious while Master Lin taught me the values of being open, smooth and stylish – clearly, two very different approaches! Master Lin was one of the superior students of Master Chen Chao Shun who was in his nineties at the time. From what I gather it sounded as if Master Chen had been assigned a post within the Green Standard Army (Standing Infantry during the Qing dynasty which had originally been formed from the Ming and other Chinese army units). Master Chen was also skilled in fist techniques and kicking strategies. After the Xinhai Revolution (in 1911) which ended the Qing Dynasty Master Chen opened a Chinese medicine shop and worked as a doctor. The movements that I often practice — such as "White Ape Emerging From Its Cave" and "Five Tigers Crossing The Forest" — were handed down through his sect.

In 1963 I passed the Entrance Exam and became a student at Xiamen University. One day, in order to prepare for the provincial level contest, Mr. Hong Zheng Fu (the head-instructor of the provincial level wushu team/group) came to Xiamen University and invited me to participate in the contest. But I was too young and inexperienced and had an exaggerated opinion of my own ability so expecting to shine I lost to a senior and more experienced martial arts master. Unexpectedly, Master Lin Du Ying, a well-known martial art master from Xiamen City, sought me out and invited me to "communicate" with him. From that time onwards I greatly benefited from a less than fortunate situation (my losing at the contest); for each Sunday, as long as I was not busy with my academic studies, I would learn quanfa from him. What Master Lin taught me was not nanquan, but beitui. I also learned Taijiquan which was initially introduced to me through a Mr. Fan Ting Yue who was one of my university teachers. At that time he was teaching me General Discussion Literature. Mr. Fan and I often went to Nanputuo temple to learn Taijiquan.

My experience in martial arts involved nothing more than sheer hard work and ongoing training and had nothing to do with Chinese divination as described within the novels of the well-known Hong Kong writer Mr. Jin Yong, nor the fantastic legendary tales for which my country is now world-famous. But I did allow me to become physically stronger and far healthier. In 1968 I engaged in some farming work where I was able to carry fresh grain weighing in excess of seventy kilograms; with a carrying pole over my shoulders and would run for miles! Later on I worked for a newspaper where I worked more than ten hours each day oftentimes not finishing until very late at night. This was the result of my quanfa training where I was taught all-year round during the hottest of days and the coldest of days. As such was the discipline.

In my youth I enjoyed so much martial arts training, I once wrote a paragraph within the *Fist Manual* stating, "When meeting-up with friends I always learned martial arts in a humble and sincere manner. If I came across a Taoist devotee or a Buddhist monk who lived in seclusion within the city area I always asked for their guidance in an amiable manner, and wherever I went I would leave the trace of my fists and my kicks."

Later on, as I became more experienced, I would meet and make many friends from both China and from overseas who would come to Quanzhou in search of the origin of nanshaolin. Therefore, I was able to make comparisons which brought me to such awareness that wushu is not only a kind of art and skill but also a blood vessel within a national civilization and culture which was also a resource for Quanzhou's development — a bridge that would provide communications of international proportions. During the 1980s I was elected Chairman to a wushu association and so since that time I have focused my attention upon the promotion of wushu (quanfa) communications, theory, study and research.

In recently years Quanzhou city has been declared by the government as a Minnan Cultural Ecology Conservation District. Nanshaolin Wuzuquan was listed by the Fujian Provincial Government as an "Intangible Cultural Heritage." With Taizuquan being one style of quanfa within the composite art called Wuzuquan, it has been handed down *by word of mouth only* during the course of hundreds of years. Regretfully, some aspects have been lost. But each time I recall when my teacher, Master Dai, was ill towards his final days, I can still see him sitting at his desk writing and editing his Fist Manual to which he would ultimately entrust me. In a world that has become fickle and impatient and where traditional quanfa has oftentimes become polluted with innovations and endless confusion between what is the flower and what is the grass, all of this has inspired me to prepare this book. This idea was supported by my wife, Hui Ping, and my daughter, Ruo Heng, who have always been at my side during the endless photo-shoots (amidst the hottest of the summertime days) that mow appear within this volume.

Confucius considered it worrysome if one learns but does not speak of (teaches) such lessons. If the traces of the Six Classics are barely seen, the country will be difficult to manage; if the essence of the Six Classics are well understood, the country would be difficult not to manage. I have not taught quanfa for quite some time now, but I have produced this volume. Whosoever understands this will not be critical.

It has taken me three months to complete this book. Many of my friends helped me along the way: Chen Ying Jie, a young photographer, helped with the photos while well-known artists Lin Jian Pu and a Wu Yong An, together designed the cover, the binding and the layout. Wu Shao Jie categorized and edited the photos while Ye Xiu Ping helped with the input. The Quanzhou Evening Paper Publishing Factory printed the first copy whilst Chen Ri Sheng, Lin Po Shui, Cai Jin Xing, Xu Qing Hui, and Lin Shao Rong offered consultancy. She Chang Qing and She Li Feng from the Quanzhou Shaolin Temple helped also helped with the photos. This book is published and was released by the Xianggang Tiandi Dushu (Hong Kong Heaven-Earth Book) Publishing House through my friendship with Sun Li Chuang, the vice chief-editor who worked as this book's duty-editor. This publication was sponsored by Chen Zu Chang from the Philippines. To all this individuals I offer my sincere and heart-felt thanks!

Zhou Kun Min
September 08, 2007
Yu Xun Tang (Yu Xun Building)
in Fang Cao Yuan (Fang Cao Garden)

泉州太祖拳

TRANSLATOR'S NOTES

Preface by Zheng Dao Xi

1. "Minnan" is a Chinese term referring to a people, a language and a culture that lay southwards from Fuzhou City's River Min. The Chinese character "min" is the "min" of "Minjiang" meaning "river." Minjiang means River Min, while "nan" means south or southern. The River Min was (and remains) the largest river and the longest river of Fujian province. Fuzhou City is the provincial capital of Fujian within which lies, to the south, Quanzhou City.

Preface by Han Jian Zhong

1. This reflects the Chinese concept of "wen and wu" — the literary and the martial. In Japan this equates to the brush and the sword while the western world would be more familiar with the notion of yin and yang. Each of these four descriptive concepts reflect and describe Balance.

2. Quanzhou's southern Shaolin temple is actually called "Dong Chan Si," which literally translates to "East Chan (Meditation) Temple" where the Chan is reflective of what the Japanese were to "repackage"/ interpret later on as Zen.

Lin Sao's Poem

1. Lady Gong Sun was the most famous sword dancer of the Tang Dynasty.

2. A parable meaning that one aspiration goes afar.

Chapter 1

1. This refers to martial arts taught to farmers when they were not engaged in farming (that is to say, in their spare time) and so, in their own opinion, the quanfa

discipline they were practicing was not being taken so seriously (by themselves) which demonstrated very well their sense of modesty.

2. In Chinese: Jiu hou tu zhen yan means, "When the wine is in, the truth is out!"

3. I do find it interesting that within this book the art "Taizuquan" is often translated into English as "Grand Ancestor Fist" whereas within Wuzuquan, this art is often referred to as "Emperor Fist." I wonder why it is not referred to, in both cases, as "Great Emperor Fist"?

4. Ancient Chinese emperors called themselves descendants of the dragon in order to distinguish themselves from ordinary folk.

5. In China the turtle and the tortoise are symbols of longevity.

6. This quote sounds like a direct reference to the Ngo Ki Lat ("five parts power") concept found within Wuzuquan which "reminds" the practitioner to utilize one's whole body when punching and, indeed, effecting each and every technique.

7. Yongchun is the alleged home of Yongchun Baihequan (White Crane Fist of Yongchun Village) which is now an hour's drive up in the hills from Quanzhou City. Yongchun Baihaiquan is one of the five styles that form, collectively, Wuzuquan.

8. Duhu is a title of the highest administrative commanding officer in the border area.

9. As well as any instructional manual can "teach" an art such as quanfa.

10. The Triads actually have their roots in within Fujian province.

11. Jinjiang is another area (they call it a city) of Quanzhou City and is the town where Quanzhou's international airport is located.

12. "shimu" translates to "ten mu" with "mu" being a unit of size, length and area while "Laonong Chan" translates to "old farmer Chan" who was a Chan sect Buddhist monk.

13. Commonly referred to in the west as, simply, "Iron Palm."

14. "She" is the title surname given to every Buddhist monk inherited from Buddha.

15. One "jin" equates to half a kilogram.

16. The term "Liugiuquan" refers to a hostel-type dwelling (guan) where individuals from the Okinawa islands would stay when upon their arrival into China via Quanzhou. In days gone by the Okinawas were referred to as the Liuqiu Islands by the Okinawans while the Fujianese referred to the Okinawas as "Liugiu." Students of Okinawan Goju-ryu Karatedo and Okinawan Uechi-ryu Karatedo may well be aware of the liugiuguan that existed for some time in Fuzhou, but to discover there was also a liugiugua in Quanzhou is going to be quite a revelation!

17. The "Thirty-Six Families" episode of 1393.

18. In fact, the Kong Han school was opened within the world's oldest "Chinatown" — that which is known locally as Ongpin. Ongpin was established in 1594 and is also famous for being home to The Philippines' oldest kung-fu school, Beng Kiam.

Chapter 2

1. This falls in-line with the Wuzuquan concept of there being ten "chien" (power, strength) forms that the beginner will learn first so as to develop a strong foundation and a firm understanding of Wuzuquan principles together with preparatory strength and power.

2. Shizizhan is the name of a Taizuquan form meaning, we are told, "Character Ten Battle," but the form quoted within this book (shizi) does not use the appropriate Chinese characters for the "Character Ten" translation. Within this book the character for "ten" does appear, but then the second Chinese character is either incorrect; or represents another Taizuquan form which my research has not permitted me to track down. During my research into the actual translation of "shizi" I encountered another possible meaning (translation), yet the fact that Taizuquan contains another form using the term "character" — namely, tianzizhan ("Heaven Character Battle") leads me to suspect that "Character Ten Battle" (shizizhan) is

an accurate translation. Interesting to note, though, that the "shi" meaning "ten" is sometimes translated as "cross" which might just be a Westerners' description as to how the character appears. During the course of my research never have I found "cross" to be an actual definition of the Chinese character "十".

3. Could this be where the corkscrew punch (typical and symbolic of karate) came from?

4. There is no singular or plural, as such, with the Chinese language.

5. The two "jian" characters used in Shuangjian (double sword) and Shuangjian (double truncheon) are spelt the same way in pinyin but appear differently as actual Chinese characters.

6. Known in the West as the "Iron Sand Palm" or simply "Iron Palm."

Chapter 3

1. In the West this refers to the crown (of the head).

2. Ziwu refers to the meridians within one's body. "Zi" is an ancient Chinese compass point representing 0° north while "wu" refers to noontime. But there is a third Chinese character which is sometimes used to describe "ziwu" and this is "xian" which means line or thread. This is the same "xian" used in Chinese term "tiexian" meaning "iron wire" or "iron thread."

Chapter 4

1. While the "three-seven horse" and the "four-six horse" refers to the front foot: rear foot weight ratio (distribution) within the sanzhanma, the expression "bu ding bu ba" I encountered during my Crying Crane and White Crane studies in Fujian where I was told this expression means, literally, "not a T-shaped (budting) stance nor a Chinese Character Eight-shaped (buba) stance." "Budingbuba" therefore appears to be somewhat and somewhere in-between these two physical expressions.

2. This kind of footwork is often referred to in Chinese martial arts as "follow step."

3. Also translated as "Three Clicks," this might well be about the rhythm and the timing.

Chapter 5

1. This reference to "cartilage" appears four times within the narrative of this sanzhan form description and each time it appears it is used to describe the gongbu (or gongjianbu) stance/posture familiarly known in the West as the "bow and arrow stance". But while this reference to cartilage makes no sense in a literal capacity, what I can extract from this term is "a twisting and stimulating of ligaments, tendons and fascia that is prompted by various upper limb, lower limb and spine/torso-oriented postures, stances and movements". This question of cartilage needs to be resolved and will be in due course as research continues along with a deeper understanding of the Quanzhou quanfa.

2. Jia means to press and squeeze from both sides.

3. While fengyu means, literally, "wind and rain", this Chinese term also refers to "trials and hardships" which is precisely what sanzhan is (as is life, itself!).

4. Within Wuzuquan, "Inviting Fist" is called "Enticing Hands".

5. General Guang is otherwise known as Kuang Gong - the God Of War.

6. The text does not speak of this, but one must turn to the right and so effect a right "bow and arrow" stance.

7. It would thus appear that within Taizuquan "swallowing" and "floating" amount to the same expression whereas it is my understanding that Wuzuquan differentiates between these two concepts.

8. It would thus appear that within Taizuquan "spitting" and "sinking" equate to the same expression whereas it is my understanding that Wuzuquan differentiates between these two concepts.

9. This ties in with what I have been told about the Wuzuquan sanzhan - that the actual sanzhan, by definition, is the three forward steps and the three backward steps while the "opening (salutation) effected by way of the even/level horse (pingma) is called qikun (or, by some, babutou). The closing part of the form (from the movement immediately prior to the double step and double arm lock/strike/break) also goes under a different name and so is not technically part of the sanzhan form!

10. While this book states upon more than one occasion that there are no wasted movements within Taizuquan, the pulling back of the right hand (fist) appears to serve no useful purpose here as the elbow strike could easily be delivered by way of "short power."

11. The text does not appear to state if the left continues to step backwards — or the right foot moves forwards from the interim hanging stance — in order to form the right horse stance. Having read the caption for #27 I am concluding that here, in #24, the left foot continues in moving backwards to form the right horse stance.

12. The notion of the click (here, a literal translation) reflects a very light touching or tapping of the toes upon the ground.

13. Bagua (or Baguazhang) is an internal Chinese (Daoist) martial art and so it would seem that the above referencing of "xia bagua" recognizes a similarity of movement and motion as found within Baguazhang.

Chapter 6

1. Where taels and catties are ancient Chinese units of weight, this idiom reflects the notion that a small amount of effort can offset, control and defeat a great strength or power. Skilled horse-riders will know only too well that holding the reigns lightly can be enough to control a horse far greater (stronger) than any human being.

2. The character used here by the author literally means "to kill."

3. It is my belief that this is a reference to a rather grim image, of a vanquisher having just terminated his adversary through decapitation and is now holding his victim's head up high by the victim's hair for all to see!

4. Houfa, Xianzhi — to move late yet arrive early! To attack before the enemy can react (or even act!). To move after the enemy has moved and yet to "arrive" first! This wonderful Chinese idiom that means to exert the very most while doing the bare minimum. In story-telling this equates to giving the reader the maximum amount of information (in order to propel the story forward) while using the least amount of dialogue.

5. This has a military connotation

Chapter 7

1. This is a direct reference to Quanzhou City.

2. Literally, "West Street" (xijie) with "hou" being a title awarded by the government.

3. This I find this very interesting. Earlier in this book we understand that within Taizuquan floating and swallowing are one of the same as are sinking and spitting yet here we understand that within Xingzhequan these four concepts are, actually, four concepts and not two wit alternative names.

4. The Chinese term "chi" as it appears here refers to an ancient Chinese measurement. Over the past few centuries the length of one chi has varied somewhat with variations even being somewhat inter-provincial, but a realistic benchmark approximation puts 1 chi somewhere between 30cm and 35cm.

5. Qichigun refers to a cudgel (gun) measuring seven chi (qichi)

6. The zhang'ergun is a cudgel measuring approximately 3.96 metres long.

7. My understanding of this is a tonfa-like instrument/weapon.

The Bible of Ngo Cho Kun

In *Chinese Gentle Art Complete*, Alexander Lim Co pours scholarship and more than 50 years' experience in Ngo Cho into the first-ever illustrated publication, and English-language translation, of this historical book on Fukien Five Ancestor Boxing. Long held as the "Bible of Ngo Cho Kun," this treatise on Five Ancestor Fist Kung-Fu has been a treasured keepsake among lineage holders of the style. Originally published in China 1917 by Yu Chiok Sam, one of the "Ngo Cho Ten Tigers," or leading disciples of the art's founder Chua Giok Beng, the book saw only a limited print run. It has been out of print for over 90 years!

This special Tambuli Media edition presents all of the original Chinese text in 244 pages, along with a new Foreword, Prefaces, an Appendix and precise English translation illustrated with over 725 clear photographs demonstrating techniques and training methods. Contents include:

- Single Short-Hand and Long-Hand Techniques
- Double Short-Hand and Long-Hand Techniques
- Kneeling and Evading Techniques
- Nine-Section Brocades
- Nine-Rotary Methods
- 18 Scholars Methods
- Solo and Partner Fighting Drills
- 38 Solo Empty-Hand Forms
- Six Weapon Art Categories

"I congratulate Sifu Alex Co for translating this rare and important book. All practitioners of Ngo Cho should have this at their side!"
—GM Benito Tan, Philippine-Chinese Beng Kiam Athletic Association

"Not only is Ngo Cho Kun rarely seen in print format, it is rarely openly taught here in the West. This translation is an absolute gem for Chinese martial arts enthusiasts the world over. A welcomed addition to the martial collectors shelf."
—The Ground Never Misses

www.tambulimedia.com

Kong Han Ngo Cho

Ngo Cho Kun, also known as Wu Zu Quan or Five Ancestor Fist kung-fu, is one of the most popular styles of Southern Fist in China. Currently, it is the official style of the Southern Shaolin Temple in Quanzhou, China. The founder of this dynamic art, Chua Giok Beng, had 10 disciples, each developing his own branch of the system. This book presents the core training of the Kong Hang Athletic Association branch of Dr. Lo Yan Chui, passed down and currently headed worldwide by Sigong Henry Lo, and in Canada by Sifu Daniel Kun.

Kong Han Ngo Cho: Forms, Weapons and Fighting begins with a historical presentation of the development of the various lines of Ngo Cho—each with a different focus on the representative systems of Tai Cho, Crane, Monkey, Monk, and Damo. The book then delves into the fundamental training that sets the basis for mastery of this style. Empty hand techniques, internal organ qigong exercises, solo forms, two man forms, training sets, fighting applications, weapon forms and applications, and full-contact lei-tai competition training are all presented in this comprehensive volume.

"A most welcome addition to the sparse reference materials on the Fukien art of Ngó Chó Kûn. I congratulate Sigong Henry Lo and Sifu Daniel Kun on a job well done." —Grandmaster Alex Co, Beng Kiam Athletic Club

"Kong Han Ngo Cho covers a lot of ground—most notably Kong Han's curriculum up to O-Duan—making this a most valuable resources on this dynamic art."
—Dr. Mark Wiley, International Beng Hong Athletic Association

www.tambulimedia.com

The Way of Ngo Cho Kung Fu

This is the first authoritative book on the art of the Ngo Cho Kun (Five Ancestors Fist), depicting its early history, development, and its embodying principles and techniques like the basic fist set "Sam Chien" (Three Battles) the advanced form "In Tin Tat" (Entwining Kick), and a complete listing of all Ngo Cho Kun solo empty-hand forms.

This book is a must for all practitioners of this style as well as other kung-fu enthusiasts. It was written under the able supervision of second-generation Grandmaster Tan Ka Hong from the original Chinese text. Great efforts have been exerted to arrive at the roots of the style.

This book offers more than 200 photographs and illustrations and aims to bring the more than 150 years of Ngo Cho tradition within your reach. It was written in both English and Chinese, lending ample touch to its authenticity, and so as to reach a wider range of kung-fu aficionados.

Translated and edited by Mr. Alexander Lim Co, with the full cooperation of the members of the Beng Kiam Athletic Club (the oldest kung-fu school in the Philippines), this book promises to bring you the authentic forms of Ngo Cho Kung-fu.

"The Way of Ngo Cho Kung Fu is one of the first books in English on the rare art of Fukien Five Ancestor Boxing. Out of print for over 30 years, this faithful reissue keeps the dual Chinese-English format and serves as a historical reference for every Ngo Cho Kun practitioner."
—Dr. Mark V. Wiley, International Beng Hong Athletic Association

www.tambulimedia.com